COVENANT RELATIONSHIPS FOR RADICALS

Amsterdam Series in Baptist and Mennonite Theologies

The Amsterdam Series in Baptist and Mennonite Theologies (ASBMT) is an academic series rooted in the Believers' Church tradition (Anabaptist-related, Free Church, Peace-Church). Ecumenically engaged and international in orientation, it provides a platform for both younger and established scholars, delivering monographs as well as single-author and edited books. It hosts a wide spectrum of academic fields while at the same time holding to a narrow focus on themes that are of particular importance to and characteristic of the Baptist and Mennonite traditions.

The series is supported by the Dutch Baptist Seminary, the Mennonite Seminary Amsterdam, the Amsterdam Centre for Religion and Peace & Justice Studies, and the International Baptist Theological Study Centre Amsterdam (IBTS). The chairs of the Dutch Baptist Seminary, the Mennonite Seminary, and IBTS (all residing at the VU University Amsterdam) oversee the series.

Scholars who wish to be considered for publication in the series should contact the Managing Editor at ASBMT@ibts.eu.

VOLUME 3

Covenant Relationships for Radicals

Baptists, Community Organizing, and Social Justice

Richard Weaver

Foreword by Paul S. Fiddes

PICKWICK *Publications* • Eugene, Oregon

COVENANT RELATIONSHIPS FOR RADICALS
Baptists, Community Organizing, and Social Justice

Amsterdam Series in Baptist and Mennonite Theologies

Pickwick Publications
An Imprint of Wipf and Stock Publishers
199 W. 8th Ave., Suite 3
Eugene, OR 97401

www.wipfandstock.com

PAPERBACK ISBN: 979-8-3852-5391-3
HARDCOVER ISBN: 979-8-3852-5392-0
EBOOK ISBN: 979-8-3852-5393-7

Cataloguing-in-Publication data:

Names: Weaver, Richard, author. | Fiddes, Paul S., foreword.

Title: Covenant relationships for radicals : baptists, community organizing, and social justice / Richard Weaver ; foreword by Paul S. Fiddes.

Description: Eugene, OR : Pickwick Publications, 2026 | Series: Amsterdam Series in Baptist and Mennonite Theologies | Includes bibliographical references.

Identifiers: ISBN 979-8-3852-5391-3 (paperback) | ISBN 979-8-3852-5392-0 (hardcover) | ISBN 979-8-3852-5393-7 (ebook)

Subjects: LCSH: Covenant theology. | Baptist Union of Great Britain. | Baptists—Great Britain. | Community organization—Philosophy. | Citizenship. | Democracy. | Civil society.

Classification: BT155 .W42 2026 (paperback) | BT155 (ebook)

VERSION NUMBER 05/18/26

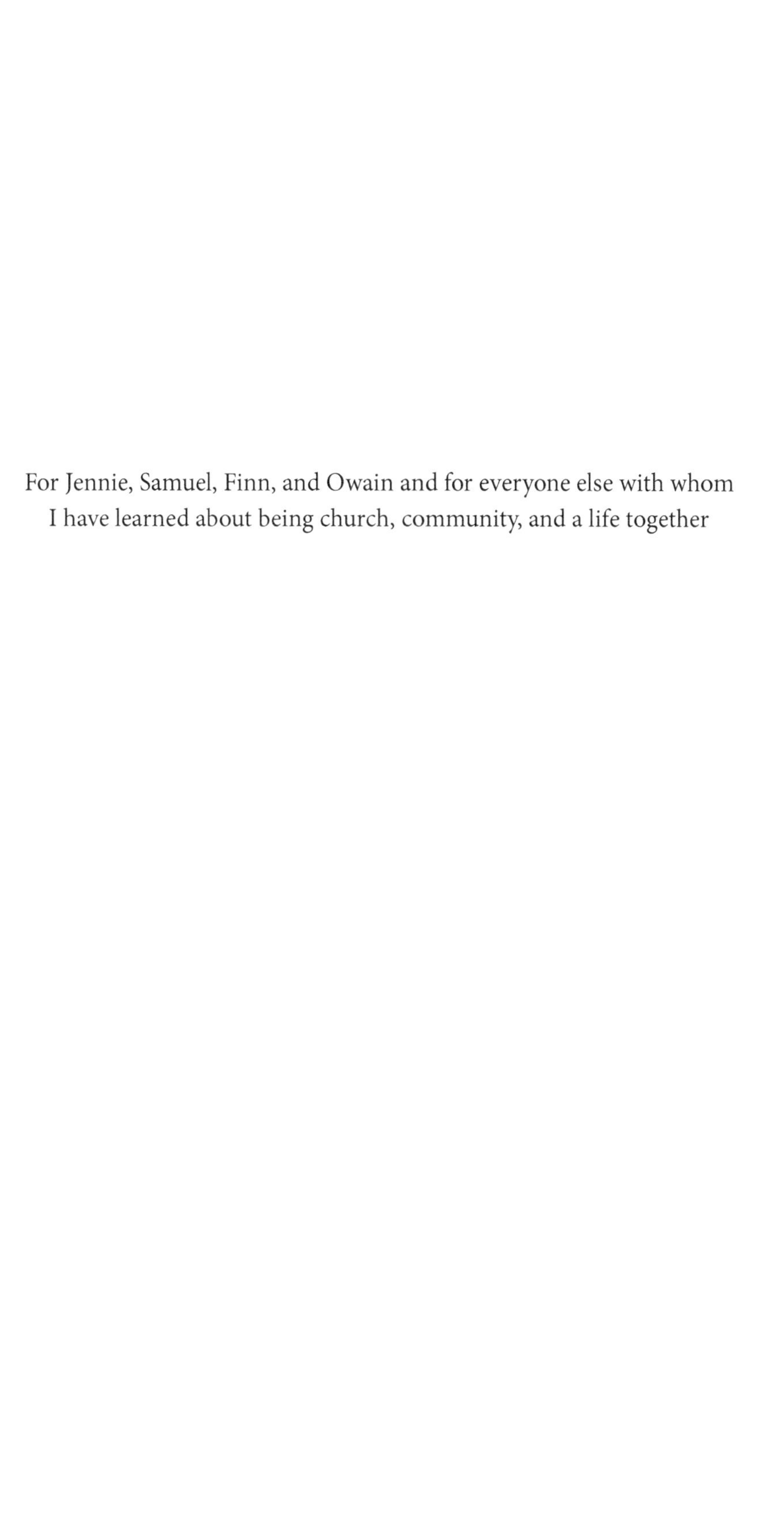

For Jennie, Samuel, Finn, and Owain and for everyone else with whom I have learned about being church, community, and a life together

Contents

Foreword

by Paul S. Fiddes

Just over forty years ago, a group of five Baptist theologians gathered in the senior common room of Regent's Park College in Oxford to discuss a writing project. They met under the (painted) eye of Dr. George Pearce Gould, a former principal whose portrait hung over the fireplace, and who was—despite his mild manner—a radical Baptist of his time. He had pressed the case for women to be recognized as ministers of the Baptist Union of Great Britain, and in 1920 admitted to Regent's Park College the first woman to be formed for ministry in a Baptist college (Violet Hedger). The five who met together were also hoping to do something radical, to help Baptists to rethink the whole nature of their life together and enable them to share more deeply in God's mission in the world.

They aimed to revive and renew the idea of "covenant" among Baptists, a guiding principle that had lapsed in Baptist memories not only in Great Britain but worldwide. Covenant was historically a binding by solemn promise of church members with each other and with God, and it explained why Baptists originally dissented from the established religion of the Church of England in their relation to the state and wider society. By the late twentieth century, however, it was generally little regarded among Baptists, even though many of their churches had founding covenants. The title of the small book that the five published in 1985 sums up their concern: *Bound to Love: The Covenant Basis of Baptist Life and Mission*.[1] Three of them in particular were active in the next two decades, speaking and writing about covenant (often together), and advocating its cause in the Council of the Baptist Union as well as on the ecumenical scene.[2] By the turn of the millennium the Baptist Union of Great

1. The co-authors of *Bound to Love* were Paul S. Fiddes, Roger Hayden, Richard L. Kidd, Keith W. Clements, and Brian Haymes.

2. The story is told, and the movement is analyzed, in Goodliff, *Renewing a Modern*

Britain had produced *Covenant 21*, a service for churches in its fellowship taking up the traditional covenant promise to "walk together before God and watch over each other," applying this to members' participation in the local church, associations of churches, and the union itself. In 2013 the Baptist World Alliance, holding in fellowship some 178,000 churches in 134 countries and territories, introduced a "Covenant on Intra-Baptist Relations," thereby giving an ecclesial tone to its international communion of national unions and conventions.

The group, gathered in 1983 (of which I was one), would have been both amazed and exhilarated to know that an able Baptist scholar and social activist of the next generation would write a book in 2025, drawing upon the idea of covenant to illuminate methods for achieving social justice, and would show its relevance not only for the gathering of a local church community, but for the organizing of a wide range of community organizations beyond the church. Such is the remarkable book which Richard Weaver has written, and which follows this foreword.

This book does in fact refer to *Bound to Love*, and other writings by members of that group over the succeeding years. But it breaks completely new ground in bringing covenant into relation with community organizing, a social movement that came to the UK in the 1980s. In a double movement of thought, Richard Weaver shows how this movement can give structure and direction to Baptist concerns for social justice, while at the same a Baptist theology of covenant can also shape community organizing.

In an original, and highly illuminating, piece of research the author provides an analysis of addresses given at assemblies of the Baptist Union of Great Britain and the Baptist Union of Wales, as well as resolutions chosen for debate, from the late 1980s to 2010. He examines these sources to understand how and to what extent Baptists were relating to each other and to other church denominations, to other institutions in civil society, and to government. The result, which Baptists in those unions (and without doubt also Baptists worldwide) need to heed, is to show that while there were many expressions of concern for social justice, there was a failure to develop a consistent social ethic and, especially, to devise means to put into practice the theological insights that were found. His argument is that a weaving together of covenant theology and the methods of community organizing will produce precisely the strategies that are needed. His careful examination of the historic origins and driving impulses of community organizing provides confidence that such a partnership is possible. His account makes only too clear that it is desirable.

Denomination.

This book is an outstanding example of a significant, recent development in Baptist reflection on the full meaning of the Baptist heritage of covenant. One reason why the idea of covenant dropped out of Baptist attention for more than a century before its revival in the period of the 1990s was that it had become inward looking and parochial, concerned only with the inner life of the church and the relations of its members towards each other. During the seventeenth century, the affirmation that Christ was the covenant maker for the church was understood as a challenge to unjust powers of the state that were—in the eyes of Baptists and other Dissenters—usurping the authority of Christ, especially in denying people of all faiths and none the freedom of religion and belief. Covenant had a political dimension to it. During the great movements for social reform in the nineteenth century, and because of a growing commitment to ecumenism, covenant, however, now seemed to have less social relevance than it had. Recently, the universal scope of covenant has been recovered, with application to urgent issues of the day. In fact, this note was sounded in *Bound to Love* itself. Brian Haymes, for example, wrote: "Covenant is the basic term that proclaims God's desire to be in relationship with all humankind," and urged that it is covenant that should enable us to see that we can affirm the uniqueness of Jesus while "allowing for the work of God in other lives, in people of other faiths."[3] He appealed, as increasingly have done, to the Hebrew idea of a universal covenant with Noah. Though he did not spell this out, we should take note that God declares a covenant with "every living creature of all flesh that is on the earth" (Gen 9:16).

It is this universal desire of God for covenant relationship, not only with Israel and the church of Jesus Christ, but with all people and every creature in the organic world, that is the theological basis for developing a covenant shape to community organizing. Richard Weaver is unpacking in practical terms the insight that was already there in the renewal of covenant in the 1980s. Other Baptists are doing this too. David Gregory has been urging a vision of God's universal covenant as a motivation for caring for the environment, halting species extinction and seeking to moderate the disastrous results of human-made climate change. We need, he argues, a paradigm shift "to a wider vision . . . of covenant relationships that more adequately reflect the situation that the relationships between God, individuals and communities are also entwined with the life of the natural world."[4] Out of his pastoral experience of working with the homeless in Southend-on Sea, UK, Dan Pratt has argued that we must develop a pattern of church in which there is room for the homeless and the marginalized within covenantal life; even where people cannot make

3. Fiddes et al., *Bound to Love*, 66, 72.

4. Gregory, "Towards a Baptist Eco-Theology," 31–32.

the conventional covenant promises there must be a circle of covenant which embraces them.[5] Others have followed through the insight of Brian Haymes that we should discern a covenant relationship of God with members of other faiths, even though the detail of this is mysterious to us.[6] We should take seriously the fact that both Judaism and Islam regard themselves as living in covenant with God, and we will then also find signs of covenant in other faiths that do not explicitly make it part of their thinking.

The clue, I suggest, is to recognize that God makes many *different* covenants in our world, not a single, homogeneous covenant. There is no lowest common denominator of covenant, no standard model. So there is something altogether distinctive about the covenant God makes through Christ with the church. This alone is created through the preaching of the word of the gospel, and sealed with the sacraments of baptism and the Lord's Supper. This particular covenant relation has an essential part to play within God's mission in the world, and those who make these covenant promises are called to cooperate with God in bringing in a new creation of love, justice and peace. But God is also at work through Christ, often in a way hidden from us, in covenants with others which take other forms. This, I suggest, is why the church can gladly cooperate with others in movements for social justice.

Richard Weaver puts his theological and sociological finger on the nub of the issue when he claims that Baptists will never develop and practice a proper social ethic until they learn to work, not only with *individuals* who do not hold the same Christian faith, but with *organizations* outside the church that are working for peace, justice, and social cohesion. Writing from an Anabaptist perspective, Stuart Murray has similarly urged Baptists to make partnerships with non-Christian agencies for social action, writing that "partnership involves recognition both of common goals and the distinctive contribution each can make," and affirming that a vision of the kingdom of God requires us to "explore fruitful partnerships with agencies, communities, organizations and individuals who may not acknowledge Jesus as Lord but exhibit 'kingdom values' in their relationships, activities and concern for social transformation."[7] What Richard Weaver does, uniquely in this book, is to take the case-study of community organizing to work out practical forms that this partnership may take, which are applicable beyond one particular network. This makes the book essential reading for all those asking what "partnership" means in concrete situations. Moreover, by showing how community organizing has informed other faith communities' social justice work, particularly in

5. Sutcliffe-Pratt, *Covenant and Church*, 28–39.

6. Fiddes, "Covenant and Participation."

7. Murray, *Vast Minority*, 141–58.

Anglican and Roman Catholic churches, he invites Baptists to learn from the experience of ecumenical partners.

In fact, this book is a fine example of "receptive ecumenism," allowing Baptists to learn, both from the practice of other communions of faith, and from the theological reflection that Anglicans and Roman Catholics have done on community organizing. From a large amount of such material, Richard Weaver distills the six principles of "solidarity, subsidiarity, the common good, neighborliness, listening, and 'centring the margins.'" Bringing these into interaction with covenant theology he has deepened and extended the very idea of covenant in a way that is appropriate for our own age. This is the kind of new thinking that the Baptist theologians who gathered in 1985 under the banner of *Bound to Love* wanted to promote, and the present book not only meets their hopes but exceeds their expectations.

Preface

In this book we will examine the theory and practice of broad-based community organizing, as practiced by the Industrial Areas Foundation (IAF) in the US and Citizens UK in Wales and England. We will establish a critical dialogue between this approach to social change and Baptist social justice theology, ethics, and practice with impoverished and marginalized people. Community organizing is an approach that originated in the US in the 1940s, and which came to the UK in the late 1980s. It has been adopted by churches from many denominations, by other faith traditions, and by many civic society institutions because of its perceived effectiveness as a vehicle for leadership development and collective action for social justice and the common good. Despite much theological reflection and research by Baptists and others on social justice as a key area for Christian discipleship and action by churches, there is currently little practice of social justice by Baptist churches in Wales and England. In addition, community organizing has not been well explored by these churches. This book aims to redress that gap.

As we will discover, Baptists would benefit from a stronger theological ethic for social justice. Community organizing has informed other faith communities' social justice work, particularly in Anglican and Roman Catholic churches. However, there is little UK Baptist literature on community organizing. This book brings the growing community organizing literature into contact with Baptist church theology, ethics, and practice. Ruth Gouldbourne, a UK Baptist historian and theologian, argues that too often Baptists are reinventing the wheel, rather than letting it take them somewhere new.[1] This book will explore whether engaging with community organizing can take Baptists somewhere new in their approaches to social justice issues, and so strengthen a Baptist theological ethic for the practice of social justice.

1. Gouldbourne, *Reinventing the Wheel.*

Context and Motivation for the Research

I start this book with a little bit of my own story. In academic study, this is often called *reflexivity*, and so we locate ourselves in relation to our writing and research. Thus, my own story and positionality are important in writing a book about Baptists, community organizing, and social justice. They give some idea of the context and experiences I am writing from, because where you stand affects what you see.[2] Anthony Reddie is a UK theologian who specializes in Black theology. He highlights the experience of rootedness of our contributions to theological reflection, where "context and lived experience are essential dimensions of how we should think about Christian theology and its operation and relationship to the church."[3] The South Wales Valleys context and my lived experiences are therefore important in explaining why Baptist churches, community organizing and social justice is the focus of this book.

Every story begins in a particular place at a particular time. My story starts with the town of Rhymney. My mother's family are from this town, at the top of the Rhymney Valley in the South Wales Valleys. There has been family there for around the past two hundred years. They moved from being hill farmers near Brecon to work in the Iron Works in Rhymney. Thus, as my mother says, I am—at least distantly—related to half the town! My mother's father, my grandfather Doug, was a coal miner. He took what he called "early" retirement in 1985 at the end of the 1984–85 miner's strike. Doug was sixty-five and had worked for fifty years in coal mining as a coal mining engineer fixing the machinery above and below ground. He started as a colliery blacksmith at the age of fifteen shoeing the pit ponies who worked underground. He then moved from pit to pit as the coal mines across the top of the valleys closed over the years. He was offered roles as a foreman but was keen to stay as "one of the men." Doug knew that the coal mine he was working in at the time of the miners' strike was also likely to be closed. He was also a proud union member, first of "The Fed" and then, after 1945, of the National Union of Mineworkers. Doug's younger brother, my great-uncle Howard, worked as a train driver and was a member of the National Union of Rail, Maritime and Transport Workers. Howard also retired after fifty-one years working on the railways. He started stoking coal on steam trains at the age of fourteen and then later he drove trains on the South Wales Valleys lines.

2. Good recent examples of theologians writing about social justice and churches out of their own lived experiences are contained in numerous chapters in Cloke and Pears, *Mission in Marginal Places: Praxis*; Cloke and Pears, *Mission in Marginal Places: Stories*; Larner, *Confounding the Mighty*.

3. Reddie, "Baptist Identity," 230.

From both Doug and Howard I learned about their passion for social justice from a trade union perspective and its importance for maintaining strong communities. They learned about democracy through the unions and their meetings. These often took place in the chapels. They went to see their MP and founder of the National Health Service, Aneurin (Nye) Bevan, speak at outdoor events ahead of the UK general elections in 1945 and 1951. These included when Bevan famously spoke from the balcony of the town hall in Tredegar. Having left school at fourteen, Doug and Howard continued their education in democracy and other subjects through the miners' institutes and workmen's institutes in Tredegar and Bargoed in the South Wales coalfields. I learned about the importance of democracy and social justice from them. I also learned from them about the comradeship of coal miners and the sense of community in coal mining villages and towns. I learned this from members of my family who were shaped by growing up in these communities. Coal mining was dirty and dangerous work but it provided these villages with love, safety, and well-paid work. The miners' strike changed all that in the 1980s.

Idris Davies was a twentieth-century Welsh poet born in Rhymney. He is also a distant relative. He was my great-grandmother's cousin on my mother's side of the family. In one of his best-known poems he wrote, "There's a concert in the village to buy us boots and bread. / There's a service in the chapel to make us meek and mild."[4] Davies was writing about an earlier miners' strike in Rhymney. However, it could equally be applied to the strike in 1984–85 and the tensions in these communities. He contrasts the practical support provided within communities during miners' strikes with the response of chapels to the issues facing the communities.

I was a regular visitor to Rhymney visiting grandparents, Howard and other family from childhood and into my thirties. This experience helped me appreciate the negative impact on communities, both immediately and over the following years, when the main employer, coal mining, shuts down rapidly where there are few alternative forms of employment. I began to understand from family and from the experience of their neighbors about social injustices and their impact on communities and their institutions. These injustices included the high rates of poverty and unemployment, insecure and low-paid work, increase in drug and alcohol problems, and a declining belief among people that it was possible to change things for the better in their communities. The miners' strike started on March 6, 1984. And just a little over forty years to the day I am writing this preface.

I also learned about the importance of democracy and social justice from a Christian faith perspective from my parents, and from being part of

4. "Gwalia Deserta," in Davies, *Collected Poems*, 33.

Baptist churches. I spent much of my childhood not in Wales but in England. My father is a Baptist minister. From when I was six to sixteen years old, we lived as a family in the manse next to the church building in the center of a large council housing estate in Rushden, a small town in Northamptonshire. There too, the main employer, in this case shoe factories, also closed down over a short period in the mid-1980s. I was at infant and junior school with children whose parents were unemployed or in low-paying insecure jobs. Our estate faced many of the same challenges as Rhymney. I was told as a child that Rushden was close to the location which inspired the slough of despond in John Bunyan's *Pilgrim's Progress* and the comparison seemed apt. In the midst of this, I observed how my parents led a Baptist church that sought to respond to the social injustices faced by our neighbors and to be a church looking outwards to the local community. Many of the congregation were also from the estate and had lived experience of poverty and other social injustices. The church was also very involved in working with other churches in the town and with other organizations to tackle social justice issues. The church grew from a congregation and membership of around thirty people to one of more than two hundred people over ten years.

When we moved as a family to Oxford, we joined a Baptist church in the south of the city. The church met in a small modern building on a side street in an economically more impoverished part of the city. During my time as a member and then as a trustee and church secretary, Anne Wilkinson-Hayes was the minister. Anne had worked as the social action lead for the BUGB. She was instrumental in getting the church (and me) involved in social justice initiatives both locally in Oxford and globally, particularly through Jubilee 2000. This was an international campaign to cancel the unpayable debts of the world's poorest countries ahead of the new millennium. Alan and Ellie Kreider, Mennonite theologians, were part of the church, as was Sian Williams, who later married Stuart Murray. Murray, another Baptist theologian, was writing and teaching on Anabaptist thinking and practice. Several members of the church were part of an Anabaptist study group, which met in my parents' home. The church was also actively involved in working ecumenically, particularly with two Anglican church congregations in the same part of south Oxford. After university, and back in Oxford, I became a volunteer coordinator with the Gatehouse, a homeless project in the city center set up by churches in Oxford. I learned much about the issues faced by homeless and vulnerably housed people in the city. I also gained a fresh perspective of how regular "guests" and the people I got to know well during my time volunteering were often invisible to many others in the city who remained oblivious to them and the issues they faced. I became passionate about housing and homelessness issues, as well as issues facing the asylum seekers who were among the guests at "The Gatehouse." I came to realize that the Baptist churches in Wales and England which had shaped my faith and my involvement in social justice had been "unusual" Baptist churches among churches at the time and even now. These churches had been actively involved in social action and social justice, through looking outwards to their communities and seeking to respond to the injustices people were experiencing.

Prior to my involvement with "The Gatehouse," and between school and university, I had spent a year with the Baptist Missionary Society (now BMS World Mission). As part of this, I spent six months as part of a team of young people in Brazil. We spent time with several Baptist churches in the south of the country. These churches were meeting on the edges of cities or in small rural villages among impoverished and marginalized people. I gained some understanding of the immense economic poverty many in these communities were facing as well as the high levels of government corruption. In many places the physical closeness between extreme wealth and extreme poverty was very evident. Despite this, there often seemed to be obliviousness to this by economically richer people. There also appeared to be a lack of relationships between people from both sides of the community, even in the church congregations. I learned much from, and was much influenced by, the leading role that young people were playing in their churches and their passion for engaging with their communities and sharing the gospel. I also came to realize how little these churches were engaging in tackling social justice issues. I learned that many in the congregations of these small Baptist churches had "converted" from Catholic churches and had rejected what they saw as practices of Catholics. This included dancing, drinking alcohol, smoking, attending Carnival . . . and tackling social justice issues. Mission was narrowly understood as evangelism and the focus was on church growth. Reflecting later on this experience, I realized I wanted Baptists in Brazil, and elsewhere, to learn from the engagement of Roman Catholic churches in social justice, rather than doing the opposite of whatever Catholics do.

After studying and working with very rural communities in the high Andes in Peru, I worked for a Christian international development organization. This was initially with partner organizations in Central America, and then in a campaigning role. I led the organization's global advocacy work around climate change as a justice issue for several years. Campaign wins were rare and only very slow progress was being made at an international level towards a binding and just international climate agreement through ongoing UN climate talks and summits. I and others, both in my organization and beyond it, were on the look-out for approaches that were making change on justice issues. It was in the midst of this search that I discovered community organizing.

I have researched and written this book from a "position on the edge of the inside."[5] I will explore and critique community organizing as an insider, as someone who has been closely involved in it since 2011. I will also critique Baptists and their approach to social justice as an insider. I grew up in some unusual Baptist churches, in that they were teaching about and practicing social action and social justice as a key part of mission. I then became frustrated that not all Baptist churches are like this. I did not realize how different my experience of Baptist churches had been until I entered a different context. I have been involved in leadership roles in Baptist churches in Wales and England, including as a deacon (now a trustee) and as a church secretary. As a community organizer with Citizens UK, I organize with a range of education, faith, union, and community organizations. In organizing with churches, this has mostly been with Anglican and Roman Catholic churches and schools and colleges, but only rarely with Baptist churches. There are currently more community organizers in Citizens UK who are Baptists (including three who are or have been Baptist ministers) than there are Baptist churches in membership of Citizens UK alliances. When I first encountered community organizing, I do not recall seeing any Baptist churches present. This did not bother me at the time, but the relative lack of Baptist church involvement in organizing has increasingly bothered me over time. I started to wonder why that is and whether community organizing could provide a way for Baptist churches to be more involved in tackling social justice issues and making positive change in local communities. Hence this research and book.

Research Question and Sub-Questions

The overall research question for my doctoral thesis asked how an investigation of the theory and practice of community organizing can help form a more adequate theological ethic for the practice of social justice by Baptist churches in Wales and England.

In addition to answering this main question, the thesis also sought to answer several sub-questions:

- What is community organizing and how has it developed in the United States and in Wales and England?

5. Center for Action and Contemplation, "Edge of the Inside."

- How have churches that have embraced community organizing understood and used it?
- What can be learned from theological reflection on community organizing by theologians and organizers in the US and UK? Who do they reference and who has influenced them?
- To what extent has a theological ethic for the practice of social justice within Baptist churches in Wales and England developed during the period when community organizing was developing in England and Wales?
- What could Baptist churches in Wales and England learn from the practice of community organizing?
- What would Baptist social justice theology and ethics look like if it included lessons learned from community organizing?

Methodology and Research Process

We will undertake a critical analysis of the available literature throughout the study. We will do this to examine the philosophy and practice of community organizing. A literature review will also tell the story of the development of community organizing first in the US, and then in the UK. In addition, this review of the literature examines how churches have got involved in it, and how they have understood and used community organizing. A literature review will also be used to examine current theological reflection on community organizing by theologians and organizers in the US and UK. A review of available documents related to the Baptist Union of Wales (BUW) and the BUGB and their annual assemblies will be done. A critical analysis of the writing of four UK Baptist theologians will be undertaken. This literature review of Baptist union documents and the writings of theologians will be used to determine the development, and overall state, of a theological ethic for the practice of social justice within Baptist churches in Wales and England during the period when community organizing was developing there.

While this will primarily be a literature study, we will engage with other practitioners, ethicists, and theologians. I also include several stories. As we will discover, stories are important in order to get a better understanding of what is going on through community organizing. Therefore, as part of the methodology for this research, we will include stories from community organizing in Wales and England to explain the approach. These stories will also help provide a deeper understanding of the experience and learning of churches engaged in organizing. In addition, we will tell the story of Baptist assemblies of two unions, and Baptist theological writing from the late 1980s to 2010. In doing this, we will focus on the development of a shared theological ethic for the practice of social justice among Baptists in Wales and England.

Methodologically, I have done reflexive practice on my experience of community organizing and my involvement with Baptist churches. I will use this experience and reflection to anchor the book. In doing this, I am being explicit about my own positionality in the research. I am bringing an insider understanding of two worlds into my research, that of Baptists and of community organizing, and their approaches to social justice.

This study will argue for the importance of listening to marginalized and impoverished people to strengthen the theological ethic of social justice in Baptist churches in Wales and England. I recognize that I have lived in a range of communities and contexts. For the last fourteen years this has largely been in South Wales, in and around the South Wales Valleys. I have been actively involved in three Baptist churches in this area. It can be argued that these communities have been, and are, oppressed and marginalized within the UK and are currently among the most economically impoverished. My research in this study is informed by living and working and worshipping in this context. Thus, this study will seek to understand how focusing on the perspectives of people currently on the margins can strengthen a theological ethic. Some words from Idris Davies's poem "Gwalia Deserta" are helpful:

> O what can you give me? Say the sad bells of Rhymney.
> Is there hope for the future? Cry the brown bells of Merthyr.
> Who made the mineowner? Say the black bells of Rhondda.
> And who robbed the miner? Cry the grim bells of Blaina.
> They will plunder willy-nilly, say the bells of Caerphilly.
> They have fangs, they have teeth! Shout the loud bells of Neath.
> To the south, things are sullen, say the pink bells of Brecon.
> Even God is uneasy, say the moist bells of Swansea.
> Put the vandals in court! Cry the bells of Newport.
> All would be well if- if- if- say the green bells of Cardiff.
> Why so worried, sisters, why? Sing the silver bells of Wye.[6]

These words highlight that how things look depends on where you are. Rhymney, Merthyr, and Blaina are towns that were built on coal mining. These were among the communities that were most impacted by strikes and mine closures. In contrast, Cardiff, Brecon, and the Wye Valley were areas of relative economic prosperity and less directly affected by the coal-mining strikes.

6. "Gwalia Deserta," in Davies, *Collected Poems*, 34–35.

Therefore, they show the different perspectives of communities in the South Wales coalfields compared to towns and cities outside of this area. As we will explore, this also highlights how churches outside of, or with little relationship with, impoverished and marginalized communities understand the issues facing these communities.

Structure of the Argument

In the first half of the book, we explore the development of community organizing first in the United States and then in England and Wales (ch. 1). We then investigate how churches have understood and used community organizing (ch. 2), and then have reflected theologically on their practice of it, extrapolating six principles from this current theological reflection (ch. 3). These six principles are solidarity, subsidiarity, the common good, neighborliness, listening, and centering the margins. These principles are drawn from theological reflection mainly by Catholic and Anglican theologians.

In the second half, we proceed to examine the development of a theological ethic for the practice of social justice within Baptist churches in Wales and England. In dialogue with these six principles, we explore how Baptists have engaged with them in developing a Baptist ethic for the practice of social justice during the period when community organizing was developing in England and Wales. We cover the period from the late 1980s to 2010, thus considering the period from the launch of the first community organizing alliances in Wales and England to the formation of Citizens UK (chs. 4–5). In chapter 4, we focus on what was being discussed at assemblies of the BUW and the BUGB. In chapter 5, we explore the main themes in the writing of four UK Baptist theologians and how these engage with the six principles. Chapter 6 will then propose a way forward for Baptist social justice theology and ethics through engagement with community organizing and the six principles. I will seek to develop the rudiments of a Baptist theology and practice for social justice that brings both community organizing and Baptist thinking together in a new synthesis.

Acknowledgments

TO JENNIE, SAMUEL, FINN, AND OWAIN. Dw i'n caru chi cymaint, a dw i mor falch ohonoch chi. Dw i'n edrych ymlaen at yr antur nesaf.

To Mum and Dad, my sisters Liz and Jo, my grandparents, and Great-Uncle Howard, from whom I have learned so much about the importance of social justice in the South Wales Valleys, across the UK, and globally. A particular thanks to Dad, for the loan of many useful books and always being willing to discuss ideas as my thinking developed over the years and in the course of my research.

To people in all the Baptist churches I have been a member of and involved in, and in particular to Anne and Mark Wilkinson-Hayes, Alan and Ellie Kreider, Sian Murray-Williams, Anthony and Amanda Clarke, Jeanette Turner, Paula Hughes, and Rosa and Francis Hunt.

To current and former staff, research fellows, and fellow students at IBTS and the Vrije Universiteit Amsterdam, and in particular to the members of the ethics research group and the 2020 cohort.

To current and former colleagues and students at Coleg y Bedyddwyr Caerdydd/Cardiff Baptist College and Cardiff University.

To current and former colleagues and leaders at Citizens Cymru Wales and Citizens UK.

To Alexis Pacheco, Javier Barrios, Serguem Jessui Silva, and all those from whom I learned about the practice of liberation theology in Nicaragua, El Salvador, Honduras, and Brazil.

To staff at Undeb Bedyddwyr Cymru/Baptist Union of Wales in Caerfyrddin/Carmarthen and the Angus Library, Regent's Park College, Oxford, for your welcome while I was researching the archives of the two Baptist Unions and the *Baptist Times* newspaper.

To my supervisors, David Gushee and Jim Purves, for all your encouragement, guidance, and insightful comments.

To Dion Forster, Stefan Paas, Henk Bakker, Paul Fiddes, and Sondra Wheeler, for your excellent comments and questions as members of my doctoral board at the Vrije Universiteit Amsterdam.

To Paul Fiddes, for his foreword to this book based on my doctoral thesis.

Abbreviations

BMS	Baptist Missionary Society
BUGB	Baptist Union of Great Britain
BUILD	Baltimoreans United in Leadership Development
BUW	Baptist Union of Wales
COF	Community Organizing Foundation
COPS	Communities Organized for Public Service
CST	Catholic Social Teaching
EBC	East Brooklyn Congregations
IAF	Industrial Areas Foundation
TELCO	The East London Communities Organisation
WIN	Washington Interfaith Network

Chapter 1

The Development and Practice of Community Organizing in the US and UK

1.1 Introduction

It was a cold clear evening in Clapham Junction in late 2011 as we gathered for the South London Citizens Delegates' Assembly and I encountered broad-based community organizing in the UK for the first time. I had been invited to be part of the delegation from St Peter's, an Anglican church meeting on the Winstanley Estate on the "wrong side of the railway tracks" in Clapham, southwest London. I was living in Wales and working in London for part of the week at the time and St Peter's had become my "midweek" church. I often stayed with friends who had moved into a flat in one of the tower blocks to be an "intentional mission community" in the large social housing estate, seeking to build relationships with people from across the estate. The Delegates' Assembly was held in Battersea Arts Centre, an iconic venue locally. I was struck by the number of people there. The main hall was packed with around four hundred people. I was very struck by the diversity of the participants, and the central involvement of faith institutions. It felt like South London with people of many ethnicities, religions, and economic backgrounds there, but all gathered together in one meeting. I had not seen a gathering like this before. There were groups from Roman Catholic and Anglican parishes and primary schools, mosques and Jewish synagogues, high schools and university student unions, and tenants and residents' associations. There was a roll call of all the institutions present—more than fifty of them in total, collectively representing tens of thousands of people. Leaders from each member institution loudly announced how many were there from their organization, how their involvement was part of them putting their faith or values into action, how much they paid each year in membership dues to be part of South London Citizens—and proclaiming their excitement at being there for the Delegates' Assembly. It felt powerful.

We were all there to decide together on the priorities for this Citizens UK chapter for the London mayoral elections in May 2012. The gathering was just months after the nights of widespread rioting in South London and elsewhere in the UK in August 2011. Institutions were still trying to work out how best to respond. The rioting had shocked many churches and other groups into seeking to build stronger relationships with those on the other side of the tracks in Clapham and in other parts of the city. People directly affected by social justice issues shared their personal experiences through testimonies. They made clear asks for what they wanted to change and for solutions to issues such as low wages, knife crime, and families living in overcrowded and damp rented accommodation. Jimmy Mizen, a sixteen-year-old Catholic teenager, had been stabbed to death in a bakery on his way home from school a few years before. His parents, Barry and Margaret Mizen, shared powerfully how his death had inspired them, their Roman Catholic parish, Jimmy's Roman Catholic school, and many other organizations in South London to persuade local shops and businesses to become CitySafe havens. The program had begun to help reduce the number of young people dying violent deaths in South London and they wanted the London mayor to take further action.[1] These were problems that I was also passionate about and had sometimes heard about on the news. However, in this assembly those directly affected were not being talked about and on the margins. Instead, they were playing central roles in the campaigns and were on stage speaking powerfully about these social injustices and what they were doing to tackle them. I resolved to find out more about South London Citizens and broad-based community organizing.

In this chapter I will look to describe what underpins the practice of community organizing I witnessed in that South London Citizens Delegates' Assembly—gathering power by uniting diverse people and institutions in a

1. For more on the story of the Mizen family and the CitySafe campaign, see Ivereigh, *Faithful Citizens*, 47–51.

common cause and by building relationships with those who have power. As part of this, I will draw on my personal experience. Having attended the Delegates' Assembly and some further events, I went on to do a six day residential training course in community organizing run by Citizens UK in East London in 2013. I then joined the leadership team to develop and launch two Citizens alliances in Wales, and became a community organizer in Wales with Citizens UK in July 2015.

However, the practice of broad-based community organizing did not begin in London or Wales, but in the United States. That is where our story begins.

The chapter is divided into four main sections. Section 1.2 will focus on the origins of community organizing in the United States. Section 1.3 examines major developments in broad-based community organizing in the United States and the deepening connection with faith institutions. Section 1.4 then examines the development of broad-based community organizing in the United Kingdom. Then section 1.5 focuses on the contemporary practice of broad-based community organizing in Wales and England.

1.2 The Origins of Community Organizing in the United States

Saul Alinsky, a community activist and political theorist, initially developed the practices of building power through community organizing in Chicago in the 1930s. Alinsky wrote two key books on community organizing, *Reveille for Radicals* and *Rules for Radicals*. The first of these books describes the political philosophy and approach of community organizing. Mary Beth Rogers, a US writer and political organizer, describes *Reveille for Radicals* as a blueprint for developing power organizations among poor people in urban neighborhoods.[2] Alinsky continually agitates for a politics rooted in people's lives:

> I start from where the world is, as it is, not as I would like it to be. That we accept the world as it is does not in any sense weaken our desire to change it into what we believe it should be.[3]

Alinsky argues effectively that thinking of the two "worlds"—the present and the promised future—in dialogue together leads to action. In *Rules for Radicals*, his second and final book, Alinsky aims to demonstrate how community

2. Rogers, *Cold Anger*, 86.
3. Alinsky, *Reveille for Radicals*, 32.

organizing practices enable people to, as he writes, "organize for power: how to get it and use it."[4] For Alinsky:

> Power is the very essence, the dynamo of life. It is the power of the heart pumping blood and sustaining life in the body. It is the power of active citizen participation, pulsing upwards, providing a unified strength for a common purpose.[5]

Rogers understands that Alinsky's basic philosophy came directly from Thomas Jefferson's concept of neighborhood wards as small groups of people who could meet regularly to work out everyday problems. Alinsky wanted to make this democratic system work by organizing to build people power.[6] Nicholas von Hoffman, a community organizer and a friend and colleague of Alinsky, notes that democracy was Alinsky's passion. Alinsky understood democracy as the best political means available, not as an end in itself, but to achieve the values of freedom, equality, justice, peace, and the right to dissent.[7]

Von Hoffman argues that *Rules for Radicals* demonstrates Alinsky's passion for ethics. He notes that the book "is a treatise on how men and women of action, people who do not shun power or its uses, can be both effective and ethical." Von Hoffman goes on to argue that "Alinsky was a rare, maybe a unique ethical teacher because he was a man from the trenches who spoke with the benefit of experience which professors and ministers of religion ordinarily do not have." Both of Alinsky's books contain the word "radical" in their titles. Von Hoffman understands that Alinsky's "frequent use of the word *radical* came . . . from a desire to make a distinction between those who talk a good game (liberals mostly in Saul's estimation) and those who play one (radicals)."[8]

In developing these practices of community organizing, Alinsky was influenced by a number of experiences. This certainly included the 1930s and the impact of the financial crash and the Great Depression.[9] In addition, he grew up in a Jewish family and neighborhood. The beliefs and practices of Judaism helped form him, for example, the shtetl tradition of communal self-organization, and the story of the Exodus and of Jeremiah "seeking the welfare of the city."[10]

4. Alinsky, *Rules for Radicals*, 10.
5. Alinsky, *Rules for Radicals*, 51.
6. Rogers, *Cold Anger*, 83–85.
7. Von Hoffman, *Radical*, 57.
8. Von Hoffman, *Radical*, 181.
9. Alinsky, *Reveille for Radicals*, viii.
10. Bretherton, *Resurrecting Democracy*, 23.

Luke Bretherton has studied community organizing extensively.[11] In *Resurrecting Democracy*, Bretherton describes how Alinsky employed ethnographic research methods to study organized crime and the mafia in the Back of the Yards area in Chicago. Through this research, he came to see the importance of neighborhoods as areas "within which meaningful social identities and structures were forged." He also came to see the importance of trusting and of strong personal relationships between people.[12] Alinsky discerned that relational power—the power developed through relationships between people and organizations—is the only means available to act for those unable to access economic or state power. Alinsky also learned the importance of local knowledge. He understood that this was developed through sustained attention to people in a community, while simultaneously seeking to develop understanding of the relationships and social transformations going on within these communities.[13] In addition, Alinsky learned the importance of building on the values of reciprocity, mutuality, and cooperation that were practiced in labor organizing. Through engaging with labor organizers, Alinsky developed an understanding of how to organize large public assemblies. He also learned how to focus attention on the issues prioritized by people living in an area, how to raise money, and how to recruit member organizations.[14]

Alinsky highlights the importance of faith in people as a key to building power:

> Believing in people, the radical has the job of organizing people so that they will have the power and opportunity to best meet each unforeseeable future crisis as they move ahead to realize these values of equality, justice, freedom, the preciousness of human life, and all those rights and values propounded by Judeo-Christianity and democratic tradition.[15]

Alinsky formed close relationships with Bishop Bernard Sheil, from the Catholic Archdiocese of Chicago, and Jacques Maritain, a Roman Catholic philosopher. Von Hoffman highlights the importance of the relationship with

11. Luke Bretherton first became involved in community organizing in London and worked closely with community organizing in the US. He has an academic focus on theology and politics. Bretherton's key books in relation to community organizing and its practice include *Christianity and Contemporary Politics*; *Resurrecting Democracy*; *Christ and the Common Life*. In 2020 he started a community organizing podcast: *Listen, Organize, Act!*

12. Bretherton, *Resurrecting Democracy*, 26.

13. Bretherton, *Resurrecting Democracy*, 28.

14. Bretherton, *Resurrecting Democracy*, 31.

15. Alinsky, *Reveille for Radicals*, xiv.

Maritain and notes that Alinsky learned from him about the importance of the common good. Alinsky also learned from Maritain about "the source of authority residing in the people," and the importance of building on this.[16] Alinsky both influenced, and worked closely with, the Catholic Church in the US. He founded the IAF in 1940 with board members including Bishop Sheil.[17] The purpose of the IAF was "to restore the democratic way of life to modern industrial society."[18]

Rogers notes that Catholic churches became the backbone of these early Organizing initiatives. She highlights the support of Bishop Sheil and Monsignor John O'Grady who thought community organizing could help urban churches to survive.[19] Rogers also highlights that many urban Protestant churches also supported the IAF. Bretherton notes that an interactive dialogue between community organizing and liberal Protestantism developed from the late 1960s onwards in the US. This occurred as more Protestant clergy participated, with the work of Reinhold Niebuhr a particular point of reference.[20] However, Alinsky underlines why he doesn't use Christian ethics with churches:

> In a mass organization you can't go outside of people's actual experience. I've been asked, for example, why I never talk to a Catholic priest or a protestant minister or a rabbi in terms of the Judeo-Christian ethic or the Ten Commandments or the Sermon on the Mount. Instead, I approach them on the basis of their own self-interest, the welfare of their church, even its physical property. If I approached them in a moralistic way, it would be outside of their experience, because Christianity and Judeo-Christianity are outside of the experience of organized religion.[21]

Thus, for Alinsky, it was a church's self-interest in continuing to have a presence, rather than Jesus' teaching on tackling injustices, that helped church leaders engage with community organizing. Alinsky goes on to argue that people "don't like to step abruptly out of the security of familiar experience; they need a bridge to cross from their own experience to a new way."[22] He argues that community organizing can provide that bridge for churches and

16. Von Hoffman, *Radical*, 139.
17. Pierce, *Reveille for a New Generation*, 107.
18. Rogers, *Cold Anger*, 83.
19. Rogers, *Cold Anger*, 86.
20. Bretherton, *Resurrecting Democracy*, 90.
21. Alinsky, *Reveille for Radicals*, xvi.
22. Alinsky, *Reveille for Radicals*, xxi.

leaders in churches. At the same time, he is being very harsh in his criticism of organized religion in living up to Judeo-Christian teaching. As Von Hoffman underlines, Alinsky understood "the duality of religious institutions and the people who ran them."[23] For example, in teaching about tactics for making change, Alinsky highlights the need to "make the enemy live up to their own book of rules. . . . They can no more obey their own rules than the Christian church can live up to Christianity."[24] So, Alinsky appears to be very sceptical about churches living out the gospel and Jesus' teachings.[25]

It may, therefore, seem surprising that the first people's organization formed by Alinsky in the predominantly Catholic Back of the Yards area of Chicago "included all of the churches . . . of this community."[26] However, Alinsky does not highlight why as Catholics or churches they were involved, beyond the ability of people to participate in democracy through their involvement. Alinsky does recognize that:

> The churches were among the few institutions that remained voluntarily in those poor neighborhoods, already organized and providing people with at least some understanding of the dynamics of group participation.[27]

Thus, this provides a good reason why Alinsky's approach to community organizing focused on churches. This also presents a good rationale for churches to get involved.

Importantly, Alinsky was focused on building alliances of *institutions*, such as churches, rather than of individual people. He understands that by doing this, organizing is not a threat to any individual existing institution. Similarly, he notes that churches, and other existing community organizations, may well be hostile towards a new people's organization in the community because they see it as "a basic threat to their own identity and security."[28] Alinsky appears to argue that churches feel threatened because they have not been doing well at developing leaders or acting for justice so far. Alinsky thus concludes *Reveille for Radicals* in 1946 with this stinging provocation:

23. Von Hoffman, *Radical*, 159.

24. Alinsky, *Reveille for Radicals*, 128.

25. In contrast, what the IAF has done since the 1970s, and the focus of Citizens UK, has been to seek to do this and to address organizing in the context of Jesus' teaching and biblical teaching.

26. Alinsky, *Reveille for Radicals*, 48.

27. Rogers, *Cold Anger*, 87.

28. Alinsky, *Reveille for Radicals*, 85.

> Organized religion has too often followed the road of other people's institutions. . . . The result has been that today much of organized religion is materialistically solvent but spiritually bankrupt.[29]

In an afterword to the 1969 edition of the book, Alinsky follows up on this and writes:

> These words could just as well have been written twenty-three minutes ago instead of twenty-three years ago. A few years ago we witnessed a commitment, a leadership and great contribution by organized religion at the beginning of the civil rights movement, but this burst of energy seems to have waned.[30]

Alinsky then ends with a challenge to the church: "It must now address itself to its role of being a vital catalyst in creating those circumstances . . . whereby people will have the ability to act and the power to operate as free citizens in a free society."[31] We will examine the extent to which churches have responded to this challenge through their engagement in community organizing later in this chapter, in sections 1.3—1.5, as well as in chapters 2–3.

It is noticeable that many of the early IAF community organizers had theological training. For example, Edward Chambers, a Roman Catholic and one of the first community organizers with Saul Alinsky, had studied at a Benedictine seminary and had also spent time with Dorothy Day, and the Catholic Worker Movement, before becoming an organizer with Alinsky.[32] Chambers himself describes how he travelled to Europe where he encountered the French priest-worker movement and was "radicalized by Europe's progressive Catholic leaders," and ultimately did not become a Roman Catholic priest.[33] Rogers highlights that at the time she was writing her book, "about one-third of the IAF's permanent organizers were nuns, priests, ministers or former associates of religious-oriented organisations."[34]

Thus, we observe that community organizing practices were initially formed from three main traditions: Judaism, the labor movement, and Christianity. Roman Catholic parishes and unions played key roles in these early alliances organized by Saul Alinsky. These alliances won campaign victories. However, they often did not remain together as alliances for long and were often only organizing among specific neighborhoods in a city. Von Hoffman

29. Alinsky, *Reveille for Radicals*, 200.
30. Alinsky, *Reveille for Radicals*, 221.
31. Alinsky, *Reveille for Radicals*, 223.
32. Chambers, *Roots for Radicals*, 91–94.
33. Chambers, *Roots for Radicals*, 90.
34. Rogers, *Cold Anger*, 178.

notes that in the late 1960s and before his death in 1972, Alinsky recognized that organizing in a specific neighborhood made less sense than it had earlier.[35] As we will discover in the next section, community organizing alliances started to become ones that brought together churches and other institutions from across the diversity of a city. Thus, these alliances were organizing institutions in a much larger geographical area, rather than within a specific neighborhood.

1.3 Major Developments in Broad-Based Community Organizing in the United States

Edward Chambers, Ernesto Cortes, Michael Gecan, and Arnie Graf were among the lead organizers of the IAF in the 1970s in the United States. These were four key figures in the development of broad-based community organizing and the 'modern IAF.' Following Alinsky's death, Chambers and Cortes undertook a self-conscious engagement with Catholic Social Teaching (CST) and sought to produce a theological basis for community organizing.[36] They came to understand community organizing as emerging from the intertwined values of family and religion.[37] The IAF produced a booklet in 1978 entitled *Organizing for Family and Congregations* which was largely written by Michael Gecan. This was a foundational document for the post-Alinsky IAF. The front piece of *Organizing for Family and Congregations* includes this verse from 2 Tim 1:7: "God did not give us a spirit of timidity but a spirit of power and love and self-control."[38]

The lead organizers of the IAF also undertook a critical reflection on its practice. Bretherton names four theologians in particular with whom these organizers engaged during this process: James Cone, Stanley Hauerwas, Walter Wink, and Walter Brueggemann.[39] Bretherton highlights that "on the theological side, Walter Brueggemann's work was felt to be the most relevant and significant."[40] Bretherton then stops here and adds no more detail. In chapters 2–3 I will analyze further the connections made in the current literature with these and other theologians.

35. Von Hoffman, *Radical*, 184.
36. Sec. 3.1.2 examines the influence of CST on community organizing.
37. Bretherton, *Resurrecting Democracy*, 41.
38. Pierce, *Reveille for a New Generation*, 372.
39. Bretherton, *Resurrecting Democracy*, 42.
40. Bretherton, *Resurrecting Democracy*, 43.

Covenant Relationships for Radicals

Chambers, in *Roots for Radicals*, updates Alinsky's *Reveille for Radicals* and *Rules for Radicals* and outlines a more humane and values-driven dimension to organizing. Michael Cowan argues that "community organizing in its modern form was invented by Alinsky, but the most significant figure in its spread and development in the last half of the twentieth century was Ed Chambers."[41] Alinsky focused on power politics. Through using this, churches and unions were able to bring lots of people together, and thus generate more people-power than their opponents in campaigns. In contrast, Chambers, with his theological training, thought religious ideas and traditions might provide important values to sustain participatory politics.[42] He considered what community organizing meant to people in churches:

> We worked with people in the churches, and their language was the language of the gospel. Their language was nothing like Alinsky's language. His language was power talk. Tough, abrasive, confrontational, full of ridicule. And those are really non-Christian concepts.[43]

From this engagement with churches, Chambers found a way of bringing these two different languages together. He focused on the tension between the world as it should be, with its language of love and justice, and the world as it is, with its language of power.[44] Community organizing then enables churches, and other organizations, to work for love and justice in the world as it is where power dominates.

Chambers takes spirituality very seriously in broad-based community organizing. He writes in much more religious language than Gecan, Cortes or Graf.[45] As we noted earlier, he was central to introducing theological engagement and reflection among community organizers in the US. Many of the organizers were themselves part of churches as well as predominantly working with churches from a wide range of denominations. Chambers asserts that broad-based community organizations "exist to act for justice with power."[46] As Chambers notes, in the 1980s the IAF began to build broader and deeper alliances. These alliances were not just organizing poor people but involved middle class people too.[47] This move was also about shifting to form

41. Michael Cowan, in Chambers, *Roots for Radicals*, viii.
42. Warren, *Dry Bones Rattling*, 47.
43. Von Hoffman, *Radical*, 159.
44. Chambers, *Roots for Radicals*, 16–20.
45. Stout, "Blessed Are the Organized."
46. Chambers, *Roots for Radicals*, 60.
47. Chambers, *Roots for Radicals*, 59.

long-lasting alliances. These alliances were ethnically diverse and involved institutions across a number of communities rather than just within one local community.

Ernesto Cortes, a Roman Catholic and lead organizer with the IAF, led the transformation of the community organizing approach to be more relational.[48] This involved deeper and more lasting connections with institutions, and a greater focus on training community leaders.[49] Cortes studied theology in graduate school and engaged mostly Protestant theologians such as Reinhold Niebuhr, Paul Tillich, and Dietrich Bonhoeffer. Cortes then went on to study CST.[50]

Cortes has not yet written a full book on community organizing. However, *Cold Anger*, written by Mary Beth Rogers and published in 1990, is structured around his life and influence and is based on interviews with Cortes.[51] This also makes it an earlier source than several of the other key texts cited on community organizing. Rogers writes from the perspective of her long-standing involvement in politics in Texas where Cortes is located. In introducing the book, she provides a good alternative description of what community organizing had become by this time:

> A new intervention in politics by working poor people who incorporate their religious values into a struggle for power and visibility. It is about women and men . . . who promote public and private hope, political and personal responsibility, community and individual transformation. Even joy.[52]

The work of the political philosopher Hannah Arendt has been influential in community organizing. Rogers remarks that "what Hannah Arendt called

48. Ernesto Cortes was the founding lead organizer of Communities Organized for Public Services (COPS) in San Antonio Texas in 1974, the longest-running current IAF alliance. COPS and other IAF alliances in Texas have had a major impact on incorporating the Latino population into the political landscape in that state. Cortes became the co-executive director of the national IAF after the retirement of Ed Chambers and continues to oversee the development of the West/Southwest IAF (Pierce, *Reveille for a New Generation*, 139).

49. Warren notes that the IAF insists upon calling all of its participants "leaders" to emphasize their connections to fellow congregants and neighbors. The IAF involves clergy and many lay leaders and has been good at encouraging women to emerge as leaders, "women who have historically shouldered the burden for community caring" (Warren, *Dry Bones Rattling*, 31).

50. Warren, *Dry Bones Rattling*, 58.

51. Another book, which I explore further later, based on conversations with Ernesto Cortes and from organizing stories is Stout, *Blessed Are the Organized.*

52. Rogers, *Cold Anger*, 1.

the joy of public happiness is in Ernie Cortes contagious. The public square belongs to everyone, he says; fill it![53] In highlighting the focus on building power through organizing, Rogers quotes Cortes where he argues that "we organize people around their values—not just issues. The issues fade and they lose interest. But what they really care about remains—family, dignity, justice and hope. And we need power to protect what we value."[54] In chapter 2, we will explore what this has meant for churches in understanding power and their values and interests. We will also explore how community organizing has enabled them to act on them through their relationships with others.

A major focus in community organizing is on strengthening institutions in civic society such as churches, schools and colleges. Cortes, in *Rebuilding Our Institutions*, highlights that it is in these intermediary institutions that we learn the habits and practices needed for a vibrant democratic culture.[55] In highlighting the need to strengthen these mediating institutions, Cortes notes that "the real conversations of engagement—of listening, and particularly of listening to another person as someone with a different perspective, a different point of view, a different story or history—rarely take place anymore."[56] Cortes argues for *mediating organizations* that emphasize practices which "teach the customs and habits necessary for the negotiation of competing values."[57]

Michael Gecan, a Roman Catholic, was a community organizer with the IAF for more than forty years. Gecan describes community organizing as the work of enabling people to come together to build power to effect democratic change where they live and work. Through this, people are able to contribute to building community.[58] Gecan argues that the role of clergy is to model the four main tools of community organizing, namely individual meetings, teaching and training, power analysis, and action and evaluation. The role of clergy is thus also to develop others to model these tools. For Gecan, community

53. Rogers, *Cold Anger*, iv.

54. Rogers, *Cold Anger*, 31.

55. Cortes, *Rebuilding Our Institutions*, 3. A version of this short book was published under the title "Toward a Democratic Culture."

56. Cortes, *Rebuilding Our Institutions*, 6.

57. Cortes, *Rebuilding Our Institutions*, 27.

58. Luke Bretherton, "What Is Community Organizing?" Michael Gecan was the lead organizer of East Brooklyn Churches (EBC) in New York City in the 1980s when this alliance conceived and implemented the Nehemiah Plan that rebuilt the East New York community with more than six thousand new, owner-occupied homes. Gecan became a co-executive director of the national IAF after the retirement of Ed Chambers and oversaw the development of the Metro IAF (Pierce, *Reveille for a New Generation*, 117). Three key books by Michael Gecan are *Going Public*; *Effective Organizing*; *People's Institutions in Decline*.

organizing enables people to build relationships across difference and across boundaries. It therefore puts pressure on institutions to think through how they relate to others across difference.[59]

Gecan and Jonathan Lange highlight a much-used phrase in community organizing which originated with Chambers. This phrase states that "all organizing is dis-organizing and re-organizing."[60] They note, in writing about (and to) trade unions,

> In many cases, your vision is not new; it has been around a while and perhaps has lost some of its cutting edge. The original members who had the courage to take on their employers and demand recognition for their union are often long gone. Many of the newer and younger workers don't know that history of struggle to establish the union and therefore take it for granted.[61]

Much of this could also be applied to churches, including Baptist churches and their early experience of persecution and struggle. We will explore this further in chapters 4–5.

Arnie Graf is a very experienced Jewish community organizer with the IAF. Although there is little in the organizing literature about its links to the US civil rights movement, Graf highlights his involvement in this movement in the 1960s. Through this he came to be involved with community organizing.[62] This social justice movement and the speeches of Martin Luther King Jr., himself a Baptist minister, are drawn on by many community organizers and leaders.

A much less well-known leader of the US civil rights movement was Bayard Rustin. Rustin understood that the experience of powerlessness is often as corrupting as the concentration of power in the hands of the few.[63] Martin Luther King is quoted as saying that "power is not only desirable, but is necessary to implement the demands of love and justice."[64] Graf highlights that Ella Baker, one of the founders of the US civil rights movement, focused on the tradition of community organizing and the emphasis on the long-term development of leadership in ordinary women and men.[65] One area where community organizing is drawing on the development of the civil rights

59. Gecan, "Change Maker Chat."
60. Lange and Gecan, *Using the Tools*, 6.
61. Lange and Gecan, *Using the Tools*, 5.
62. Graf, *Lessons Learned*, 10.
63. Long, *I Must Resist*.
64. King, *Where Do We Go*, 37.
65. Graf, *Lessons Learned*, 12.

movement is when it is described as slow, patient, and respectful work. In *I've Got the Light of Freedom*, Charles Payne argues that in "overemphasizing the movement's more dramatic features, we undervalue the patient and sustained effort, the slow, respectful work, that made the dramatic moments possible." Payne notes that Ella Baker called this "spadework."[66] I note the influence of the US civil rights movement in the development of the IAF and particularly on the involvement of Black Baptist churches.

Graf was a co-executive director of the IAF. As an organizer, he helped to rebuild a key IAF alliance—Baltimoreans United in Leadership Development (BUILD)—in Baltimore, Maryland. Monsignor Clare O'Dwyer and Revd. Vernon Dobson, minister of Union Baptist Church, played key roles in this rebuilding process.[67] Baltimore was the first predominantly African American city that the IAF had entered, seeking to build a broad-based organization, since the late 1960s. Graf highlights the central role of leaders and members from Union Baptist Church, a Black Baptist church in Baltimore, in actions that helped to build the power and membership of BUILD and then to go on to win the living wage campaign in Baltimore.[68] As Lange highlights, BUILD was predominantly built up of Black-majority Protestant and Roman Catholic churches. These churches initially did a lot of service provision among poor communities. However, many of the people accessing these services during the week were not part of the church on Sundays. A key area was therefore to build deep relationships between these groups as part of the living wage campaign. Many of these meetings happened in the basement of Union Baptist Church. These meetings, and the involvement of the churches, created the political space to win change through the introduction of a living wage in the city.[69]

Graf also organized another IAF alliance—Washington Interfaith Network (WIN)—in the District of Columbia. It is striking that many of the Baptist churches involved in WIN, in the BUILD alliance, and in other IAF alliances are those where the majority of members and congregations are African American. It is not hard to see the reasons for engaging Black-majority churches to build people power to bring about change in a predominantly African American city. As Graf highlights, "The only thing I was certain of from the start, was that any effort in DC had to begin with the Black church."[70]

66. Payne, *I've Got the Light*, 264.

67. Pierce, *Reveille for a New Generation*, 145.

68. Graf, *Lessons Learned*, 119.

69. Bretherton, "Campaigns as Public Action."

70. Graf, *Lessons Learned*, 128.

Samuel Freedman, in his book *Upon This Rock*, writes powerfully about Revd. Johnny Ray Youngblood, minister at St Paul Community Baptist Church in Brooklyn, New York, and chair of EBC. Freedman describes EBC as an IAF alliance of fifty-two churches and one synagogue.[71] This book is a very detailed description of a Black Baptist church involved in community organizing. It details the struggles and challenges facing the church and its leadership as well as those facing the broader community.

Youngblood was central to organizing for the Nehemiah affordable housing program. The program was named after the biblical prophet of a Jewish nation staggering home from forced exile which then rebuilt Jerusalem.[72] Freedman describes how Youngblood was the "unwitting originator" of the program, after Gecan heard him preach from the book of Nehemiah.[73] Youngblood preached that "to rebuild oneself was to rebuild the community, and to rebuild the community was to rebuild oneself."[74] From the stories Gecan tells in his book *Going Public*, it appears that Youngblood and the St Paul Community Baptist Church were central to EBC and its success as an alliance. Chambers also highlights the Nehemiah housing program as a key example of the power of broad-based community organizing. He describes it as a story of imagination and hope coming together in a poor area, becoming a model for communities throughout the US.[75]

Warren, in picking up a theme in Graf, Pierce, and Gecan's writing, highlights the central importance of the involvement of Black Baptist churches in IAF alliances.[76] They all draw heavily on the Black Baptist church experience of involvement in broad-based community organizing and their key involvement in IAF alliances, such as EBC in New York City and BUILD in Baltimore. However, they do this without dealing in any depth with the theological engagement of these churches with community organizing.

Graf argues that a "universal principle" of broad-based community organizing is the necessity of people and their institutions to demand real respect and recognition rather than grudging tolerance in the public arena.[77] Through seeking this recognition, Graf includes a helpful summary of important social,

71. Freedman, *Upon This Rock*, 19.

72. Freedman, *Upon This Rock*, 19.

73. Freedman includes the story of the Nehemiah housing campaign (*Upon This Rock*, 332–40).

74. Freedman, *Upon This Rock*, 319.

75. Chambers, *Roots for Radicals*, 27.

76. Warren, *Dry Bones Rattling*, 66–67.

77. Graf, *Lessons Learned*, back cover.

economic, and political changes that powerful IAF alliances have created.[78] These include: EBC in New York City and the Nehemiah Plan that rebuilt the East New York community with more than six thousand new, owner-occupied homes; BUILD and the living wage in Baltimore; and COPS, which changed the political dynamic of San Antonio, Texas, and won better facilities in economically poor areas. The names of these and other alliances, such as WIN and Greater Boston Interfaith Organization, also highlight the importance of faith institutions to these broad-based community organizations.

Gregory Pierce is another Roman Catholic and an organizer and leader with the IAF since 1970. He edited *Reveille for a New Generation*, a book brought together in celebration of the eightieth anniversary of the IAF in 2020. Pierce affirms the importance of convincing religious institutions that it is in their immediate and long-term interest to join together in broad-based organizations that have enough power to create pockets of the world as it should be right in the midst of the world as it is. This, he writes, helps "repair the fabric of the world."[79]

Pierce also highlights five things which now distinguish the IAF form of community organizing. First, it is fiercely nonpartisan. Second, it organizes institutions, not individuals. Third, it seeks relational power instead of dominant power. Fourth, it is committed to the training and development of leaders. Fifth, it is uncompromising in demanding of itself an openness to radical diversity in its membership.[80]

Bretherton argues that this move to a deeper engagement with faith institutions was not a fundamental change of emphasis for the IAF, but a systemization and making explicit what was already central in the origins of Alinsky's approach to community organizing.[81] However, much of the available literature by IAF organizers and academics suggests that there was indeed a fundamental change of emphasis in developing much deeper engagement with faith institutions. Mike Miller, a Christian, another very experienced community organizer in the US, argues that Alinsky's approach has therefore been revised, modified, expanded and elaborated to meet new circumstances and with new priorities. "Faith-based" community organizing focuses on religious congregations as the principal building blocks of "people power." This approach "draws upon the moral, and social and economic justice teachings of the world's great religions. . . . It engages deeply with the life of religious

78. Graf, *Lessons Learned*, 14–15.

79. Pierce, *Reveille for a New Generation*, iv.

80. Pierce, *Reveille for a New Generation*, 105.

81. Bretherton, *Resurrecting Democracy*, 42.

congregations, using action in the world on behalf of justice as a tool to renew and revitalize them."[82]

Bretherton notes that Mark Warren, a US sociologist and anthropologist, in *Dry Bones Rattling*, and Richard Wood, a US sociologist, in *Faith in Action*, both emphasize how community organizers themselves generate theological reflection and outline different responses to involvement in community organizing within different kinds of congregations and denominations. Warren focuses on the multiracial dynamics of an IAF alliance. In contrast, Wood examines the multidenominational and ecumenical aspects of community organizing.[83] We will examine the theological reflection generated by organizers and leaders in chapter 3.

In *Blessed Are the Organized*, Jeffrey Stout, a US religious studies academic, studies community organizing through several stories from across the US. He argues that the details of the stories are important in drawing out the principles. Importantly, Stout then highlights that almost all the literature on organizing is not concrete enough to convey a full picture of what is going on through the organizing.[84] Angus Ritchie, an Anglican vicar and director of the Centre for Theology and Community in the UK, highlights that Stout's study of Organizing in the US offers a number of striking examples of the adaptability of community organizing to Roman Catholic as well as Black Baptist churches.[85] Romand Coles, a political theorist and ethicist, also made a study of the IAF in his book *Beyond Gated Politics*. As with much of the work of Stout and Bretherton on community organizing, this work is also focused on how organizing supports democratic practices.[86]

In this section we have observed how powerful civil society alliances involving churches and others have won change on justice issues and developed leaders in their communities. However, we could ask to what extent it is possible to transfer broad-based community organizing to another context. Or to put it another way, we could ask how community organizing would need to adapt to another context, both geographically and culturally and with a different church context. We will find out in the next section as we explore the development of this form of community organizing in the United Kingdom.

82. Miller, *Community Organizing*, 1.

83. Bretherton, *Resurrecting Democracy*, 14.

84. Stout, "Blessed Are the Organized."

85. Ritchie, *Inclusive Populism*, 47.

86. Another book by Romand Coles referenced by Bretherton and Ritchie in writing about organizing and democratic practice is Hauerwas and Coles, *Christianity, Democracy.*

1.4 The Development of Broad-Based Community Organizing in the United Kingdom

In this section we will trace the progression in the UK from the development of early alliances and the Community Organizing Foundation (COF) in the late 1980s and early 1990s, to London Citizens in the mid-2000s, and then to the formation of Citizens UK ahead of the 2010 UK general election. A paper in 2021 setting out the foundations of Citizens UK highlights that the work at Citizens UK is influenced by a heritage which draws on both the IAF and the US civil rights movement. The paper also highlights the rich history in the UK "of people organizing for power and change such as the Levellers, the abolitionists, the Chartists, early trade unionists like the match girls and dock strikers, and the suffragettes."[87]

Graf highlights that the COF, which went on to become Citizens UK, was founded by Neil Jameson after he spent time with Chambers in Chicago and with Gecan in New York City. Graf also understands that key to the development of community organizing in the UK was Jonathan Lange. As an IAF organizer, for several years from 2000 onwards Lange spent two to three weeks, three or four times a year, with Neil Jameson and other UK organizers.[88] Warren produced an in-depth study of community organizing in the UK in 2009. In this he sets out to discover how a US organizing strategy has worked in the very different social and political context of the UK.[89] It is important to note that Warren wrote this before the greater prominence gained by Citizens UK following the global economic crisis in the late 2000s. Warren describes how Neil Jameson, a British Quaker and a social worker, travelled to the US in 1977 where he met IAF organizers and attended IAF community organizing training there.

Neil Jameson led the development of broad-based community organizing in the UK and was founding director of Citizens UK. Jameson envisioned this as "not faith led, but faith inspired."[90] Similarly, Bretherton describes the founding of broad-based community organizing in the UK as a "faithful and pluralistically secular act in which Christianity played a crucial catalytic role, hosting what became in practice a common life politics."[91] Bretherton argues that in Citizens UK explicit "religious" language and beliefs are present

87. Jonathan Cox, phone call, Dec. 1, 2021.

88. Graf, *Lessons Learned*, 179.

89. Warren, "Community Organizing in Britain," 99.

90. Bretherton, *Resurrecting Democracy*, 77.

91. Bretherton, *Resurrecting Democracy*, 78.

alongside and feed into "secular" public reason.[92] As Bretherton notes, the previous Citizens UK logo featured people in religious and nonreligious costume holding hands around a common space defined by their relations.[93] This again highlights the importance of building relationships across difference and also the presence of many faith institutions in Citizens UK.

Several British religious leaders attended IAF training during the 1980s including Rowan Williams (who went on to become archbishop of Canterbury) as well as Barry Morgan (who went on to become archbishop of Wales).[94] The influential Church of England *Faith in the City* report in 1985 led to the formation of the Church Urban Fund which then provided funding for community organizing and the COF.[95]

The first community organizing alliance formed in the UK was in Bristol with the central involvement of Neil Jameson.[96] Communities Organised for Greater Bristol was launched in 1989 with twenty-six members. All of the members were religious institutions, and primarily Anglican.

At about the same time as the development of this alliance in Bristol, Warren describes how Sister Mary MacAleese founded the UK's second community organizing alliance in Liverpool.[97] The Merseyside Broad-Based Organisation was launched in 1992 with forty-one members. The members were mostly Roman Catholic, with some Muslim organizations.

These successes in Bristol and Liverpool were accompanied by a growing group of supporters within the Roman Catholic and Anglican church denominations. This support led to community organizing alliances being formed in the 1990s in Sheffield, North Wales, the Black Country, and East London.[98] However, as Warren notes, a number of these alliances struggled to form strong local foundations. Thus, in 1999 the alliances in North Wales, Liverpool and Sheffield either withdrew from the COF or folded.[99]

One of the alliances which continued was in East London. This alliance went on to play a significant role in the expansion of community organizing again in the UK. The East London Communities Organisation (TELCO) was formed in 1996. It grounded a community organizing alliance among the

92. Bretherton, *Resurrecting Democracy*, 83.

93. Bretherton, *Resurrecting Democracy*, 102.

94. Jim Barnaville, Roman Catholic Archdiocese of Cardiff, online meeting, Feb. 22, 2021.

95. Commission on Urban Priority Areas, *Faith in the City*.

96. Warren, "Community Organizing in Britain," 105.

97. Warren, "Community Organizing in Britain," 106.

98. Warren, "Community Organizing in Britain," 106.

99. Warren, "Community Organizing in Britain," 110.

large and growing Muslim population in East London as well as among the area's historic Roman Catholic community. The membership was made up of a large number of Roman Catholic parishes (with many in the congregations from Ireland and West Africa), several Anglican parishes, and a number of mosques. Thus, this diverse membership made the alliance both multi-faith and multiracial.[100]

Bernadette Farrell is a Roman Catholic leader, a former leading Citizens UK organizer, and a songwriter. She played a key role in the development of community organizing in East and South London, and in encouraging the strong involvement of Roman Catholic institutions in these alliances. Farrell drew on the historical involvement of the Roman Catholic Church in communities and the struggle for social justice, including the key role of Cardinal Manning in the East London dock strikes.

Austen Ivereigh, in his book *Faithful Citizens*, provides a helpful guide to how community organizing translates the principles of CST—including solidarity, subsidiarity, intrinsic human dignity, participation, and the option for the poor—into concrete victories on social justice issues. He tells stories of the involvement of Roman Catholic parishes and schools in major London Citizens campaigns in East London and across the city around the living wage, housing and immigration. Through these, Ivereigh highlights how Citizens UK has brought about significant changes through applying CST and community organizing in its political actions. Ivereigh identifies that the values and vision of CST are made real through the method of community organizing.[101] As noted earlier, we will examine in more depth the influence of CST on community organizing in chapter 3.

Notable campaign successes by TELCO on the living wage[102] and on securing commitments for communities in East London for the London 2012 Olympics led to expansion of community organizing into South, North, and West London and the formation of London Citizens in 2006.[103]

Graf reveals that the living wage concept came from IAF organizer Jonathan Lange's meetings with hundreds of low-wage workers in Baltimore. Through these meetings, Lange and the workers developed the living wage

100. Warren, "Community Organizing in Britain," 107.

101. Ivereigh, *Faithful Citizens*, 4.

102. The living wage campaign was launched by TELCO in 2001. It became a focus area for Citizens UK. The organization formed the Living Wage Foundation to encourage businesses to accredit as Living Wage employers. By July 2024, this campaign had won over £3 billion of additional wages, lifting over 460,000 people out of working poverty across the UK.

103. Warren, "Community Organizing in Britain," 111.

campaign together.[104] Graf argues that most of the universal principles of community organizing have been translated easily to the UK and other countries.[105] This includes how a campaigning focus on tackling low wages has also been translated into a living wage movement in the UK.

Warren highlights some clear differences between community organizing in the UK and the US at that time. He contrasts the local focus of alliances in the US, as well as their focus on raising dues and developing large numbers of local leaders in member institutions, with the national profile of Citizens in the UK, which lacks a wide and deep leadership base and does not raise enough in membership dues.[106]

However, we also observe the similarities between the US and the UK with the key role that faith institutions played in the formation of alliances and their ongoing involvement in community organizing efforts. Mosques and other Muslim institutions played an important role in the development of TELCO in East London as well as in other alliances in England and Wales. Reflecting on this, leaders and organizers in Citizens UK produced a useful resource on Islam and community organizing.[107]

Jane Wills has written extensively about Citizens UK work, particularly in East London.[108] In *Faith in Action*, Wills argues that community organizing "has successfully brought faith organisations and faithful people into public and political life" and that religious organizations have been at the heart of this work.[109]

In East London, Wills highlights that faith organizations and their leaders explained their engagement on the basis of a number of factors. These were their strong commitment to relationship building across differences, their own religious traditions, and a desire for getting things done.[110] Wills observes that faith organizations have been able to build relationships with other faiths at the local level based on love and respect and common ground. Importantly, Wills notes that community organizing has also enabled these faith organizations to engage with people who they wouldn't otherwise be able to.[111]

Wills highlights that for Anglicans in East London, the Church of England is the established church and so already has access to power. However,

104. Graf, *Lessons Learned*, 185.

105. Graf, *Lessons Learned*, 195.

106. Warren, "Community Organizing in Britain," 113.

107. Ali et al., *New Covenant of Virtue*.

108. For example, Wills, "Faith in Action"; Jamoul and Wills, "Faith in Politics."

109. Wills, "Faith in Action," 19.

110. Wills, "Faith in Action," 19.

111. Wills, "Faith in Action," 27.

community organizing provides authentic connection to people who live in the parish. In contrast, she argues that Roman Catholics already have a strong tradition of solidarity with poor people through CST.[112] However, Wills also highlights that the most marginalized and vulnerable people are often the least connected to institutions. Importantly, these are the people who need social justice the most.[113]

I observe in Wills's work a question as to whether community organizing can rebuild the faith institutions and other civil society organizations on which it depends. This is in the context of declining numbers of people regularly participating in these institutions. It is also in the context of people gathering together as churches and other faith institutions from increasingly big geographical areas, rather than predominantly from the surrounding local community. Wills concludes that in terms of developing meaningful relationships and social change at the neighborhood scale, faith institutions "can play a part in this work, but they will not provide the scale or depth of support required to reconfigure relations of power."[114] This is a challenge to churches and other faith institutions. I will explore this further later in this book.

Grace Davie, in *Religion in Britain Since 1945: Believing Without Belonging* and in her later book, *Europe: The Exceptional Case*, focuses on the sociology of religion in Britain. Her work is useful for outlining the overall church context in Wales and England in which community organizing has developed and continues. She remarks that "taking faith or religion seriously is becoming, increasingly, the exception rather than the norm in British society."[115] Davie goes on to note that British people retain some sort of religious belief even if they do not see the need to belong through attending churches on a regular basis. She argues that religious organizations, despite their minority status, continue to be a significant feature of contemporary British society. In *Europe: The Exceptional Case*, she picks up on the theme of believing without belonging and comments that while there is considerable persistence in believing, there is considerable decline and secularization and yet still a latent sense of belonging.[116]

Elaine Graham's view of the crisis of postmodernity is that it is not just about belief but about "the exercise of civic power, participation and citizenship."[117] In addition, she highlights that this is in a context where the

112. Wills, "Faith in Action," 29.

113. Wills, "Faith in Action," 39.

114. Wills, "Faith in Action," 41.

115. Davie, *Religion in Britain*, 69.

116. Davie, *Europe*, 5.

117. Graham, "Practical Theology," 107.

preeminence of a Christian way of life in the UK can no longer be taken for granted, thus picking up on Davie's conclusions. Davie appears prescient when she remarks that pragmatic alliances of like-minded people from a range of denominational backgrounds, over relatively specific issues, are a likely outcome.[118] Davie understands that Europe's churches have become influential voluntary organizations, capable of operating in a whole variety of ways. Crucially, this places churches in the civil society sphere. She realizes that "in this sphere, churches are key players, central to the structures of a modern democracy and attract more members than almost all their organizational equivalents."[119]

Davie notes that the 1985 Church of England report *Faith in the City* pushed issues of deprivation, and particularly urban deprivation, to the top of the political agenda. She highlights that the "established church found itself speaking for precisely those elements of society least likely to be found in its pews."[120] Davie observes that clergy were often the only professionals still resident in the most deprived areas of British cities and had firsthand knowledge and could gather accurate information.[121] She notes that other institutions in civil society have also experienced similar collapses in numbers at the same time, namely political parties and trade unions.[122]

From this it could be argued that the collapse in church attendance is less about belief and more about underlying economic and social change. Davie concludes that some churches will have more difficulty than others in coming to terms with this decline, with the way in which the institution is embedded in society being important. For example, she highlights that Europe's historic churches (including Roman Catholic and Church of England) fitted easily into patterns of a preindustrial society and a hierarchical structure but have lost social control with increased urbanization.[123] To this we could add that these historic churches have also lost social control through the secular emphasis on diversity and inclusion. All of this context may well have been in the minds

118. Davie, *Religion in Britain*, 71.

119. Davie, *Europe*, 18.

120. Davie, *Religion in Britain*, 152. I have not found in the literature on theological engagement with community organizing any reference to *Faithful Cities*, which is the successor to and develops the *Faith in the City* report highlighting what churches should be doing on the ground. See Commission on Urban Life and Faith, *Faithful Cities*.

121. A good example of this is seen where Holman records the voices of impoverished people telling their own stories of dealing with poverty in Easterhouse, Glasgow. In doing so they find power and dignity as they themselves tell their own story (*Faith in the Poor*).

122. Davie, *Europe*, 21.

123. Davie, *Europe*, 141.

of Anglican and Catholic leaders in the UK from the 1980s onwards as they considered engagement in community organizing.

In recent years, the impacts of globalization and political populism and the question of how churches should respond to both have also had a growing influence on the context for churches.[124] Warren and Stout both write about broad-based community organizing in the US and the involvement of faith institutions in the context of the power of the religious right and Evangelicalism on politics there. Both see broad-based community organizing as a counteracting force against this, and against the enormous power of money and business in US politics. However, in Wales and England the context is different. Political populism has also had an impact on UK politics. However, currently there is no powerful religious right seeking to influence UK politics.

Warren, in his study of community organizing in the UK, includes a focus on religious institutions in Britain and the state of religious participation and, as he calls it, "the faith-based social capital resources available to community organizing."[125] Warren notes that overall, there was a lower percentage of the white population attending Church of England and Roman Catholic churches. In contrast, a higher proportion of those from ethnic minority groups, such as Black Christians and Bangladeshi and Pakistani Muslims, were attending religious services in the neighborhoods where Citizens was focused.[126]

Warren highlights that "the IAF itself uses the term broad-based rather than faith-based to describe its organizing work, because it wants to make clear that it does not pursue a religious agenda, and because IAF organizations include some secular institutions like schools and unions in their membership."[127] However, Warren also highlights the view of academics that the success of modern community organizing in the US lies in its ability to engage the social capital embedded in religious congregations. Warren goes on to argue that faith-based social capital is relatively weak in the UK compared to the US.

Warren includes some trenchant observations on a range of religious institutions. Denoting the Church of England as part of the establishment, Warren picks up on a tension between US-style community organizing and this context for Anglicans.[128] However, he does conclude that the "Church of England has an orientation to public engagement and a faith tradition that

124. For a detailed exploration of church responses to globalization, see Walsh and Keesmaat, *Colossians Remixed*. Two recent explorations of church responses to populism are: Ritchie, *Inclusive Populism*; and (Pope) Francis, *Let Us Dream*.

125. Warren, "Community Organizing in Britain," 114.

126. Warren, "Community Organizing in Britain," 115.

127. Warren, "Community Organizing in Britain," 101.

128. See Furbey et al., "Breaking with Tradition?"

can support progressive democratic action."[129] Warren presents the Roman Catholic Church as historically a persecuted church in the UK, and a church which has not been part of the establishment.[130] He observes that many Roman Catholic churches were ready for community organizing in the 1990s, with many priests drawing on liberation theology and CST for their theology and practice.[131] Warren concludes in his study "that the most likely religious candidates for political action through community organizing in Britain are Anglican and Catholic, but their parishes are weak."[132] Warren also highlights the lack of leaders in both Anglican and Roman Catholic churches.

An early study of community organizing in the UK highlighted that some Christian denominations have been more receptive to organizing than others. The greater relative initial success of organizing with Roman Catholic institutions than with Anglicans may also be related to how faith is practiced in poorer areas. Roman Catholics have a strong tradition of civic political engagement in the UK which, unlike that of Anglicans, tends to be based on numerical strength and mobilisation rather than establishment connections.[133]

The involvement of Anglicans in Wales and England in broad-based community organizing is linked with the recent story of the Anglican church in these nations. Bishop Adrian Newman, in his role as Church of England bishop of Stepney in East London, was a key actor in investing in broad-based community organizing in England. Newman saw community organizing as a way for the Church of England to avoid terminal decline and to find its future. Newman provided investment in the Centre for Theology and Community (initially known as the Contextual Theology Centre) to provide an evidence base for churches to grow and to live out their mission for social justice and social change.[134] Therefore, we observe that Anglican involvement in Citizens UK started with leaders who were interested in organizing and who then reflected theologically on their practices. Following this, there was the development of tools for Anglican ministers to engage in organizing. Over the last ten years, the Centre for Theology and Community has been working with churches involved in community organizing in East London.

There is now much more focus on institutional strengthening and leadership development in Anglican and Roman Catholic churches than it appears

129. Warren, "Community Organizing in Britain," 115.

130. Roman Catholic churches and Baptist churches in the UK both share this outsider status in not being the established church.

131. Warren, "Community Organizing in Britain," 116.

132. Warren, "Community Organizing in Britain," 118.

133. Furbey et al., "Breaking with Tradition?"

134. Matthew Bolton, in-person meeting, Mar. 13, 2019.

there was in the early 2000s. In his article Warren makes no mention of Baptists, Methodists, Quakers, Salvation Army, or Jewish groups.[135] He sees that the greatest potential for community organizing with faith groups "lies in the rich network of vibrant religious communities found among Britain's racial and ethnic minorities," and therefore not in the mostly white and declining Christian denominations.[136] I note that not all Baptist churches in Wales and England are white majority and many are in economically poorer areas of cities. In addition, Baptist churches have a greater focus, in theory at least, on leaders beyond the church minister. Instead, there is a focus on leadership by a much larger group of church members and deacons or trustees.

Bretherton includes a brief history of Citizens UK in *Resurrecting Democracy* (2015). Importantly, this was written in the context of the much higher national profile Citizens UK alliances gained through the response to the 2008 global financial crisis and the campaign to cap the cost of lending. He highlights that broad-based community organizing is still a relatively new phenomenon in the UK. This is in contrast to the US where the IAF was founded in 1940.[137]

As described earlier, the first alliances were formed in the UK at the beginning of the 1990s with London Citizens formed in 2006 and the formation of Citizens UK ahead of the 2010 UK general election. The antislavery movement in the UK and the long campaign to end the Atlantic slave trade, the Suffragettes, the London dock strike in 1889 and its catalytic effect on the emergence of the labor movement, and Chartism are sometimes cited as part of the prehistory of community organizing in the UK.[138] As Bretherton notes, churches played a key role in the antislavery movement, the Chartist movement,[139] and the London dock strike. Chartism is an area which resonates deeply with me in my organizing. Recalling the family background I described earlier, I understand that it is highly likely that family members

135. More recently there has been involvement from synagogues and other Jewish institutions in broad-based community organizing in the UK. A key resource for a Jewish approach to community organizing is Jacobs, *Where Justice Dwells*. In addition, Clifton et al., *Marching Towards Justice*. In this short book the authors highlight how community organizing can enable the Salvation Army to return to its justice-seeking roots.

136. Warren, "Community Organizing in Britain," 122.

137. Bretherton, *Resurrecting Democracy*, 76.

138. Bretherton, *Resurrecting Democracy*, 76.

139. Chartism was a working-class movement, which emerged in 1836 and was most active between 1838 and 1848. The aim of the Chartists was to gain political rights and influence for the working classes. Chartism got its name from the People's Charter, which listed the six main aims of the movement. The Chartists were particularly strong as a movement and with significant support in Northern England, the West and East Midlands, and the South Wales Valleys.

were involved in the Chartist movement. In addition, I understand that they were involved in the Chartist march on Newport in 1839 from Rhymney and Tredegar, and other towns and villages in the South Wales Valleys.

Bretherton argues that community organizing is best understood as an extension and development of American populism. In his description of political populism and community organizing, these develop political space, provide popular education, develop a broad base of local leaders, and focus on the common good.[140] However, he perceives that the roots of community organizing in American populism are a hindrance when transplanting it to the UK:[141]

> The constant danger in the British context is . . . that community organising will become reduced to a technique or method or political mobilization as it struggles to embed itself in the lived traditions and values of its member institutions, divorced as it is from any wider cultural-historical frame of reference with which participants can instructively identify community organising.[142]

I will explore further how community organizing connects to lived church traditions and values in chapters 2–3.

Much of Bretherton and Stout's preoccupation in *Resurrecting Democracy* and *Blessed are the Organized* is with how community organizing helps strengthen democracy and democratic action. In examining church engagement with broad-based community organizing, it is important to briefly examine how churches teach about democracy and democratic action. Bretherton highlights that, in the 1930s and 1940s, William Temple, then archbishop of Canterbury; Jacques Maritain, a Roman Catholic philosopher; and Reinhold Niebuhr, a US Protestant theologian, "all claimed that while Christians do not need democracy to practice their faith, democracy enshrines central Christian commitments, and so democracy should be an aspirational feature of political order for Christians."[143] Warren argues that:

> The expansion of democratic action follows from a right understanding of religious teachings. Most of scripture is about the relationship of the community to the poor. So, if you probe religious teachings deeply, they lead you to a democratic life.[144]

140. Bretherton, *Resurrecting Democracy*, 52.
141. Bretherton, *Resurrecting Democracy*, 54.
142. Bretherton, *Resurrecting Democracy*, 55.
143. Bretherton, "Recovering Democratic Politics," para. 8.
144. Warren, *Dry Bones Rattling*, 192.

Thus, religious traditions teach democratic action. Stout notes that priests are responsible for the spiritual formation of their congregations which includes teaching them their responsibilities as citizens. Stout goes on to argue that "the church must hold the people and their rulers responsible for the injustices they have perpetuated and permitted. At times, it is a pastor's responsibility to speak prophetically on the church's behalf."[145]

Bretherton argues that, in the UK, community organizing enables church as church to play a part in democratic citizenship, "because it is not derived from a British Christian subculture and so it is not constrained by a memory of exclusion of religion from the public sphere or the very real history of the Establishment's exclusion of both Nonconformists and Roman Catholics from holding office."[146] In England, the Church of England is the established church. In contrast, the Church of England in Wales is disestablished. The Roman Catholic Church is not the established church in either nation and so is already outside of formal power structures. In the US there is no established church. However, it can be argued that parts of the Church have a stronger influence on politics in the US than in England and Wales.

Warren, Bretherton and Wills all provide their analyses of religious institutions in Britain in relation to their state of participation and their relative power as institutions. I will develop their analysis of faith institutions and the conclusions they come to by analyzing churches' understanding and use of community organizing in chapter 2 and also later in this book.

There is no mention in the literature of Baptist church involvement in the formation of these early alliances in England. In seeking to build powerful civic society alliances, community organizers and leaders were seeking to bring together institutions which they saw as organizing large numbers of people and able to pay membership dues. From this, it appears likely that one reason Baptist churches were not involved is that they did not appear in the power analysis of key civic society institutions in an area, whereas Anglican and Roman Catholic churches and dioceses did.

Despite the continuing decline in regular church attendance, Roman Catholic and Anglican churches and church schools are still largely the key institutions within communities of high social deprivation and are still the institutions which organize people and organize money. As a result, over time, there have been more Citizens UK organizers who understand how to engage with Anglican and Roman Catholic churches rather than with Baptist churches. Conversely in the IAF, because of the strong involvement of Black-majority Baptist churches there appear to be more organizers who understand

145. Stout, *Blessed Are the Organized*, 200–201.

146. Bretherton, *Resurrecting Democracy*, 102.

how to organize with these churches. Through this research, I hope to provide more understanding about community organizing with Baptist churches in Wales and England.

1.5 The Contemporary Practice of Broad-Based Community Organizing in Wales and England

In the context of growing populism in UK politics, and ongoing division in communities following the referendum vote in 2016 to leave the European Union, many see community organizing as a way to come together locally across difference and work on common issues. As in the US, the focus in the UK is on advancing relational power through developing community leaders, strengthening institutions and making change. There are currently more than 450 institutions in membership of Citizens UK alliances in Wales and England.[147] These broad-based organizations include educational, union, and community groups as members in addition to faith institutions. As in the US, churches and other faith institutions provide the backbone of these alliances. Currently in the UK, the Roman Catholic Church, Church of England, and Church in Wales are the most engaged. These churches have the most financial and leadership investment in broad-based community organizing. In chapters 2–3, I will develop further how churches, as institutions, and church denominations, have understood and reflected theologically on broad-based community organizing.

Matthew Bolton, the current executive director of Citizens UK, took over the leadership of the organization from Neil Jameson in 2018. In *How to Resist*, he asserts that "the fundamental aim of Community Organizing is for people to build and use power, to have control over decision-making and to hold the state and market to account."[148] He includes personal stories of his involvement as a community organizer and stories of campaigns to illustrate the key principles of broad-based community organizing. This is done in a similar way to a number of the books written by organizers in the US.

Unlike Neil Jameson and many of the other experienced current Citizens UK organizers, Bolton did not come to community organizing with a strong personal faith. Thus, in contrast to other organizers, he does not personally see organizing as a key part of people living out their faith in public life. In *How to Resist*, there is little on the importance of faith institutions to community organizing. However, as in the books by US organizers, many of the

147. Citizens UK, *Annual Report 2020.*

148. Bolton, *How to Resist*, 8.

organizing stories in the book show their central involvement in winning change on the living wage and other issues.

In launching two Welsh alliances in 2014 with the tagline "Organizing for power, social justice and the common good," strong links were made with an understanding that community organizing is standing in a long and proud tradition of action for power, social justice and the common good in Wales. Ecclesiastes 1:9 was used as a refrain: "What has been is what will be, and what has been done is what will be done; and there is nothing new under the sun," and in Welsh, "Does dim byd newydd dan yr haul." The examples used in this launch assembly included, first, working people in the industrial age who resisted exploitation by forming trade unions—organizing people for change. Second, the example of ordinary people raising subscriptions to build chapels so they could worship in their own tongue and tradition—organizing money to own their own institutions. Third, the Chartist leaders of the Newport Rising (John Frost, Zephaniah Williams, and William Jones) who in 1839 sent shock waves through the establishment by organizing thousands to protest at the denial of the right to assembly. Fourth, the example of Welsh communities who were at the forefront of organizing the modern labor movement, and who elected Keir Hardie the first Labour MP to give working people power in the UK Parliament.

Arnie Graf introduced Ed Miliband, leader of the UK Labour Party from 2010 to 2015, to community organizing in 2011. Miliband provides a great demonstration of the power of stories of change. He attended Citizens UK national leadership training in October 2015 a few months after losing the 2015 UK general election. In his book *Go Big*, published six years after this training, Miliband accurately recounts a story he heard as part of this training:

> One of the organizers of the course, Jonathan Cox, the director of Citizens Cymru Wales talked about some work he had done with young members of the British-Somali community in Cardiff. Young people in this community had felt stigmatised and alienated for many years. Citizens Cymru had begun by asking them what they wanted to change. It turned out that one of the things that really animated them was that there were three Nando's in Cardiff but none was halal so they couldn't eat there. Nando's had many halal restaurants in the rest of the UK, and even one ten miles away [in Nantgarw] in a part of Wales with few Muslims, but not in Cardiff. In fact, though it has the largest Muslim population in Wales, not a single chain restaurant in the city centre or fashionable Cardiff Bay made any kind of halal provision.
>
> Ali Abdi, a local youth worker, built a team of young people which set about campaigning for a halal Nando's in Cardiff with

> the support of Citizens Cymru. They wrote letters to the company, which led nowhere, but eventually got them to agree to a meeting after eighty young people—including four who ran, walked, cycled and took the train dressed as chickens—marched to the nearest branch [in Nantgarw]. The Nando's bigwigs came to Cardiff armed with a PowerPoint presentation explaining why it wasn't practical to have a halal restaurant there, but in the event they never got to deliver it.
>
> The locals asked if they could start the meeting by sharing why they loved Nando's so much, gave the visitors Welsh cakes they had baked (which they explained they couldn't themselves eat because they were fasting for Ramadan) and made their case for a halal branch. In response the bigwigs committed Nando's to working with the young people and promised to think about their proposal and come back to them—the kind of thing people in positions of authority say to avoid confrontation. The locals said how pleased they were at this response and that they hoped to celebrate Eid al-Adha (the second festival of Eid, around two months after Eid al-Fitr, which marks the end of Ramadan) at a halal Nando's in Cardiff. But, they said, if that wasn't possible they would recruit the Bishop of Llandaff, the Archbishop of Cardiff and the general secretary of the Muslim Council of Wales to dress up as chickens and do their own "chicken run" to Nando's on Eid.
>
> The execs went pale. Unbeknown to them, the young people were employing Saul Alinsky's ninth rule of organizing: "The threat is usually more terrifying than the thing itself." It works. The bigwigs didn't fancy hosting a bishop in a chicken suit; the young people won their campaign, and Nando's now boasts on its website about its halal branch in the Cardiff Old Brewery Quarter.[149]

Miliband clearly loves this story, as do I. I have told it many times to inspire others to organize in their communities. I started this chapter with a story and include this one here as they both demonstrate a number of key focus areas of community organizing in the UK. These areas include working across difference, putting faith into practice in organizing, and involving those who often feel powerless and on the margins of communities and institutions and enabling them to play a central role in bringing about change. Miliband describes how this story helped him understand a different model of leadership:

> While the standard model of political leadership revolves around the charismatic individual, community organizing leadership is

149. Miliband, *Go Big*, 215–16.

> much more collective and empowering. Train people in methods for making change happen, and anyone, whatever their self-image, can become a leader.[150]

I will examine this focus on leadership development again in chapter 2.

Eighteen months after the launch assembly, Citizens Cymru Wales organized the Governance of Wales Accountability Assembly in March 2016. As with the launch assembly, this was hosted by Tabernacl Y Hayes, a large Welsh Baptist chapel in central Cardiff. At the accountability assembly seven hundred people, from thirty-six of the forty electoral constituencies across Wales, came together six weeks ahead of the May 2016 Senedd (Welsh Parliament) elections. The leaders of the four political parties in the Senedd at that time attended; Andrew R. T. Davies for the Welsh Conservatives, Carwyn Jones for Welsh Labour, Kirsty Williams for the Welsh Liberal Democrats, and Leanne Wood for Plaid Cymru (the Party of Wales). Leaders from the alliance set out their six Citizens priorities for the next Welsh government before hearing how these politicians would respond to these priorities. The first ask was to make Wales a living wage economy, including through making sure that Living Wage accreditation spread across the whole public sector and to every organization in receipt of Welsh government funding.[151] Leaders from Citizens member institutions, including cleaners and care workers, shared their personal experience of low pay and the importance of the living wage for them and their communities. Michelle Kazembe recounted her experience:

> While studying at Swansea University, I was working as a part-time cleaner. I am well aware of the gruesome early morning shift and that it's more preferable than the night. I am fully aware of the conditions buildings are left in. I know the pressure that comes with having to complete the large task in such a short amount of time and the little appreciation that comes from the management. . . . I heard from a grandmother [and fellow cleaner] overjoyed at the news of the birth of her first grandchild yet at the same time overcome with sorrow because she had to save up money for six months just so she can afford the travel to London on top of everything else she was juggling.[152]

All four of the party leaders were asked whether, if they became first minister of Wales after the elections, they would work together with Citizens to make Wales a living wage economy. Not a small ambition. Six weeks ahead of an

150. Miliband, *Go Big*, 217.

151. Citizens Cymru Wales, *Governance of Wales*.

152. Citizens Cymru Wales, *Governance of Wales*, 30–31.

election, all four party leaders said yes to this request and committed to work with the alliance on this and the other priorities raised.

Following the elections, a delegation of leaders from the alliance met with Carwyn Jones, who had been reelected as first minister. Over the following years the Citizens alliance met regularly with the first minister, and others in the Welsh government. One significant result of holding politicians to account for their commitments at this assembly was that Welsh government funding ensured social care workers in Wales were paid the living wage. In addition, Kirsty Williams became cabinet secretary for education in the Welsh government following the elections. She did not forget the commitments she had made publicly at the assembly. Williams became a key ally in working with Citizens Cymru Wales to ensure all ten Welsh universities became accredited Living Wage employers. I will examine further the practice of accountability assemblies in community organizing in chapter 2.

Jason Wood, a sociologist at Nottingham Trent University in the UK, led research into the impact of new citizens' alliances between 2018 and 2020. He highlights the lack of academic research into the impact of Citizens UK broad-based community organizing.[153] The research led by Wood shows how community organizing reweaves the social fabric of local communities. Using the analogy of weaving, local civic society institutions, such as churches, mosques, schools, colleges and housing associations, are the "warp" and the relationships between community leaders are the "weft." Continuing the weaving analogy, the "shuttle" is the community organizer working with the leadership team of each Citizens UK alliance. The "shuttle" is the connecting instrument. It is sharp at both ends and connects the big and little strands, the local alliance and the central Citizens UK.

Wood describes the practice of community organizing by Citizens UK as "the UK's evolving adoption of Saul Alinsky's approach to broad-based community organizing."[154] However, as highlighted above, what was adopted and then adapted in Wales and England was not the original model developed by Alinsky. Instead, it was the model developed by Chambers and Cortes and others which emphasized the central role of churches. In this model of community organizing, churches became increasingly important to shaping the practices of the alliances. Wood notes that there is a different relationship between government and citizens in the US compared to the UK. Despite this, Wood notes Citizens UK's success of forming alliances with broad-based membership.[155] He concludes:

153. Jason Wood, online meeting, Nov. 2, 2020.

154. J. Wood, "Power to Act," 203.

155. J. Wood, "Power to Act," 205.

> The cumulative impact of such work [broad-based community organizing] might be found in deeper-rooted civil society institutions, which, through their democratic engagement, may in turn contribute to healthier levels of diffuse support—and influence over—the levers of social change.[156]

As community organizing continues to grow and develop in Wales and England, it should be possible to measure its long-term impact on churches and other institutions. In addition, it should also be possible to assess more fully the earlier concerns expressed by Warren and Wills on the ability of churches and other faith institutions in Wales and England to contribute to the development of sustained and significant people-powered change in economically impoverished areas of these nations.

1.6 Summary

The literature review in this chapter reveals the key focus of broad-based community organizing in both the US and UK on developing leaders, strengthening institutions, and making change. The roots of community organizing are in specific places and community institutions, and in leadership by local people themselves. We note how the historical and current context of churches and civic society has influenced the development of broad-based community organizing in both the US, and in Wales and England. It may be that context is key.

For example, Black Baptist church involvement in the US was specific to their particular contexts and experiences. But the Baptist experience and theological engagement with broad-based community organizing is not dealt with in any depth in the current literature. This is despite Baptist involvement in the US underpinning and playing a central role in several of the key campaigns of the modern IAF, notably the living wage campaign in Baltimore and the Nehemiah housing program in New York City.

The literature raises a number of perceived difficulties in importing an approach developed in the US church and civic society context into very different contexts in Wales and England. Despite this, from the literature, there appear to be many similarities between broad-based community organizing in the US and Wales and England, and the approach appears to have been successful in developing powerful broad-based civic alliances in Wales and England.

156. J. Wood, "Power to Act," 214.

However, we have observed some significant differences between the US and UK experience. First, Citizens UK has been able to organize and act to win change at a UK-wide level, for example changing UK government policy on wages, immigration and refugees. In contrast, in the US the focus is on citywide or statewide action. Second, the alliances in Wales and England appear to have a much deeper involvement of mosques and other Muslim institutions, as well as synagogues and other Jewish institutions, in comparison to the alliances in the US. However, it is important to note that the investment by Christian churches and schools, particularly Anglican and Roman Catholic ones, in the UK is much greater than that from other faiths. Third, and significantly, community organizing in the UK is still relatively new, with Citizens UK now organizing for around thirty years, compared to the more than eighty years of experience of the IAF in organizing in the US.

Continuing this journey through broad-based community organizing, the next chapter will focus on how it has been taken up by churches in Wales and England and what it means for their practice of social justice.

Chapter 2

Churches' Understanding and Use of Community Organizing

2.1 Introduction

In chapter 1 we learned about the story of community organizing in the US and UK. Having unpacked the narrative of the development of community organizing, this chapter will focus on how churches have got involved in it and their understanding of community organizing.

Broad-based community organizing is seeking to reweave the fabric of civic society by improving and bringing back a relational culture to our institutions. In the last chapter we observed how churches and other faith institutions were key to broad-based community organizing from the outset. We traced the increasing focus on organizing with faith-based institutions in both the US and in the UK. We also traced the current situation where religious institutions are now the backbone of broad-based community organizing in both the US and Wales and England. As we noted in chapter 1, the names of the alliances reflect the influence of faith institutions. For example, Jeffrey Stout highlights that an IAF alliance in New Orleans is called Jeremiah, taking this name from Jer 29:7: "Seek the welfare of the city, for in its peace you will find your own."[1] In addition as we observed, also in chapter 1, one of the major

1. Stout, *Blessed Are the Organized*, 21.

campaign successes of broad-based community organizing in the US is the Nehemiah housing program.

Bretherton highlights that churches have been the key institutions involved in the IAF since its inception in 1940. He goes on to highlight research by Richard Woods and Brad Fulton which reveals that as of 2021 more than 5000 community-based institutions are involved in community organizing in the US. Around 3500 of these are religious congregations spread across all denominations, with tens of thousands of individuals involved. However, Bretherton asserts that "despite being one of the most significant forms of democratic politics to emerge over the past fifty years, community organizing is little understood either within or outside of the church."[2] Community organizing is often best known for its social justice campaigns and the public actions that are part of these campaigns. These are very visible and often accompanied by media attention. However, as he highlights, much of the other work that organizing does such as building relational power through one-to-one and house meetings is nether visible nor well understood outside of those involved in organizing.[3] A useful comparison is to consider what goes on inside a church congregation and in church services compared to how the congregation is seen and understood by the wider community. Therefore, the stories we tell about how change unfolded through community organizing should include this often unseen work.[4]

In Doing Justice: Congregations and Community Organizing, Dennis Jacobsen, a Lutheran Church pastor in Milwaukee, writes about congregation-based community organizing in the US.[5] Jacobsen argues that:

> Although the practices and principles of Congregation-based Community Organizing have been heavily influenced by Alinsky,

2. Bretherton, "Recovering Democratic Politics," para. 26.

3. Bretherton, "Campaigns as Public Action."

4. A good example of this is the story of how the movement to abolish slavery grew in the UK recounted by Adam Hochschild in his book *Bury the Chains*. The title of the book comes from a story of a group of enslaved people in the town of Falmouth, Jamaica, who immediately following the emancipation of enslaved people in the British Empire on August 1, 1838, placed their slave whip and chains in a coffin and buried the coffin in a Baptist churchyard (348–49). In addition, intriguingly the US subtitle of the book is *Prophets and Rebels in the Fight to Free an Empire's Slaves*. This alternative subtitle provides useful language in thinking about the role of churches in bringing about change; in the language of freeing enslaved people in an empire, and with Christians following in the line of the prophets (who were also rebels) in the Old Testament, Jesus, and on to Martin Luther King Jr. and many others.

5. This is another term for broad-based community organizing used in the US and signifying that this is a form of organizing where all (or almost) all of the institutions involved in an alliance are churches.

> most laity and clergy engaged in these organisations have never read any of his writings, and may never have heard of him. A more direct connection is felt to the civil rights movement and to the work of Dr. Martin Luther King Jr.[6]

This is important to note as we consider how churches in both the US and UK have understood community organizing. As we observed in chapter 1, Citizens UK emphasizes that its approach to organizing is influenced by both the broad-based community organizing of the IAF and the US civil rights movement, in which Martin Luther King Jr. was a preeminent leader. One area that is important in drawing on the US civil rights movement is that it was driven by the faith of its leaders and the involvement of churches, and crucially that it was successful in winning significant change. As Jacobsen notes, "The historic success of the civil rights movement encourages those who still hope that the church can signify the Kingdom of God in an oppressive society."[7] For Jacobsen, congregation-based community organizing joins the values and principles of Martin Luther King Jr. to the methodology of Alinsky. So, we will consider in this book how community organizing practiced by churches draws on both Alinsky's and King's teachings on power.

This chapter will focus on how churches from different denominations understand and use key practices of community organizing. This chapter is divided into five main sections. Section 2.2 will examine how church engagement in community organizing has led to a fuller articulation of the values on which it is based. I will also highlight that the initial interest in community organizing for churches may also be driven by other interests.

Building relational power is a key area in community organizing and the focus of section 2.3. Then in section 2.4 I will examine how tools and practices to build relational power have been understood by churches. I will also consider some of the comparisons made between these and other church practices, particularly that of Anglican and Catholic churches—picking up from Wills, Warren, and Bretherton and their analysis of this in chapter 1. Section 2.5 will examine how institutional structures have influenced churches' involvement in community organizing. Finally, in section 2.6, I will highlight one way community organizing aiming to build relational power in a congregation has been put together in the UK.

6. Jacobsen, *Doing Justice*, 24.

7. Jacobsen, *Doing Justice*, 24.

2.2 Values and Community Organizing

As I highlighted in chapter 1, one area which struck me from my first experience of community organizing in London was the number and range of churches and other faith institutions involved. I was struck by their openness at the assembly in underlining how community organizing connected strongly with their values and enabled them to put these values and their faith into action.

Cold Anger describes the transition in the IAF towards an understanding of self-interest that made room for the values and vocations of member institutions. In Cortes's words, "Organizing became about *values and vision* as well as *action and issues*."[8] As Miller highlights:

> Connecting community action to religious faith is a powerful experience. When that connection is made, people are not only addressing a local issue, they are also acting as Jesus would have them act.[9]

Thus, through community organizing, congregations become a place where they are able to act on values of justice in ways directly connected to the pressures they, their families and neighbors are experiencing. It is also an approach to enable people to reflect on what Jesus in the Gospels, and both the New and Old Testaments, say about justice.[10]

Jeffrey K. Krehbiel was co-chair of WIN, the IAF alliance in Washington, DC, as well as a Presbyterian church minister. Krehbiel produced a very helpful resource for organizing with Christian churches called *Reflecting with Scripture on Community Organizing*.[11] Krehbiel believes that the church is called to be a community of alternative values and practices that bears witness

8. Ritchie, *Inclusive Populism*, 77; emphasis in original.

9. Miller, *Community Organizing*, 36. Mike Miller is a very experienced organizer in the US who worked with both Saul Alinsky and Ed Chambers. Miller had previously organized with the Student Nonviolent Coordinating Committee (SNCC), the principal channel of student commitment in the US to the civil rights movement during the 1960s, and also with Cesar Chavez on the farmworker movement in the US (Bretherton, "Saul Alinsky—Part 2").

10. Miller, *Community Organizing*, 37.

11. The four reflections in this short book are Krehbiel's: "Attempt to engage the Bible with my experience in organizing, and engage my organizing with the Scriptures. . . . The Bible can illume the work of community organizing and how organizing can create a window into the biblical text" (Krehbiel, *Reflecting with Scripture*, 9). In using these reflections for group study, Krehbiel recommends a Bible study method which is an adaptation of Wink's *Transforming Bible Study* to seek to find where "we find the living God addressing us at the point of our and the world's need" (45–47).

to the gospel in common life. Krehbiel argues that community organizing offers hope for the renewal of the church itself through how a congregation can impact its local community and strengthen its own membership at the same time.[12]

As Bretherton highlights about the early involvement of the Catholic Church in organizing with Alinsky in Chicago, the initial self-interest of the archdiocese was that community organizing provided a way of "Americanizing" their largely immigrant clergy and overcoming ethnic enclaves that were developing within the church.[13] So, we note that the initial self-interest of churches in being involved in community organizing may not be social justice or the common good. Instead, it may be to build stronger relationships with others in their neighborhood, to work with those of another faith, or to develop leadership skills among clergy and lay people.

We can trace a similar story with the initial significant investment by the Church of England in organizing in England. As we noted in chapter 1, an Anglican bishop saw community organizing as a way for the Church of England to address its self-interest to avoid terminal decline and to find its future.

Community organizing has indeed helped address the denomination's concern for church growth. A study by the Centre for Theology and Community of churches in East London involved in community organizing showed that together the Anglican congregations studied had doubled in size.[14] Significantly, this was from new people who were not already going to another church. The majority of people were also from those who were able to walk to church, so leading to stronger local parishes. The report also demonstrated that this growth came from church leaders taking a strongly relational approach. Taking this approach led to them thinking carefully about the interests of the people coming, and to thinking of the church as a place where people can learn about community. Involvement in social justice campaigns, for affordable housing and leadership development then came from this.[15]

Hannah Rich, in *Growing Good*, a 2020 report for the Church in England, argues that social action can be a route to church growth in both numerical and spiritual terms.[16] The report strongly affirms community organizing. She

12. Pierce, *Reveille for a New Generation*, 171.

13. Bretherton, *Resurrecting Democracy*, 35.

14. Green, *Church Growth in East London.*

15. Angus Ritchie and others at the Centre for Theology and Community have produced a number of reports and resources to encourage churches' involvement in broad-based community organizing: Ritchie et al., *Just Church*; Clifton et al., *Marching Towards Justice*; Ritchie and Hutt, *From Houses to Homes*; Ritchie, *People of Power*; Rodrigues, *Realities Are Greater.*

16. Rich, *Growing Good*, 12.

reveals that social action, through community organizing, leads to church growth when it enables congregations to develop meaningful relationships with those they would not otherwise have met, or who might not otherwise have come into sustained contact with the church.[17]

In relation to both Catholic and Anglican churches, Ivereigh understands that a major development in modern organizing is the focus on parish development and so strengthening institutions that have often been seen as becoming weaker.[18] As Ritchie understands, a feature of community organizing that makes it particularly attractive to religious institutions is that it strengthens member institutions. For him, this is "an achievement that serves the interests of the wider alliance as well as the individual congregations."[19]

Jay MacLeod produced an early practical and theological evaluation of community organizing in the UK. MacLeod recognizes that the engagement of congregations in the IAF led to a fuller articulation of the values on which both community organizing and churches are based:

> The key word in church or broad-based organising is values. People are still organised around issues based on self-interest, but church-based organisations are also built upon the values, visions, beliefs and commitments which stem from religious traditions. Even old-school organisers are coming to appreciate that churches work better from their own values and vision than from self-interest. Self-interest has yielded to the values of justice, concern for the poor, the dignity of the person, participation and respect for diversity as a motivation for involvement.[20]

Therefore, for MacLeod, the ability to put into practice these values has become more important than the narrow self-interest of churches to grow numerically, or at least to arrest decline, and to find new leaders to run church-based activities.

Bretherton notes that the philosopher Alasdair MacIntyre makes the distinction between institutions and practices. Practices (such as education) need institutions (such as schools, colleges, and universities) to sustain them. However, institutions can often become the enemy of good practice. Instead, they seek the external goods of money, status, and power to keep the institution going and in doing this they undermine their practices.[21] In community

17. Rich, *Growing Good*, 13.
18. Ivereigh, *Faithful Citizens*, 43.
19. Ritchie, *Inclusive Populism*, 52.
20. MacLeod, *Community Organising*, 4.
21. Bretherton, "Institutions."

organizing, institutions are challenged to live up to their values. In addition, community organizing helps disorganize institutions and reorganize them and get them moving in a different direction. This will mean becoming more outward rather than inward-focused with stronger relationships and more focus on the wider community. I will develop this further in chapter 6 where I will outline some implications of engaging in community organizing for the practice of Baptist and other churches in building relationships and working together with others based on their values.

2.3 Building Relational Power

Krehbiel highlights that the "basic vocabulary of community organizing . . . is troubling to many church leaders. . . . For many Christians, the vocabulary of faith and the vocabulary of organizing seem to be at odds, if not in outright contradiction."[22] Thus, Krehbiel highlights that, despite many faith organizations seeing community organizing as their best way to work for social justice and the common good, "there has always been a tension between the 'actions' of community organizations and the 'values' of the religious groups, mostly revolving around issues of tactics, power, and accountability."[23]

Bretherton highlights the emphasis in community organizing on building power and the development of an alternative power structure to that which already existed.[24] Thus, an understanding of and focus on power is at the heart of broad-based community organizing. How churches view power and how they understand, or not, their own power affects the relationships formed inside and outside churches and is therefore crucial for their engagement with the wider community and in broad-based community organizing. Ritchie highlights a common truth within organizing, "that those who need change the least are the ones most likely to problematise the issue of building power."[25] Related to this, Stout argues,

> Most people do not view their situation in terms of power relations. It is not in the perceived interest of the dominant to teach people how to conceive of and perceive power. Indeed the dominant would often prefer that power remain invisible and unmentioned. If ordinary people view it as something inherently bad and

22. Krehbiel, *Reflecting with Scripture*, 7–8.
23. Krehbiel, *Reflecting with Scripture*, 5.
24. Bretherton, *Resurrecting Democracy*, 46.
25. Ritchie, *Inclusive Populism*, 31.

> not the sort of thing one would like to acquire and exercise, so much the better from the perspective of the dominant.[26]

Therefore, to challenge dominant power we need to be able to talk about power constructively. Bretherton highlights that many people, including in churches, are overly suspicious about power, and they feel that power is remote for them; their experience is often of entrenched dominant power.[27] However, in *Doing Justice*, Jacobsen underlines,

> To the powerless, the Bible frequently promises power. . . . We find that we cannot run away from power once we take the ethical teachings of Jesus seriously. These teachings draw us into a life of compassion and righteousness that seeks justice.[28]

Bretherton understands that we aspire to live in the world as it should be where justice prevails and love rules. However, as we noted in section 1.3, organizing for power is needed to go from the world as it is to the world as it should be. Jacobsen, writing out of his experience of congregations involved in community organizing, argues,

> Sometimes the world as it should be can have limited, positive impact on the world as it is. It is likely to happen only when love enjoins power in the interests of justice, and this assumes a willingness to engage the rough and tumble public arena of the world as it is.[29]

Building on this, Graf quotes Pastor H. Lionel Edmonds, a senior minister of Mt. Lebanon Baptist Church in Washington, DC, who was very involved in WIN, the IAF alliance there. Edmonds understands that "power is not owned by the oppressor. Power belongs to those who possess the capacity to think in a creative and organised way and then to act with strength and precision."[30]

Using a quote that is often employed in organizing, Jacobsen recognizes that in seeking justice in the public sphere we learn the truth of Frederick Douglass's maxim, "Power yields nothing without a struggle. It never has and it never will."[31] Then, Jacobsen argues, we experience the distinction Reinhold Niebuhr made in *Moral Man and Immoral Society*: "As individuals, men believe that they ought to love and serve each other and establish justice between

26. Bretherton, *Resurrecting Democracy*, 40.
27. Bretherton, "Ability to Act."
28. Jacobsen, *Doing Justice*, 40.
29. Jacobsen, *Doing Justice*, 12.
30. Pierce, *Reveille for a New Generation*, 167.
31. Jacobsen, *Doing Justice*, 40.

each other. As racial, economic and national groups they take for themselves whatever their power can commend."[32] I will return to these connections between church practices and community organizing practices for social justice in chapter 3, and then in the second half of this book in relation to Baptist churches.

Broad-based community organizing focuses on building relational power. Engagement with Walter Wink, a US biblical scholar and theologian, on the concept of relational power was helpful in the development of community organizing. In *Engaging the Powers*, Wink provides a reading of the New Testament and the ministry of Jesus as exemplifying creative, nonviolent resistance and the use of relational power to bring about change.[33] Warren highlights how the IAF distinguish between two kinds of power—unilateral (as power over others) and relational (power with others to be able to act collectively). The IAF took this distinction from Bernard Loomer.[34] His writing on power has also been influential on organizing in the UK, particularly in the understanding of power with or relational power.[35] His article on "Two Conceptions of Power" distinguishes between power over and power with.[36] Relational power is mutual or shared power. For Loomer, love is in play in relational power where the quality of relationship and trust in the relationship are key.

Chambers argues that relational power is infinite and unifying, not limited and divisive. Thus, as you become more powerful, so do others in relationship with you. Conversely, as others who you are in relationship with become more powerful, so do you. Importantly, everyone has relational power, however marginalized and impoverished they are. In the book of Exodus, the Hebrew people experience Pharaoh's dominant power. In contrast, at Mount Sinai there is the building of relational power. Bretherton understands the vertical and horizontal dimensions of building relational power. He outlines the horizontal dimension as the relationships with existing and new member institutions of an alliance. The vertical dimension is the relationships with those with the power to make change on an issue.[37] There is an interesting

32. Jacobsen, *Doing Justice*, 40.

33. Other key books by Walter Wink on power are *Naming the Powers*; *Unmasking the Powers*; *Powers That Be*.

34. Warren, *Dry Bones Rattling*, 68.

35. Loomer, "Two Conceptions of Power."

36. Although the distinction between power with and power over originates with Follett, *Creative Experience*. Hannah Arendt also sketched a conception of relational power in her book *On Violence*. See also Arendt, *On Revolution*, 105–98.

37. Bretherton, *Resurrecting Democracy*, 138.

comparison to be made between this conception of relational power and Baptist understandings of covenant relationships. I will develop this further in chapters 5–6.

Every faith institution has power. They organize people and money every week. Graf argues that if churches and other organizations want power, then people need to organize their own people and money so that they can deliver them consistently and persistently.[38] In institutions you cannot avoid power held through hierarchies. The perception of power depends on the type of church. However, to disrupt unjust power structures in the world takes power. Community organizing builds power in communities and disrupts these power structures by bringing mercy, justice and discipleship together.

In regard to building power through organizing for the common good, Stout highlights that broad-based organizing is seeking to build bridges across lines of geography, class, race, ethnicity and religion where the well-being of the city as a whole is in the interest of each individual and group in the city.[39] He notes the convergence of interests in the common good with the need to build power but with fewer and weaker institutions. He highlights that more and more effort needs to be devoted to "reweaving the social fabric," through strengthening the relational life of institutions.[40]

Although Stout is writing about broad-based community organizing in the US, the same is true of the context in Wales and England, particularly in relation to churches. Therefore, with churches providing the backbone of alliances, community organizing is focused on organizing institutions that are in decline. So, it could be argued that community organizing is investing in groups which may disappear. We could ask the extent to which engagement in community organizing is able to halt or reduce rates of decline of faith institutions. We could also ask whether looking outwards helps churches grow—numerically and in leadership across the church. As we observed in section 2.2, there have been some studies in England which suggest that community organizing has led to the growth of some churches.

An early action as part of the living wage campaign in East London highlights how building relational power can make a bank live up to its values:

> A nun walks into a bank in central London on a Friday lunchtime. But she is not alone. Sister Una McCreesh and a group of nuns from a Roman Catholic convent in East London queue up for the tellers. Sister Una is the head teacher of a school. One day a pupil had written in his book that his mother was dead. It turned out he meant

38. Graf, *Lessons Learned*, 23.

39. Stout, *Blessed Are the Organized*, 37–38.

40. Stout, *Blessed Are the Organized*, 38.

> that she had three jobs, early morning, all day, and in the evening, and he so never saw her. Having heard numerous stories like this, Sister Una and others decided to act on low pay which was affecting this boy's family and many others in their community. Through their understanding of the gospel, the nuns put their faith into action. They wanted to persuade HSBC to pay the real living wage as it was a significant local employer. HSBC wouldn't give them a meeting, so they stored up the collection plate money for several weeks and took it into the bank's busiest branch to pay it in.
>
> There are about 1500 parishioners and the collection plate money was mostly in small coins. So, there was a large amount of money to be counted. This tied up one teller, while the other teller had a queue of nuns and other people each saying they would like to open a bank account. They caused enormous queues and the bank could not get any other business done that day. Because of their action, they got their meeting with senior staff at HSBC. After several further actions by leaders from Roman Catholic and other faith groups, this campaign was successful in winning significant change with their communities when HSBC agreed to pay the real living wage.

This story of Sister Una McCreesh and the campaign which led to HSBC becoming Canary Wharf's first Living Wage employer is also told in *Just Love*, a book by Angus Ritchie and Paul Hackwood, then director of the Church Urban Fund.[41] This story of building relational power and developing leadership by nuns and members of congregations from a variety of churches contributed to winning change on a justice issue. It involved teams of people, and leaders were developed through taking action together.

2.4 Tools and Practices to Build Relational Power

I will focus on how tools and practices to build relational power have been understood and used by churches, and their perceived usefulness both inside a congregation as well as in the wider community. I will focus on one-to-one relational meetings, house meetings, and accountability assemblies. Through these I will consider how churches have understood community organizing's approach to leadership development.

One-to-one relational meetings can be understood as the most important practice in community organizing. Everything builds from these. In *Realities Are Greater Than Ideas*, Rodrigues describes the practice of community

41. Ritchie and Hackwood, *Just Love*, 57–61.

organizing from the perspectives of parishes involved. This resource makes use of Pope Francis's teachings to address the questions of why and how Catholics are called to organize. It also shares stories and lessons from the last twenty years of Catholic involvement in broad-based community organizing in the UK.[42] Rodrigues is keen to examine what organizing offers the church and what the church offers to organizing.[43]

In considering what organizing offers the church, Rodrigues highlights that the tools and practices of community organizing enable Catholics to embody something of the gospel. Rodrigues maintains that distinctive Catholic Christian engagement in organizing will be suffused with prayer and regular reflection on the Gospels, and it will start with our encounter with God. Rodrigues goes on to assert that this engagement will recognize and be attentive to the activity of God in people and in actions, for example in one-to-one conversations. Rodrigues describes one-to-ones as "sacramental encounters," recognizing that genuine respectful and open encounter is at the heart of our faith; we encounter Christ in our meetings with each other if we know how to listen.[44] The one-to-one conversation enables people to encounter others in their community face to face and so helps embody a culture of encounter. Rodrigues also argues that this captures something of the way Jesus encountered others.[45]

House meetings are another key practice in community organizing for listening and developing leaders. Cortes describes these meetings as "the crucible of democracy." In this understanding, democracy depends on people being able to deliberate together and develop knowledge and wisdom together. Bretherton argues that most people do not usually have access to these spaces where house meetings build relationships between people in a neighborhood or geographical area.[46] House meetings can be places of encounter for people from different backgrounds but with overlapping concerns and visions for their community. In house meetings relationships are developed between people. Decision-making that takes place in these meetings puts people directly affected by issues at the center of discussions and decisions.

In considering what the church offers to organizing, Rodrigues notes that churches, by embodying a rich culture of encounter, can help ensure that organizing is rooted in deep listening to those on the margins, through one-to-one conversations and house meetings. Therefore, through the use of these

42. Rodrigues, *Realities Are Greater*, 4.
43. Rodrigues, *Realities Are Greater*, 3.
44. Rodrigues, *Realities Are Greater*, 35.
45. Rodrigues, *Realities Are Greater*, 26.
46. Bretherton, "Other Basic Tool."

practices, churches will be rooted in the realities of peoples' lives rather than just ideas about what their lives might be like.

Rodrigues describes Cortes's understanding of house meetings as small group meetings which are about relationship building, telling stories and developing narratives, while also inquiring into the deep concerns affecting people's lives.[47] A house meeting can be described as a small group conversation to understand what is happening in a neighborhood. It is a tool for solidarity to bring people from different parts of an area together. House meetings in institutions such as churches can build relationships and create imagination and energy. Rodrigues notes this will be intertwined with theological reflection and prayer and provide a communal time for reflection on how the community can act on an issue. In churches, house meetings have been included in weekly prayer meetings in Roman Catholic churches and these house meetings often start and end with prayer.[48] I observe some similarities with house groups in Baptist churches and with the Baptist practice of church meetings. I will explore this further in chapter 6.

Accountability assemblies are large public gatherings bringing together member institutions of an alliance to share their priorities for making change on social justice issues with decision makers from business and government. The purpose is to seek to build accountable relationships with these decision makers on these priorities in order to bring about change. Community organizing makes much use of religious language. For example, in assemblies as well as in one-to-one conversations and house meetings, people sharing their experience of an injustice is described as them sharing their testimony on this issue. Sharing testimony is seen as sharing private grief or pain around a social injustice in a public setting. Therefore, in this practice, private religion becomes public. A private faith is being publicly expressed and lived out in public.

Rodrigues highlights that community organizing enables people on the margins of society to come into the center of politics and public life. He notes that organizing is about "including the poor in society not just as a matter of justice and responsibility, but also because we can become enriched and learn by listening to them."[49] Organizing offers occasions for the church to work with those who are often beyond its walls.[50] People who are on the margins of their communities or institutions often play central roles in public actions and assemblies to bring about change on issues which grieve and anger them personally, as well as others in their community. Rodrigues recognizes that

47. Rodrigues, *Realities Are Greater*, 17.

48. Bretherton, "Other Basic Tool."

49. Rodrigues, *Realities Are Greater*, 30.

50. Rodrigues, *Realities Are Greater*, 19.

community organizing develops these people as grassroots leaders and so, "gives the most excluded and often disillusioned communities the confidence that public engagement could be successful and indeed enjoyable, and builds relationships of solidarity and trust across communities."[51] This is what I observed in my first experience of Citizens in London. This is also what we observe in the Nando's story in section 1.5, and the story of the living wage action in the bank in section 2.3.

Krehbiel highlights that "a fundamental assumption of organizing is that every community has within it leaders capable of acting on their own behalf in relationship with others. The goal of organizing is to find and cultivate those leaders."[52] Therefore, Krehbiel maintains that this challenges how leadership is often understood by church leaders. It also challenges how a church engages with the community outside its door. The wider community is seen to have resources and not just needs.[53]

Identifying and developing the leadership of people on the margins of communities and institutions through organizing is in contrast to what Krehbiel identifies as "the tension in our culture . . . between what biblical scholar Walter Brueggemann calls the myth of scarcity and the liturgy of abundance." Krehbiel, in reflecting on the account of the feeding of the five thousand in Mark 6:30–44, highlights that Jesus directs the disciples to have the crowd sit down in groups of fifty to one hundred and comments that in that moment the crowd becomes a community. This changes the dynamic when the crowd is organized into a community and is able to look more deeply and discover the abundant resources already present.[54] The worry over scarcity drives people "to imagine that their needs will be met only if each person fends for himself or herself."[55] The myth of scarcity leads to isolation whereas the liturgy of abundance is celebrated in community. Jesus pushes his disciples into community in the feeding of the five thousand, where their leadership is still critical. It is they who organize the crowd. But it is in relationship, in the context of community, that leaders are identified and developed, the resources flow and there is common action together.[56]

It can be argued that we live in increasingly socially fragmented communities. Miller notes that churches are often the only values-based, stable

51. Rodrigues, *Realities Are Greater*, 11.
52. Krehbiel, *Reflecting with Scripture*, 16.
53. Krehbiel, *Reflecting with Scripture*, 16–17.
54. Krehbiel, *Reflecting with Scripture*, 13.
55. Krehbiel, *Reflecting with Scripture*, 15.
56. Krehbiel, *Reflecting with Scripture*, 15.

organizations in many low-income communities.[57] Miller argues that, in churches, community organizing begins with people sharing with one another about their faith and their concerns, and then reaching out in wider circles to their neighbors. This can also be understood as the move from sharing in a one-to-one conversation to sharing in a house meeting and then in an accountability assembly. Thus, as Miller notes, "organizing begins with the life experience of people in the congregation and it then enables them to construct a believable vision that connects their faith to action in the world."[58] However, Miller argues that "many congregations fail to function as communities . . . [there is] little sharing of people's core concerns."[59] Through community organizing, congregations are called to take on a special responsibility for their neighborhood. This responsibility is to activate their neighbors from passivity to participation and to move from a sense of powerlessness to one of self-empowerment through relationship-building and the beginnings of a deeper community.[60]

In *Dry Bones Rattling*, Warren opens this study of the IAF alliance in San Antonio, Texas—COPS—with the story of Father Al Jost praying with other COPS leaders ahead of a major assembly where the alliance was calling for affordable housing, job training and school reform. Father Al spoke that day about

> the story of Ezekiel's prophecy of the valley of dry bones, a symbol of a community in ruins, physically and spiritually, a community without hope and in despair. Father Al spoke of the bones beginning to rattle, to come together, of sinews forming, and flesh and blood growing. He told of a great army emerging as a symbol of the community coming together to rebuild itself.[61]

Picking up from the analysis of Davie highlighted in section 1.4, David Barclay, from the Centre for Theology and Community, comments that such weakened communities are a result of the "withering of the public sphere," with the rapid decline in membership of public institutions such as political parties, trade unions and faith groups.[62] He notes that "where neighbours might have previously interacted in a number of different places—from trades unions to voluntary associations or local places of worship—now there are fewer opportunities

57. Miller, *Community Organizing*, 16.
58. Miller, *Community Organizing*, 20.
59. Miller, *Community Organizing*, 21.
60. Miller, *Community Organizing*, 22.
61. Warren, *Dry Bones Rattling*, 3.
62. Barclay, *Making Multiculturalism Work*, 19.

for meaningful relationships to be formed which cross boundaries of belief, tradition and culture."[63] He then highlights how this has led to the disappearance of the soft skills to make connection across difference possible.

Barclay highlights the work of Danielle Allen, a US academic, on political friendship as a relational process of working together in spite of differences. He goes on to highlight that Citizens UK and community organizing, in helping people act on their own interests, is a key catalyst for building such political friendships and community.[64] He notes that suspicion of religion as a motivation for engagement makes it harder to build the political friendships needed in our communities. Barclay understands that community organizing enables people of faith to talk openly about their core motivations for engaging in the public sphere.[65]

Bretherton argues that those who seek to keep religious language out of the public sphere thus prevent real dialogue and encounter. Bretherton understands that "what we need is a politics that can live with deep plurality over questions of ultimate meaning and can encompass the fact that many communities and traditions can contribute to the common good—each in their own way."[66] Bretherton goes on to argue that "the hearing of others' interests and concerns in the context of ongoing relationships and the recognition that everyone . . . occupies the same mutual (not neutral) ground foster the sense that in each other's welfare we find our own."[67]

Barclay argues that taking action together, combined with sharing core motivations and testimony, can help people develop "deep" public identities and so break down the division of the public and private realms in society.[68] He quotes Anna Rowlands, a UK Catholic theologian, who recognizes that community organizing "doesn't place barriers around religious identities in the way that lots of other forms of political advocacy would do, so it sees as seamless the relationship between religious identities and social and political identities."[69] From this, there is a clear need to engage across difference and across boundaries. Community organizing, where people are able to share openly about their motivations for action and for being involved, should therefore be a place where Baptists who are keen on mission feel welcome and able to share their faith motivation. I will develop this further in chapter 6.

63. Barclay, *Making Multiculturalism Work*, 20.
64. Barclay, *Making Multiculturalism Work*, 21–26.
65. Barclay, *Making Multiculturalism Work*, 36.
66. Bretherton, *Christianity and Contemporary Politics*, 50.
67. Bretherton, *Christianity and Contemporary Politics*, 88.
68. Barclay, *Making Multiculturalism Work*, 45.
69. Barclay, *Making Multiculturalism Work*, 49.

2.5 Institutional Structures and Churches' Involvement

As Bretherton notes, in the Southwest IAF in the US, a number of Roman Catholic leaders and organizers had experience of working in Latin America. In these IAF alliances, engagement between the Roman Catholic Church and broad-based community organizing included a focus on liberation theology and elements of liberation theology were critically appropriated and incorporated into organizing.[70] Warren also notes that Roman Catholics in the IAF took some inspiration from liberation theology.[71] However, instead of forming base communities they instead participated within existing church structures.[72]

Stout highlights that, according to Cortes, "the liberation theology movement had essentially invited Vatican censure by allowing its own version of regularised house meetings, the so-called base communities, to develop into a second church within the church."[73] Cortes was therefore careful to shape IAF practices in a way that would not invite the Catholic hierarchy to respond negatively. Sister Judy Donovan, a former IAF organizer in California, had previously been involved in rural base communities in Brazil. Stout quotes her as saying, "Goodness and right [theology and analysis] fail all the time. There had to be a way to put our words of faith into action or, you know, what does it matter?"[74] Stout notes that Donovan came to see liberation theology as excessively abstract and idealistic, whereas broad-based community organizing is pragmatic.

As we observed in section 1.3, Black-majority Baptist churches have played a key role in broad-based community organizations in the US. This appears to be despite what could be seen as an institutional structure which could make it harder to engage them. Rogers notes significant differences between the role of a Catholic parish in a Hispanic neighborhood—with involvement in community organizing being done under the authority of the priest and a supportive bishop—and the role of a church in a Black community with the autonomy and power of the minister. Rogers recognizes that many Black pastors have had to build their own institution and their power. In comparison, Catholic priests are given a powerful position in a church.[75]

70. Bretherton, *Resurrecting Democracy*, 89.

71. Warren, *Dry Bones Rattling*, 194.

72. For a discussion comparing the IAF to base communities, see Rogers, *Cold Anger*, 136–39.

73. Stout, *Blessed Are the Organized*, 188.

74. Stout, *Blessed Are the Organized*, 189.

75. Rogers, *Cold Anger*, 174.

Baptists are not always good at associating with others.[76] Warren highlights that "in Baptist denominations, congregations are fiercely independent," although they do form associations and pastor networks are important.[77] In contrast, Roman Catholics and Anglicans have models of associating in their ecclesial structures, through the parish structure. Through these, it can be understood that churches have a sense of responsibility for everyone in their parish. Warren highlights that Roman Catholic churches have lots of lay leaders within the parish and the local neighborhood itself. He notes that this contrasts with the number of lay leaders in Black-majority and mainline Protestant churches.[78] In addition, Protestant congregations are often drawn from more than one neighborhood and not just from the neighborhood where the church meets.

One of the biggest institutional challenges appears to be that Protestant churches in the US are often meeting in more affluent neighborhoods and so struggle to connect with the interests of those in the congregation and local area.[79] I observe that this is also largely true of Baptists in the UK, although less so in Wales, where many Baptist churches are associated with working-class communities. We will investigate this further in chs. 4–5.

The parish hierarchy and the neighborhood-based parish have supported Roman Catholic involvement. In addition, the focus on lay leadership development within Catholic parishes links well with broad-based community organizing and its focus on leadership development.[80] However, I observe that there is little or no mention of what this means for changing patterns of leadership in Catholic, Anglican, and other church denominations where traditionally there has been one or a small number of people whom everyone looks to for leadership and decision-making. I agree with Warren when he concludes that "even more than faith traditions . . . institutional structure has a profound influence on the ability of religious communities to generate effective power."[81]

76. This is despite the commitment to watching over and walking with others in early Baptist confessions and declarations. These confessions and declaration were also shared convictions of churches meeting together rather than just the product of one church. I will explore this further in chs. 4–5 and also develop this in ch. 6.

77. Warren, *Dry Bones Rattling*, 201.

78. Warren, *Dry Bones Rattling*, 209.

79. Warren, *Dry Bones Rattling*, 205.

80. Warren, *Dry Bones Rattling*, 195.

81. Warren, *Dry Bones Rattling*, 209.

2.6 The Hallmarks of an Organized Church

From the engagement of churches in broad-based community organizing in Wales and England, the hallmarks of an organized church began to be articulated. Examining these is one way to put together community organizing practices to build relational power in a congregation. In *People of Power*, Ritchie identifies seven hallmarks of an organized church across very different denominations and traditions.[82] These are habits which enable a local congregation to harness the potential of organizing both for renewing their internal life and for taking action with their neighbors on issues of common concern. Ritchie's experience is that when these habits are cultivated, internal renewal and external action reinforce one another. In doing so, Ritchie argues that churches fulfil Paul's injunction to Timothy—moving from timidity to discover a new spirit of "power, love and self-discipline" (2 Tim 1:7).[83]

The first two hallmarks of an organized church focus on faithful and effective ministry. The first hallmark is that the church integrates theology, spirituality and action. As Ritchie highlights, in many congregations, community engagement and social action appear to be the passion of a small number of church members, but not part of the institution's "core business." If social action is to move from the periphery to the core of a church's life, Ritchie argues that worship and teaching will need to express the connection between the two.[84]

Rodrigues argues that an organized Catholic parish integrates theology, spirituality and action. Thus, as Rodrigues notes, "the congregations' participation in organizing flows out of their encounter with Jesus Christ. So rather than social action feeling like the passion of only a few church members on the sidelines it instead is integrated into the spiritual and sacramental life of the community."[85] Thus, the second hallmark of an organized church is a relational culture where there is regular teaching on the theological importance of relationship building.[86]

The next three hallmarks focus on planned and sustainable leadership. The third hallmark is that the church is constantly reorganizing, to renew its

82. Ritchie, *People of Power*, 23. These seven hallmarks are an updated version of the hallmarks of an "Organised Catholic Church" outlined in Rodrigues, *Realities Are Greater*, 17–20.

83. Here Ritchie is explicitly drawing on and using the same verse employed at the start of the foundational document for the modern IAF, *Organizing for Families and Congregations*, as described in ch. 1 (Pierce, *Reveille for a New Generation*, 372).

84. Ritchie, *People of Power*, 24.

85. Rodrigues, *Realities Are Greater*, 17.

86. Rodrigues, *Realities Are Greater*, 25.

focus on people.[87] As noted earlier, a phrase much used in community organizing is that "All organizing is dis-organizing and re-organizing." A congregation which has taken community organizing to its heart is in a perpetual process of being transformed.

Thus, an organized church will constantly be evaluating whether its meetings allow every voice to be heard. It will also evaluate whether people from different cultures, age groups and classes are involved in leadership. It will evaluate whether church activities genuinely reflect the concerns and values of the whole membership, and whether they are accessible to those on the margins of the church community. In addition, leadership will be understood to be about developing the capacity of others to act and to lead.[88]

In the fourth hallmark, leaders are being developed through public action. Therefore, the process used to plan, deliver, and evaluate a church meeting will be understood to be as important as anything the meeting decides. Community organizing encourages church congregations to see every part of their life as an opportunity to develop new leaders. Thus, an organized church will have an increasing number of people developing their leadership capabilities, both in the church and outside the walls of the church building.[89]

The fifth hallmark is that power and responsibility are shared. As Ritchie notes, it will take time for a new team of leaders to take responsibility for the life of the local church. When power is shared in this way, responsibility and ownership are also shared.[90]

The final two hallmarks of an organized church focus on engagement with the wider community. The sixth hallmark is that the church has an instinctive readiness to work with those beyond its walls. Organized churches engage in holistic mission, demonstrating the integrity of their commitment to the common good. They understand the need for collective power in order to realize that common good, and so act with other congregations of faith and institutions of civil society. Its members are willing to be influenced by, as well as to influence, those beyond its walls.[91]

Finally, in the seventh hallmark, a congregation tells and embodies the Christian story. Both telling and hearing one another's stories, within the congregation and in the public arena, are at the heart of the church's

87. This resonates with the phrase *ecclesia reformata, semper reformanda* (the church reformed must always be reformed) used by Dutch Reformed Church theologian Johannes Hoornbeeck (1617–66) and picked up by seventeenth-century Baptists.

88. Ritchie, *People of Power*, 26.

89. Ritchie, *People of Power*, 27.

90. Ritchie, *People of Power*, 29.

91. Ritchie, *People of Power*, 29.

culture—connecting its stories wherever possible with the biblical story. Ritchie understands that in our increasingly privatized and individualistic world, this congregation is confident, both at telling the Christian story and in embodying it—in the way it reaches out and the way it welcomes others in.[92]

Ritchie recognizes that community organizing helps people grow as disciples, seeing organizing as something that can help the church to be more faithfully the church. Thus, for him, community organizing is not just about applying an approach but as the way we do church in developing leaders, maturing disciples and acting on social injustices.

2.7 Summary

In this chapter we have explored how churches from different denominations understand and use key practices of community organizing. In section 2.2, we observed how church engagement in community organizing has led to a fuller articulation of the values on which both organizing and churches are based. Community organizing connects strongly with the values of churches and with Christ's teaching and practice on love and justice. Organizing has enabled churches to put these values and their faith into action. We also noted that an initial attraction to community organizing for churches may also be driven by other interests.

Building relational power is a key area in community organizing. An understanding of power as power with or relational power was contrasted with a common understanding and experience of power as dominant power or power over. In addition, we have explored how tools and practices to build relational power have been understood by churches. These tools include one-to-one conversations, house meetings, and accountability assemblies. We have also examined how institutional structures have influenced churches' involvement in community organizing. We observed how churches involved in organizing were inspired by Latin American theologies of liberation, but without challenging directly the existing structures and hierarchies within church denominations. We noted that institutional structure has a profound influence on the ability of churches to generate effective relational power with others. Finally, we have explored one way that community organizing practices to build relational power in a congregation have been put together in the UK.

This literature review of churches' understanding and use of community organizing reveals the crucial point that for many churches their understanding of community organizing and theological reflection on it has come from

92. Ritchie, *People of Power*, 30.

their use and practice of it rather than the other way round. The *hallmarks of an organized church*, developed by Ritchie, are based on churches' experience and use of community organizing, rather than as a theoretical framework to engage churches in organizing. This is not about convincing churches that social justice is deeply rooted in Christian faith. However, through their engagement in organizing, churches have made it a bigger priority for a congregation by moving social justice to the center of the life of the church congregation and integrating social justice in all aspects of a church congregation. In chapter 6 we will explore what this could mean for Baptist engagement in broad-based community organizing.

Bretherton argues that "a key catalyst for constructively engaging with religious discourses can be the presence of an organiser from within a particular tradition for whom wrestling with the points of connection and contention between organising and their religious beliefs and practices generates a more self-conscious process of engagement."[93] This is me! This is where I find myself and my theological engagement with broad-based community organizing, coming from a Baptist perspective. I also recognize this is also true for many of the key organizers in the US and in the UK.

Bretherton then goes on to argue that more significant is a robust relationship between key religious leaders and organizers and to be able to engage in open and critical dialogue between them on what matters to them. For me, the question remains to what extent the Roman Catholic faith of many of the early organizers in the US set the pattern for involving Catholic churches in broad-based community organizing, and the extent to which Catholic teaching and traditions have influenced the practice of community organizing. We will explore this further, and build on the themes emerging from chapters 1–2, as we focus on theological reflection on community organizing in the next chapter.

93. Bretherton, *Resurrecting Democracy*, 90.

Chapter 3

Theological Reflection on Community Organizing

3.1 Introduction

CHAPTERS 1–2 HAVE SHOWN the depth of the involvement of churches in community organizing and their understanding and use of community organizing practices. As Bretherton highlights, "Community organising continues to have a symbiotic relationship with religious beliefs and practices, in particular those of Christianity."[1] Bretherton argues that "it is churches of all denominations that have most intensively and faithfully engaged with and funded Alinsky's approach to organising, both during his life and subsequently."[2] These chapters have also shown how theological reflection and thinking has been woven into community organizing.

The theological and ethical themes explored in these first two chapters include acting on justice issues based on values, the understanding of relational power, and building relationships with others—including with impoverished and marginalized people. These themes which have emerged from churches' engagement in community organizing are not identical with, but are related to, themes within the social justice literature that preceded and

1. Bretherton, *Resurrecting Democracy*, 23.

2. Bretherton, *Resurrecting Democracy*, 35.

have developed alongside the emergence of community organizing, such as liberation theology, Black theology, and CST.

Theological reflections on community organizing therefore join a conversation about power, love and justice with those on the margins that has already been present for a while. I am considering how theologies of liberation and social justice that have already been developed are strengthened and deepened by a theology of community organizing that emerges from its practice. Community organizing has built on and reshaped the social justice literature that proceeded it. In this book, I focus on who is contributing to this literature and what they add to the conversation on a Baptist theological ethic for the practice of social justice.

This chapter will focus on how theologians and community organizers in the US and UK reflect theologically on community organizing. I am keen to explore whom they reference and who has influenced them, as well as which theologians they mostly ignore. From the community organizing literature, the three main interlocutors are Edward Chambers, Ernesto Cortes, and Michael Gecan. I focus on theological reflections on organizing from Luke Bretherton, Austen Ivereigh, Angus Ritchie, and Anna Rowlands.

The division between these two lists is complicated somewhat by the fact that the US community organizers listed above all came to organizing having completed theological study. In addition, the theologians listed have all had significant involvement as leaders (and as an organizer in the case of Austen Ivereigh) in Citizens UK alliances. Theological reflection on community organizing is going on constantly by leaders and organizers, much of which is not written down or published. I have restricted myself in this chapter to reflections on the available literature.

Ritchie describes community organizing growing out of churches on the margins who are, "working in the midst of weakness and vulnerability to build a powerful movement for social justice."[3] Ritchie emphasizes that this means "building the power of the most vulnerable and marginalised communities to achieve social change," and to grow in God's love together.[4] For Ritchie, community organizing is not just applying an approach but as the way we do church in developing leaders, fostering discipleship, acting on social injustices, and putting relationship building at the center of the life of the church. In *Resurrecting Democracy*, Bretherton contends that "community organising provides a lens through which to constructively address these concerns [economic and political turmoil, the relationship between different faiths and political life] and understand better the relationship between religious

3. Ritchie and Hackwood, *Just Love*, 101.

4. Ritchie and Hackwood, *Just Love*, 107.

diversity, democratic citizenship, and economic and political accountability."[5] Bretherton takes the term "community" in the term "community organizing" to denote "a coming together by mutual agreement of distinct institutions for a common purpose without loss of each of their specific identities or beliefs and practices."[6] Therefore, churches can bring their whole selves, beliefs, and practices into broad-based community organizing. Thus, it is not surprising that so many churches are involved.

3.1.1 Theologians Cited in the Community Organizing Literature

From the literature reviewed in chapters 1–2 we have seen that these authors were picking up the ambient voices of who was most significant in theology and Christian ethics at the time. Therefore, there are references to Stanley Hauerwas, Walter Wink, Reinhold Niebuhr, Walter Brueggemann, Paul Tillich, and Dietrich Bonhoeffer, among others, in the literature. Thus, we can ask the question of who has been woven seriously into the theology of community organizing. Going beyond periodic references to specific figures, the sources or figures that appear to be the most influential in current theological reflection on community organizing are the CST tradition that starts with *Rerum Novarum* in 1891 and goes through the Vatican II documents, and the recent work of Pope Francis which is explicitly reflective of community organizing. These are related but distinct sources.

3.1.2 The Influence of Catholic Social Teaching on Community Organizing

The theological tradition of CST has played a formative role in the development of community organizing in Wales and England. Anna Rowlands, a British Catholic political theologian with a long-standing involvement with Citizens UK in London and in northeast England, notes that CST comes into being in the context of the Catholic Church seeking to "form consciences and communities rather than wielding political power—and with the church not in the state, and the state not in the church."[7] We observed in chapter 2 the influence of CST on the US community organizer Ernesto Cortes in particular. Pope Francis's teaching has had a great deal of influence on Austen

5. Bretherton, *Resurrecting Democracy*, 2.
6. Bretherton, *Resurrecting Democracy*, 241.
7. Rowlands, *Towards a Politics of Communion*, 180.

Ivereigh, Angus Ritchie, and Anna Rowlands and their thinking on community organizing.

In *Faithful Citizens*, Austen Ivereigh reveals how broad-based community organizing expresses key aspects of CST. He was formerly a community organizer with Citizens UK and latterly has been the biographer of Pope Francis.[8] In *Faithful Citizens*, Ivereigh argues that CST principles often seem abstract and there appears to be no vehicle for translating them into action. He argues that the fuel and road map offered by CST have found a perfect vehicle in community organizing.

For Ivereigh, community organizing is so suitable as a vehicle for CST because it is "deliberately unideological, emphasising action over theory, and because it *does* politics rather than just *talks* about it."[9] Ivereigh argues that "the most important thing for community organizing is what CST teaches us about relationships: this is the key to building the power to act. Before you can act, you must first build those relationships."[10] Ivereigh claims that "the brilliance of community organising—the reason it is so effective—is that it organises around *people* [and relationships between people], not *issues*."[11] For Ivereigh this is why it fits so well with CST. CST Principles which speak most directly to those engaged in community organizing include solidarity, subsidiarity, and the common good. Rowlands explains that CST is above all an orientation towards a particular kind of social imagination and challenges our social imaginations.[12] As Rodrigues notes, through the application of CST, "the Church can remind a broad[-]based alliance . . . that '*time is greater than space*,'" and so "organise with patience and with a focus on people."[13]

Both Rowlands and Ivereigh expertly highlight what we can learn from CST and papal encyclicals from *Rerum Novarum* onwards. Papal encyclicals and other key documents produced by Pope Francis and previous popes such as *Rerum Novarum*,[14] *Gaudium et Spes*,[15] *Evangelii Gaudium*,[16] *Laudato Si'*,[17]

8. Francis, *Let Us Dream*.

9. Ivereigh, *Faithful Citizens*, 33; emphasis in original.

10. Ivereigh, *Faithful Citizens*, 160.

11. Ivereigh, *Faithful Citizens*, 5; emphasis in original.

12. Anna Rowlands, at book launch for *Towards a Politics of Communion*, Jan. 25, 2022.

13. Rodrigues, *Realities Are Greater*, 31; emphasis in original.

14. Leo XIII, *Rerum Novarum*.

15. Paul VI, *Gaudium et Spes*.

16. Francis, *Evangelii Gaudium*.

17. Francis, *Laudato Si*.'

and *Fratelli Tutti*[18] have all played a key role in engaging Roman Catholic groups in community organizing. For example, *Rerum Novarum* highlighted the importance of a just wage and Citizens UK now lives that out in campaigns for a living wage. Roman Catholic schools and parishes in Wales and England often play leading roles in these campaigns.

Six major principles that appear to be emerging most consistently in the current theological reflection on community organizing are solidarity, subsidiarity, the common good, neighborliness, listening, and centering the margins. From this list we observe the significant influence of CST on community organizing. For a start, the first three are key principles of CST. In this chapter, I will explore substantively how different figures have reflected theologically on each of these principles. There will be some inevitable blurring of the boundaries in these sections, reflecting how the principles interrelate, for example, solidarity and subsidiarity, and solidarity and neighborliness, to pick just two examples. Finally, I will analyze what is missing from the current theological reflection on community organizing. This chapter will therefore lay the groundwork for the following chapters which will focus on Baptists and community organizing in the UK, looking at where these themes are present, if at all, in the social justice theologies of Baptists.

3.2 Solidarity

Let us consider the principle of solidarity. The *Catechism of the Catholic Church* defines human solidarity in this way:

> The principle of solidarity, also articulated in terms of *friendship* or *social charity*, is a direct demand of human and Christian brotherhood.
>
> An error, today abundantly widespread, is disregard for the law of human solidarity and charity, dictated and imposed both by our common origin and by the equality in rational nature of all men, whatever nation they belong to. This law is sealed by the sacrifice of redemption offered by Jesus Christ on the altar of the Cross to his heavenly Father, on behalf of sinful humanity.
>
> Solidarity is manifested in the first place by the distribution of goods and remuneration for work. It also presupposes the effort for a more just social order where tensions are better able to be reduced and conflicts more readily settled by negotiation.
>
> Socio-economic problems can be resolved only with the help of all the forms of solidarity: solidarity of the poor among

18. Francis, *Fratelli Tutti*.

> themselves, between rich and poor, of workers among themselves, between employers and employees in a business, solidarity among nations and peoples. International solidarity is a requirement of the moral order; world peace depends in part upon this.
>
> The virtue of solidarity goes beyond material goods. In spreading the spiritual goods of the faith, the Church has promoted, and often opened new paths for, the development of temporal goods as well. So throughout the centuries has the Lord's saying been verified: "Seek first his kingdom and his righteousness, and all these things shall be yours as well":
>
> For two thousand years this sentiment has lived and endured in the soul of the Church, impelling souls then and now to the heroic charity of monastic farmers, liberators of slaves, healers of the sick, and messengers of faith, civilization, and science to all generations and all peoples for the sake of creating the social conditions capable of offering to everyone possible a life worthy of man and of a Christian.[19]

Therefore, as Ivereigh notes, CST starts from the person as a spiritual being, defined through relations with other people and with God. These relationships are of fundamental importance. Ivereigh goes on to highlight that solidarity is "strongly linked to justice, for it highlights the interdependence of all human beings, and is a commitment to seeking the good of one's neighbour, especially the most vulnerable."[20] For Pope Francis, solidarity "acknowledges our interconnectedness: we are creatures in relationship, with duties toward each other, and all are called to participate in society."[21] Pope Francis states that "the word 'solidarity' is a little worn and at times poorly understood, but it refers to something more than a few sporadic acts of generosity. It presumes the creation of a new mindset which thinks in terms of community."[22] So, solidarity means becoming "solid with," becoming "attached to." The struggle for justice and dignity of impoverished and marginalized people becomes my struggle.

Rowlands notes that solidarity enters the lexicon expressing what had been thought of in Christian usage over centuries as *fraternity* and *friendship*.[23] As Rowlands highlights, CST has been influenced by Jacques Maritain's

19. Catholic Church, *Catechism*, §§1939–42.

20. Ivereigh, *Faithful Citizens*, 167.

21. Francis, *Let Us Dream*, 53.

22. Francis, *Evangelii Gaudium*, §188. See also Rowlands, *Towards a Politics of Communion*, 261.

23. Rowlands, *Towards a Politics of Communion*, 240.

thinking on pluralism and the radical solidarity of Dorothy Day.[24] Jacques Maritain was a French Catholic political philosopher who perceived "the state as an organizational and administrative instrument whose purpose was to serve justice and the common good, but not to be elevated beyond this."[25] Day was committed to solidarity with the weak, oppressed, and marginalized, which involved challenging the actions and attitudes of powerful people and groups.[26] As we observed in chapter 1, Maritain was influential on Alinsky in developing community organizing. In addition, Chambers spent time with Dorothy Day's Catholic Worker Movement before becoming an organizer with Alinsky.

Loaves and Fishes is Dorothy Day's account of thirty years as leader of the Catholic Worker Movement and a companion book to Day's autobiography, *The Long Loneliness.* As Day and the Catholic Worker Movement demonstrate, "we have an obligation to ourselves to know what is possible for our fellow human beings to imagine, and more important, to bring into being, to realize, day in, day out."[27] From this account, we learn that Maritain was a visitor to the organization, that Peter Maurin (with whom Day founded the Catholic Worker newspaper) would have preferred to call it "Catholic Radical" as radicals get to the root of things, which includes the principle of studying together and thinking about a problem before acting.[28] From this we can observe nuggets of where the Catholic Worker Movement's approach influenced the development of community organizing. Through supporting strikes, forming houses of hospitality in cities across the US, and working together on communitarian farms, Day is describing solidarity between the movement's staff and the many impoverished people supported by the Catholic Worker Movement.

Rowan Williams, a Welsh theologian and former archbishop of both Wales and Canterbury, notes that in the last twenty to thirty years the theme of solidarity as a foundational point has come more and more into focus. Solidarity is not a term solely used in theological thinking. For example, in Wales we might think about solidarity and the labor movement and unions, and the solidarity of working-class communities. From this Williams argues that solidarity might be better seen as "a radical shared interest."[29] I find this focus on a radical shared interest helpful and important. What is important here is to be able to leap over the natural solidarity of class and neighborhood which

24. Rowlands, *Towards a Politics of Communion*, 29.

25. Rowlands, *Towards a Politics of Communion*, 181.

26. Bradstock and Rowland, *Radical Christian Writings*, 204.

27. Day, *Loaves and Fishes*, xiii.

28. Day, *Loaves and Fishes*, 7–31.

29. Williams, "Solidarity," 09:52.

you might expect and make the leap to something you would not expect. For example, think of people leaping across differences of race, class, and religion to have a radical shared commitment together.

Kenneth Leech, an Anglo-Catholic priest and community theologian, is frequently quoted in Ritchie's theological engagement with community organizing. Leech and Ritchie both reflect in their writing on their ministries in Whitechapel in East London.[30] Leech describes a minority Christian community in the middle of a large Muslim population, surrounded by an even larger population of people not connected to any faith. He argues that "in this context of plurality, diversity and confusion . . . [the] Church [was] faced now, as always, with the false polarities of ghetto or surrender, of the heroic sect surrounded by impenetrable walls or the shapeless pseudo-community of the unclear and the vague."[31] Leech makes reference to members of "the East London community group" in helping him understand community.[32] It is possible that here Leech is referring to TELCO, the Citizens UK alliance in East London.

Ivereigh links solidarity with the community organizing practice of large public assemblies and has a chapter in *Faithful Citizens* entitled "Assembling in Solidarity." Ivereigh notes that an assembly is a key event in community organizing, "a 'civic congregation' where people of different faiths and none who live alongside each other express the hopes and frustrations they share for the city, commit to working in solidarity with each other for the common good, and hold people with power to account."[33]

Leech understands that individualism is not able to sustain a genuine community of persons in relationship. Instead of individualism, a central point for Leech is "the need for a strong sense of common life, rooted in God and in human solidarity." Thus, Leech reveals that solidarity "is not about creating union out of the materials of discord, but rather of combating those forces which disrupt solidarity through a return to the source of solidarity, that is, to God."[34] Thus, this is about returning to a solidarity that is already given by God, rather than creating it.

Rowan Williams picks up on this, highlighting that we are bound together in solidarity, our interests are shared, and our good depends on one another.

30. Leech, *Sky Is Red*, 1.

31. Leech, *Sky Is Red*, 3.

32. Leech, *Sky Is Red*, 7.

33. Ivereigh, *Faithful Citizens*, 71. In this chapter Ivereigh focuses on the same London Citizens assembly in Nov. 2009 that Bretherton uses powerfully in the opening chapter of his book *Resurrecting Democracy*.

34. Leech, *Sky Is Red*, 34.

Building on this and returning to the idea of solidarity as a radical shared interest, Williams, in his 2021 Ken Leech lecture, understands that shared interest is therefore already written into what it means to be a human being. To build a humanity where everyone can support their neighbor, Leech quotes from Valerie Pitt, an Anglo-Catholic socialist and literary scholar, that it is only in the sharing of power that we can fully understand how shared interest works.[35]

Williams understands solidarity as something we all have, that was lost and can be restored in Christ. Therefore, Williams argues that life in the communion and solidarity of the church is not a new set of relations superimposed on humanity's natural life. Rather it's the release of what we have forgotten or frustrated. Thus, the release of solidarity is to give into the life of our neighbors. Rowlands understands that solidarity provides a language that enriches the church's ability to talk about its own social life and our interdependent nature. Solidarity will also mean allowing other people's dreams and hopes for a better life to become the church's own.[36] Williams argues that solidarity is not the same as the common good. Common good language can assume that we already know what is good for everyone before we start. In contrast, Williams notes that we need to discover what the common good is in a particular context and how the voices of those who have not been heard can be incorporated. Williams concludes by arguing that, in light of this vision of released or fulfilled solidarity, the church should have a commitment to walk together with people in the local community. Importantly, this is about enabling the release of a solidarity which we already have. The task is for the church to speak of this universal solidarity and to live out what has made us human together, rather than set up a rival solidarity to the society around.[37] We observe that Ivereigh connects solidarity with the practice of assembly, Pope Francis connects it with relationships, and as Rowlands highlights, solidarity with marginalized and impoverished people. Williams, drawing on Leech, connects solidarity with listening. An important thing to note here is that they are all making strong connections between community organizing practices and solidarity, a key principle in CST.

Considering all the voices we have engaged so far, henceforth solidarity will be defined in this book in the following way: *Solidarity is the rediscovery of the radical shared interest held between people in fraternal relationships, as a key part of being human. Solidarity especially means radical shared interest with impoverished and marginalized people. We were made in God for fraternal*

35. Leech, *Sky Is Red*, 159.

36. Rowlands, *Towards a Politics of Communion*, 244.

37. Williams, "Solidarity."

relationships. Anything which disrupts solidarity should be resisted. So, part of the work of solidarity is countering the disruption of solidarity.

3.3 Subsidiarity

We now turn our attention to subsidiarity, a key principle in CST but not a term used by people in day-to-day life. Ivereigh argues that subsidiarity "supports a dispersal of authority as close to the grassroots as good government allows, and it prefers local over central decision-making: Decisions should be taken and carried out as close as possible to the people they affect." He understands that subsidiarity requires people to organize, "to compel those who have the power to act [to resolve issues] to do so, at the level at which they are able to."[38]

Pope Francis "describes subsidiarity as a double movement—from 'top to bottom and bottom to top.' It is the maximization of participation and the fostering of responsibility at every level for the common good that marks a good process of subsidiarity." Rowlands goes on to highlight that for Pope Francis, "any action that sees itself as promoting subsidiarity must be simultaneously an option for the poor—both privileging a listening process to the most marginalised communities and enabling the initiative and contribution of all." Thus, Rowlands concludes that "in this sense, Francis argues there is no solidarity without subsidiarity."[39] We observe that this also picks up some of the discussion above on solidarity.

Picking up on the mention of participation (another key principle of CST), Ivereigh, with Francis, also understands that participation is one of the expressions of the principle of subsidiarity. Ivereigh highlights that participation means "a series of activities by means of which the citizen, either as an individual or in association with others, whether directly or through representation, contributes to the cultural, economic, political and social life of the civil community to which [she or] he belongs."[40] Ivereigh also ties together participation with subsidiarity and solidarity and a focus on marginalized and impoverished people in the following helpful way:

> To be "public people" is not just a right, but a Christian obligation . . . whatever the means of participation, it is also important to promote at the same time the participation of the excluded,

38. Ivereigh, *Faithful Citizens*, 169.

39. Rowlands, *Towards a Politics of Communion*, 235.

40. Ivereigh, *Faithful Citizens*, 169; quoting the *Compendium of the Social Doctrine of the Church.*

> especially of the disenfranchised—giving a voice to the voiceless: "The primary purpose of this special commitment to the poor is to enable them to become active participants in the life of society."[41]

Rowlands recognizes that subsidiarity was an animating principle for Dorothy Day's Catholic Worker Movement and for Saul Alinsky, Cesar Chavez, Edward Chambers, and Ernesto Cortes's community organizing.[42] For Dorothy Day, "The meaningful context for Christian political action was the local community and face-to-face relationships, through which both community and healthy autonomy of exchange and action for all could be pursued."[43] However, Rowlands then mentions nothing more on how broad-based community organizing understands and uses subsidiarity.

Ivereigh is helpful here. He notes that:

> Subsidiarity rejects the message many have internalized: that we are powerless to change the world around us. It is a principle which holds that not only *can* power be exercised by active local organisations holding politicians and employers accountable through assemblies, but that it *should* be exercised in this way. Rather than wait for government to introduce new legislation, local organisations should press for changes locally, where they are—at the level at which change can be effected.[44]

Subsidiarity can thus also be related to the focus on institutions in community organizing, the importance of relationships between them, and the importance of intermediary institutions. As we noted earlier, the importance of these intermediary institutions is a key theme for Cortes. Rowlands understands that in the texts of papal encyclicals, "the principle of subsidiarity focuses on people and their relationship to—and participation in—social, political and economic groups and [intermediary] associations."[45] Rowlands highlights that *Gaudium et Spes* reaffirms the need for intermediary bodies at every level of society.[46] Broad-based community organizing builds alliances of these intermediary bodies such as churches and other institutions. These are alliances of institutions rather than of individuals. Bretherton argues that "in an increasingly deinstitutionalised and atomized society, religions provide one of the few corporate forms of life available for mobilizing and sustaining the ability

41. Ivereigh, *Faithful Citizens*, 170.
42. Rowlands, *Towards a Politics of Communion*, 215.
43. Rowlands, *Towards a Politics of Communion*, 218.
44. Ivereigh, *Faithful Citizens*, 169; emphasis in original.
45. Rowlands, *Towards a Politics of Communion*, 227.
46. Rowlands, *Towards a Politics of Communion*, 199–203.

of individuals to act together in defense of their shared interests."[47] Bretherton highlights that community organizing develops a "consociationalism," or mutual fellowship, between organizations and their members.[48] Alexis de Tocqueville offered the seminal treatment of this in *Democracy in America*. Cortes understands that these intermediary institutions must be constantly rebuilt, as "it is . . . in these intermediary institutions that we are taught the habits and practices requisite for a vibrant democratic culture. . . . Without these institutions we are reduced to self-absorbed narcissism that easily appropriates the language of consumerism and individualism."[49] Cortes goes on to highlight that it is through listening to someone with a different perspective through these intermediary institutions, a different story or history, that we develop a larger vision of our neighborhood, our state or our society.[50]

Considering all the voices we have engaged so far, henceforth subsidiarity will be understood in this book in the following way: *Subsidiarity brings together the importance of action together by people and institutions on issues facing people, with the principle that decisions should be taken and carried out as close as possible to the people they affect. In addition, those who are impoverished and marginalized should become active citizens in decisions on issues which affect them.*

3.4 The Common Good

A key idea in both Catholic Social Teaching and community organizing is the common good. The *Catechism of the Catholic Church* defines the common good in this way:

> In keeping with the social nature of man, the good of each individual is necessarily related to the common good, which in turn can be defined only in reference to the human person:
>
> Do not live entirely isolated, having retreated into yourselves, as if you were already justified, but gather instead to seek the common good together.
>
> By common good is to be understood "the sum total of social conditions which allow people, either as groups or as individuals, to reach their fulfilment more fully and more easily." The common

47. Bretherton, *Resurrecting Democracy*, 2.

48. Bretherton, *Christ and the Common Life*, 389–97.

49. Cortes, *Rebuilding Our Institutions*, 3.

50. Cortes, *Rebuilding Our Institutions*, 6–8.

> good concerns the life of all. It calls for prudence from each, and even more from those who exercise the office of authority. . . .
>
> The common good is always oriented towards the progress of persons: "The order of things must be subordinate to the order of persons, and not the other way around." This order is founded on truth, built up in justice, and animated by love.[51]

Building on this definition, Francis argues, "Seeking the common good calls Christians to suffuse the political order with small, personal acts of civic and political love," and thus love is political.[52] Rowlands argues that a Christian conception of the common good is distinctive to that described by secular philosophers. For Christians, God is our first and ultimate Common Good, and where the goodness of God is a current reality and a life that we are drawn into. Rowlands highlights that for Paul the common good is the body of Christ in a life of loving God and loving neighbor. In addition, drawing on Paul, the core task in seeking the common good is to strive for unity within diversity.[53]

Ivereigh claims that "the common good—which citizens are obliged to work for—implies a high degree of participation in decision-making."[54] In *Just Love*, Ritchie and Paul Hackwood, then director of the Church Urban Fund, argue that "the common good of the community and justice are absolutely central to what it means to be a Christian."[55] As Leech puts it, "In God there is social life, community, sharing. To share in God is to share in that life."[56] Rowlands argues,

> The common good is a process[,] not a thing: It is the process through which people, with all their differences, seek to communicate about what matters to them as persons and matters to building something good which can exist between and beyond them. It is a communicative process: that's where we discover the shape of the elusive thing we call the common good.[57]

Working for the common good is a central way in which both the IAF and Citizens UK describe community organizing. For example, there is a big focus on the common good in Chambers's book *Roots for Radicals* and in the Citizens UK Foundations document. Chambers argues,

51. Catholic Church, *Catechism*, §§1905–6, 1912.
52. Rowlands, *Towards a Politics of Communion*, 169.
53. Rowlands, "Mixing Religion and Politics."
54. Ivereigh, *Faithful Citizens*, 169.
55. Ritchie and Hackwood, *Just Love*, 18.
56. Ritchie and Hackwood, *Just Love*, 19.
57. Anna Rowlands; quoted in Rodrigues, *Realities Are Greater*, 46.

> The common good of a large and diverse community can be pursued effectively only when a representative collective of institutions is bold enough to stand for the whole. It can be advanced only when real differences are bound together in a web of relationships anchored in the institutions that bring citizens and people of faith together—churches, neighbourhood groups, labour unions and other associations. Public relationships both require and bring forth the ability to live with the inevitable tensions of common life.[58]

Writing about Citizens UK Organizing in East London, Ritchie recognizes that the wider goal is to build an alliance "with an ongoing set of relationships of trust and commitment . . . [and which] develops grassroots leadership and the power of people in Britain's poorest neighbourhoods to work together for the common good."[59]

Citizens UK describes itself as political but nonpartisan, seeking to win change through forming accountable public relationships with decision makers both on the right and left of politics. Rowlands argues that the common good is a very, and perhaps frustratingly, elastic idea, and one that refuses to go away. Nevertheless, she recognizes that it is an essential idea to help us address the most challenging issues we face today. However, as Rowlands notes, there is much discussion and dispute about what the common good means, and it has been popular as an idea among both left- and right-wing groups and movements.[60]

Thus, for an organization seeking to work with faith institutions—for whom the common good is a key idea—as well as with politicians from across the political spectrum, it may well suit community organizing to leave the common good open to be defined in different ways. As noted before, churches form the backbone of community organizing alliances. Leech questions the use of common good language by churches, noting that "it is a favourite phrase in Anglican worship, and does tend to reflect a Church which is unfamiliar with, or removed from, social conflict and which thinks of itself as neutral and detached . . . the common good is something to be struggled for . . . and it cannot be achieved within the present order of things."[61] Hence, Leech argues for

58. Chambers, *Roots for Radicals*, 23.

59. Ritchie and Hackwood, *Just Love*, 25.

60. Rowlands, "Mixing Religion and Politics." In UK politics, both Blue Labour and Red Tory, as initiatives within the Labour and Conservative political parties, drew on parts of CST. See, for example, Davis, *Tangled Up in Blue*, which also covers the author's interactions with Citizens UK; and Blond, *Red Tory*.

61. Leech, *Sky Is Red*, 158.

churches to be "rooted in the communities of people who are most seriously affected by the injustices of the present system."[62]

In *Christ and the Common Life*, Bretherton makes the case for why Christians should be committed to democracy as a vital means of pursuing a flourishing life. Bretherton understands that "flourishing depends on being embedded in just and loving forms of common life."[63] As Bretherton outlines, "A guiding assumption of this book is that the richer our engagement with ways of understanding the relationship between ecclesial and political life, the deeper will be our understanding of what it means to be the church and of the nature of faithful witness."[64] It is notable that in both *Resurrecting Democracy* and *Christ and the Common Life*, Bretherton uses the term "common life" rather than "common good." In the first of these books Bretherton explains that "while talk of particular 'goods in common' or 'common goods' is wholly appropriate for a generic way of denoting a shared realm of meaning and action and commitment to the good of political association amidst enmity and rival visions of the good life, the term *common life* seems simultaneously more sober and hopeful."[65]

In the second book, Bretherton outlines that common goods can only be achieved by participating in some form of association and so are constitutive of human flourishing. Bretherton goes on to argue that "determining the common good of a family, workplace, or small-scale community is possible and necessary [for politics of the kind Bretherton outlines in this book]. . . . But beyond that scale, a claim to know *the* common good of a conurbation, region or the globe is antipolitical. It denies the plurality and contestability of moral visions in complex societies and the conflicts that arise in pursuit of divergent moral goods, all of which must be negotiated through politics."[66]

In *Journey to the Common Good*, Brueggemann argues that the concept of neighborliness can show us the way toward a greater common good. Brueggemann sees the common good as "the sense of community solidarity that binds all in a common destiny—haves and have-nots, the rich and the poor . . . that reaches beyond private interest, transcends sectarian commitments, and offers human solidarity."[67] As we have observed earlier, Brueggemann uses the language of scarcity and abundance. Here Brueggemann argues that the journey from scarcity to abundance to a neighborly common good

62. Leech, *Sky Is Red*, 161.

63. Bretherton, *Christ and the Common Life*, 1–2.

64. Bretherton, *Christ and the Common Life*, 4.

65. Bretherton, *Resurrecting Democracy*, 306.

66. Bretherton, *Christ and the Common Life*, 32–33; emphasis in original.

67. Brueggemann, *Journey to Common Good*, 1.

is one we must all make again and again to be fully human.[68] Brueggemann underlines that it is the faithful church which keeps at this task of living out a journey that points to the common good.[69]

From the different ways in which the principle of the common good has been explored, it appears that there is a lack of definition of the common good in the community organizing literature and theological reflection on it.

The common good is the well-being of the community as a whole. One tradition defines it as peace, justice and the flourishing of all. While I admire Bretherton's focus on a common life rather than the common good, I think it is a mistake to shy away from a definition of the common good. I am also not convinced by Rowlands's description of the common good as a process rather than a thing. I understand that it may be that in community organizing the best way to get to a common understanding of the common good is through a communicative process. However, the common good is more than a process, it is something concrete.

Thus, considering all the voices we have engaged so far, henceforth the common good will be understood in this book in the following way: *The common good advances towards the well-being of the community, measured by such things as justice, peace, and flourishing. It is best achieved through a communicative process involving all stakeholders in the community.*

3.5 Neighborliness

The common good is held in the relationships between people. Rowlands notes that *Fratelli Tutti* picks this up in relation to the ethical demands of neighbor love. She therefore understands "the life of the common good is to be lived in pursuit of the dual commitment to love God and to love neighbour, through which we express and are returned to our deepest longings and inherent social value. . . . In the most mundane forms of neighbour love . . . we find the threads of a connection that pulls us into something transcendent."[70]

Organizing together with others comes from a common commitment to a particular place and people and, as Bretherton notes, a commitment to encountering others and the work of re-neighboring and constantly learning how to be a neighbor.[71] He argues that community organizing helps answer some key questions that should arise if we are seeking to love our neighbor:

68. Brueggemann, *Journey to Common Good*, 31–32.

69. Brueggemann, *Journey to Common Good*, 32.

70. Rowlands, *Towards a Politics of Communion*, 123.

71. Bretherton, *Resurrecting Democracy*, 95.

What does this mean in practice; how do we address the poverty and injustice we encounter; what power relationships shape our relationships; and what power relations are important in our relations with others?[72]

Bretherton argues that often Christians have a very abstract view of loving our neighbors, but the practice of community organizing makes it very concrete. He highlights that people may have a deep, if abstract, moral commitment to loving their neighbors. However, it is through community organizing that people understand about organizing for power and what it will take for their neighborhood or area to flourish. In addition, community organizing helps clarify what it will take for peoples' dignity to be realized rather than people being acted upon by dominant power structures, and it helps effect the transformation people see in themselves and in others as they practice organizing.[73]

Power is again a key area for Bretherton. In *Christ and the Common Life*, as in *Resurrecting Democracy*, he draws heavily on his experience of learning from community organizing about the importance of power, listening and relationships. As Bretherton identifies, an "often unacknowledged side to the issue of neighbour love in politics is the question of what kind of power shapes the relationship between oneself and another and how this power is distributed."[74]

Bretherton understands that the basis of a common life is neighbor love. Neighbor love incorporates "love of the stranger, the enemy, and the friendless."[75] In this he underlines that theological reflection on politics (political theology), "gives priority to those who speak from the 'underside of history,'" and so we need to decenter to give space to the suffering and despised.[76] Bretherton suggests that "politics is not merely an arena for practicing neighbour love; it can of itself be a form of neighbour love."[77] Thus, he understands politics as a means of generating public friendship across difference. He thus reveals that "politics-as-neighbouring reweaves the fragile fabric of reciprocal relations that hold society together."[78]

Community organizing is therefore generating richer patterns of neighborliness. In understanding community organizing as being about reweaving civil society, it, "can be conceptualised as a form of tent making where a

72. Bretherton, "How Community Organising Helps."

73. Bretherton, "Ability to Act."

74. Bretherton, *Christ and the Common Life*, 1–2.

75. Bretherton, *Christ and the Common Life*, 22.

76. Bretherton, *Christ and the Common Life*, 26.

77. Bretherton, *Christ and the Common Life*, 41.

78. Bretherton, *Christ and the Common Life*, 44.

place is created in which hospitality is given and received between multiple traditions." Bretherton notes that "the encounter with others and their stories informs the sense of what it is like to live on this mutual ground, to dwell together in a given and shared urban space."[79]

In *Reality, Grief, Hope*, Brueggemann, drawing on his earlier book, *The Prophetic Imagination*, highlights that it is one thing to call for a prophetic imagination; it is quite another matter to actually have a prophetic imagination.[80] This prophetic imagination is that we should have the same imagination of the prophets to call out and confront injustice and act for justice. As Brueggemann highlights, "The prophetic tradition imagines an alliance of God and neighbor against . . . exploitation, so that there is no possibility of loving God without loving neighbor."[81] Brueggemann then underlines the importance for the prophetic church "to focus on the presence and defining importance of the neighbor, most especially the neighbor who lives at the edge of or is excluded from [a community]."[82]

Brueggemann notes that in contemporary society, and in the context of empire, there is a focus on individualism at the expense of the common good or what is needed for a common life together. He also argues that there is an "assumption that the 'neighborhood' is an unfortunate inconvenience rather than an indispensable arrangement for viable human life."[83] Brueggemann understands that the narrative of the Roman Empire also collides with the ministry of Jesus and "the Jesus movement embodied a vigorous, emancipated alternative to Rome," with its solidarity with poor people.[84] His thinking is that a narrative of the neighborhood is told and enacted from below, which then provides a foundation for a community where people love their neighbor. This then exposes the narrative of empire as inadequate. Brueggemann argues that you cannot have empire and neighborhood, equating this to Jesus' teaching that you cannot serve God and wealth.[85]

Brueggemann concludes:

79. Bretherton, *Resurrecting Democracy*, 93.

80. Although *Reality, Grief, Hope* is written later than the other books by Brueggemann which have influenced Cortes and Ritchie and others in their community organizing reflections, I find it helpful for shaping further theological reflection on community organizing, including what is being missed in the current reflections, and so I have included reference to this book here.

81. Brueggemann, *Reality, Grief, Hope*, 36.

82. Brueggemann, *Reality, Grief, Hope*, 38.

83. Brueggemann, *Reality, Grief, Hope*, 115–16.

84. Brueggemann, *Reality, Grief, Hope*, 137.

85. Brueggemann, *Reality, Grief, Hope*, 142–51.

> When it is faithful, the church—the local congregation as the defining unit of faith—is committed to an alternative unneighborly practice of the world. It does so in the face of shrill, insistent reductionism that wants to eliminate the inconvenience of unneighborly obligations.[86]

Neighborliness is not a named principle in CST. However, as we have observed, there are close links between this theme and love of neighbor, solidarity, subsidiarity, and seeking the common good. Leech recognizes that the strength of the Anglican church is in neighborhoods and argues for a parish which develops community, discovers a common life and is committed to its neighborhood. Crucially, Leech links this neighborliness and seeking the common good with common action.[87]

Thus, considering all the voices we have engaged so far, henceforth neighborliness will be understood in this book in the following way: *Neighborliness brings together a communal commitment to a particular people and place and encourages public relationships to be formed and strengthened between people. This neighbourliness is motivated by seeking to love our neighbor and incorporates love of the stranger, the enemy and the friendless. Neighborliness thus recognizes the power dynamics that exist in a neighborhood and seeks to change how this power is distributed.*

3.6 Listening

Listening is a very important practice in community organizing. Bretherton highlights that organizing begins with listening. It should be an ongoing process for churches and other institutions rather than a one-off activity. It is attentive to the experience, conditions and stories of people where they live and work.[88] Williams argues that theology begins "in the middle of things."[89] So you need to be in the middle of things with people to hear their experiences and perspectives. A commitment to listening is important, as is a commitment to understand that marginalized and impoverished people have a good understanding of the issues affecting them as well as of potential solutions. As Ivereigh underlines, "Creating time for listening, either one-to-one or in gatherings and meetings, is a prerequisite for solidarity, for we must first know

86. Brueggemann, *Reality, Grief, Hope*, 162–3.
87. Leech, *Sky Is Red*, 239.
88. Bretherton, "Other Basic Tool."
89. Williams, *On Christian Theology*, ii.

and hear each other, before we can properly engage with the world beyond the parish."[90]

In *Effective Organizing for Congregational Renewal*, highlighting the importance of building public relationships with other people through listening to others in one-to-one meetings, Gecan quotes Dietrich Bonhoeffer: "The first service that one owes to others in the fellowship consists in listening to them. . . . Those who cannot listen long and patiently will always be talking past others, and finally will no longer even notice it. . . . The death of the spiritual life starts here."[91] Later, Gecan quotes Martin Buber, that "all real living is meeting."

As we noted in chapter 2, in community organizing one-to-one relational meetings are a key approach for listening. This approach was developed by Chambers. He described these relational meetings as "one organized spirit going after another person's spirit for connection, confrontation, and an exchange of talent and energy."[92] Gecan also understands one-to-one relational meetings as a spiritual practice: "If the death of the spiritual life starts in 'talking past others' . . . then the birth of the spiritual life starts in the individual one-to-one meeting—in listening to the other person."[93] Rowlands notes that for Dorothy Day, "the meaningful context for Christian social action was the local community and face-to-face relationships, through which both community and healthy autonomy of exchange and action for all could be pursued."[94] From this we can deduce that Chambers's time with Dorothy Day's Catholic Worker Movement influenced him in the development of one-to-one relational meetings.

Ritchie understands that through listening to other people from different faith, ethnic, and social backgrounds we start to see what God sees in a situation. This then picks up Stout's argument that "what appears secular in the eyes of the average citizen has a sacred dimension in the eyes of the church."[95] Through relational meetings with other people and listening to their experiences of injustice, Stout highlights that "we experience the emotions of other people directly by being in their presence."[96] He argues that broad-based community organizations "neither exclude conceptions of sacred value from the

90. Ivereigh, *Faithful Citizens*, 168. One-to-one conversations and house meetings are two tools of organizing that were explored in the previous chapter.

91. Gecan, *Effective Organizing*, 14; quoting Bonhoeffer, *Life Together*.

92. Chambers, *Roots for Radicals*, 35.

93. Gecan, *Effective Organizing*, 14.

94. Rowlands, *Towards a Politics of Communion*, 235.

95. Stout, *Blessed Are the Organized*, 194.

96. Stout, *Blessed Are the Organized*, 152.

discussion, nor require everyone to convert to a single conception of shared value. Instead, they encourage citizens to speak openly about what matters most to them and to do so in the language most familiar to them, which is often the language of a religious tradition."[97]

Bretherton understands the importance of starting with listening which "assumes the poor have something to teach the privileged about how to live and that a common life between them is necessary to the flourishing of each and the flourishing of all."[98] He highlights that "we must listen to others who differ from us in background and belief because their experiences, their stories, who they are as people matter."[99] Bretherton understands that in churches doing listening there is *double listening*, where there is listening within the church and to neighbors in community, alongside listening to tradition and Scripture.[100]

Ritchie, drawing on his experience of organizing in East London, highlights that "the process of listening to congregation members and to the wider parish was itself understood as an attempt to discern what God was already doing in Bethnal Green, and what he had laid on its people's hearts."[101] However, it is very important that listening to people on the margins is practiced, and not just talked or written about. As Rowlands argues, we need to be able to hard wire the experiences of those at the margins into decision-making processes.[102] The next section builds on this. It explores how those on the margins become central in practice, and not just in theory.

Therefore, considering how listening has been explored so far, henceforth listening will be understood in this book in the following way: *Listening is where we should always start as churches, with listening to those in the church and to neighbors in community, alongside listening to our tradition and Scripture. Then, who we are listening to matters. Listening well will involve listening to impoverished and powerless people and those at the margins of churches and communities, and so listening for the prophetic minority.*

3.7 Centering the Margins

Addressing members of COPS, Cortes said,

97. Stout, *Blessed Are the Organized*, 235.
98. Bretherton, *Christ and the Common Life*, 78.
99. Bretherton, "Recovering Democratic Politics," para. 11.
100. Bretherton, *Christ and the Common Life*, 174.
101. Ritchie and Hackwood, *Just Love*, 23.
102. Rowlands, "Mixing Religion and Politics."

> You reach out to those who are outcast. . . . You bring people who are outside democratic society into the life of the community, and you become an instrument whereby they can develop dignity and self-respect. . . . You have truly shown . . . the passion for justice that can never be squelched.[103]

Thus, COPS is using community organizing to bring those on the margins into the center. It is demonstrating that those perceived as powerless do not have to stay powerless. Gecan understands that through organizing "the poor become less poor, the disconnected of all races and classes engage. The marginalized begin to move towards the center. The powerless gather, organize, and act."[104] In this community organizing effort in Texas, with Roman Catholic churches full of Mexican immigrants, we observe how this alliance and Cortes have drawn on Latin American liberation theology.

Liberation theology enters into the recent theological context for community organizing in both the US and UK. Liberation theology "attempts to look at reality from the underside, from the margins, through the eyes of those who do not count."[105] For Gustavo Gutiérrez, theology is critical reflection on Christian praxis in the light of the word of God. Liberation and participation of the poor are key words, and a call for social justice is central. Gustavo Gutiérrez underlines in *A Theology of Liberation* that

> this is a theology which does not stop with reflecting on the world, but rather tries to be part of the process through which the world is transformed. It is a theology which is open—in the protest against trampled human dignity, in the struggle against the plunder of the vast majority of people, in liberating love, and in the building of a new, just and fraternal society—to the gift of the Kingdom of God.[106]

Leonardo and Clodovis Boff declare that "liberation theology leads to action: action for justice, the work of love, conversion, renewal of the church, and transformation of society."[107] In both the US and UK there were Roman Catholic and other Christian leaders who had been much influenced by liberation theology. In this context, community organizing comes along and is also seen as an approach that talks about looking to the margins, and working with the marginalized and those who feel powerless.

103. Rogers, *Cold Anger*, 125.
104. Gecan, *Going Public*, 163.
105. Bosch, *Transforming Mission*, 497.
106. Gutiérrez, *Theology of Liberation*, 15.
107. Boff and Boff, *Introducing Liberation Theology*, 39.

As Bradstock and Rowland note, Gustavo Gutiérrez's earlier book *A Theology of Liberation* was instrumental in crystallizing a variety of movements in Latin American Catholicism in the wake of Vatican II and the political struggles and resulting changes in the late 1960s. Importantly, they highlight Gutiérrez's active involvement as an advocate and interpreter of impoverished people with whom he lived and worked.[108] So, a Baptist theological ethic of social justice will also need to be based on the experience of practitioners and of impoverished and marginalized people they work with.

In *A Theology of Liberation*, Gutiérrez concludes,

> We will have an authentic theology of liberation only when the oppressed themselves can freely raise their voice and express themselves directly and creatively in society and in the heart of the People of God, when they themselves "account for the hope," which they bear, when they are the protagonists of their own liberation.[109]

From this conclusion to the book, we observe how community organizing, in enabling people at the margins to be agents of change on issues they prioritize, has taken up the liberation theology of Gutiérrez and the Boffs and the popular education of Paulo Freire.[110]

In *The Task and Content of Liberation Theology*, Gutiérrez outlines the essential features of liberation theology. He highlights the call in Vatican II for the church to become the church of all, and in particular the church of the poor. From this Gutiérrez reveals three concepts of poverty—material, spiritual, and "poverty as a commitment to be assumed by all Christians, which expresses itself in solidarity with the poor and in protest against poverty."[111] Gutiérrez goes on to highlight three dimensions of liberation: political and social liberation, human liberation, and liberation from selfishness and sin. For Gutiérrez, this last dimension "is the last root of injustice that has to be eliminated. Overcoming this leads to reestablishing friendship with God and with other people."[112]

Rowlands highlights that the vision of the church of the poor articulated by Pope Francis in *Evangelii Gaudium* entails solidarity with the poor. It also entails an openness of ourselves to the poor in which we are able to learn

108. Bradstock and Rowland, *Radical Christian Writings*, 335.

109. Gutiérrez, *Theology of Liberation*, 307.

110. Freire, *Pedagogy of the Oppressed.*

111. Bradstock and Rowland, *Radical Christian Writings*, 336.

112. Bradstock and Rowland, *Radical Christian Writings*, 337.

from the poor and are willing to be disrupted and to feel uncomfortable.[113] Bretherton and Ritchie both highlight the importance of involving people at the margins. Here again we observe in this section the influence of Pope Francis's teaching on Ritchie's reflections on community organizing. Bretherton argues that Alinsky's approach enables the appearance of those who are depoliticized or excluded from decision-making processes.[114] Community organizing enables them to appear and act on their terms.[115] In *Just Church*, Ritchie, Burbridge, and Walton understand that how things look depends on where we stand. So, they highlight the need to focus on how things look to those on the margins. They argue that theology must emerge from, and speak into, this context of struggle and injustice.[116]

As Ritchie and Hackwood recognize, every community has a clear sense of who and what are at the center and who and what are at the margins. They highlight that Jesus was born at the very margins of a social order in which the Roman Empire and the temple authorities were at the center of power. They highlight Leech's understanding that this perspective of the poorest and most vulnerable formed the background to Jesus' proclamation of the kingdom of God.[117] Ritchie and Hutt highlight that the God revealed in the Bible is again and again shown to be both with and for the marginalized.[118] Drawing on Brueggemann, they include this quote:

> It is likely that our theological problem in the church is that our gospel is a story believed, shaped and transmitted by the dispossessed; and we are now a church of possessions for whom the rhetoric of the dispossessed is offensive and their promise is irrelevant. And we are left to see if it is possible for us again to embrace solidarity with the dispossessed.[119]

Later, in *Inclusive Populism*, Ritchie quotes Stanley Hauerwas, that "Christian social ethics can only be done from the perspective of those who do not seek to control national or world history but who are content to live *out of control*."[120] In the preface to *Inclusive Populism*, Ritchie notes that "Pope Fran-

113. Rodrigues, *Realities Are Greater*, 42.

114. Bretherton, *Resurrecting Democracy*, 45.

115. It is interesting to compare this understanding of enabling people to appear with how McClintock Fulkerson explores this in *Places of Redemption*, 21.

116. Ritchie et al., *Just Church*, 9.

117. Ritchie and Hackwood, *Just Love*, 98.

118. Ritchie and Hutt, *From Houses to Homes*, 18.

119. Brueggemann, *Land*, 93.

120. Ritchie, *Inclusive Populism*, 138.

cis's vision of a theology and politics rooted in the lives of the poorest citizens is an important inspiration for this book."[121] Ritchie argues that community organizing has striking resonances with this vision articulated by Pope Francis which "begins with realities, not simply ideas."[122] In *Evangelii Gaudium*, Pope Francis argues,

> Realities simply are, whereas ideas are worked out. There has to be continuous dialogue between the two, lest ideas become detached from realities. It is dangerous to dwell in the realm of words alone, of images and rhetoric. So [an important] principle comes into play: realities are greater than ideas.[123]

For Ritchie, this means not just seeing the poor as a category of person deserving of a better life but as people to engage in organizing for social justice.[124] Ritchie argues that "community organizing not only involves action by the 'suffering poor' but a movement funded by their own money is a challenge to the stereotyped narrative of powerlessness and dependency."[125]

Ritchie highlights Pope Francis's focus on *teologìa del pueblo* in the Latin American church. This theology sees impoverished people "not merely as the objects of liberation or education, but as individuals capable of living faith legitimately in their own manner, capable of forging paths based on their own culture."[126] In 2021, Pope Francis addressed an international conference of grassroots Catholics, community organizers, and academics gathering to take forward his call for the church to embrace a politics of fraternity, rooted in the life of the people with a focus on broad-based community organizing. Pope Francis calls for a politics not just for the people, but with the people, rooted in their communities and in their values:

> It is impossible for the Church to separate the promotion of social justice from the recognition of the culture and values of the people, which include the spiritual values that are the source of their sense of dignity. . . . Now, more than ever, we must build a future from below, from a politics with the people.[127]

121. Ritchie, *Inclusive Populism*, xi.

122. Ritchie, *Inclusive Populism*, 18. This phrase is itself the inspiration for the title of another publication which Ritchie collaborated on with others and highlighted in ch. 2 (Rodrigues, *Realities Are Greater*).

123. Francis, *Evangelii Gaudium*, §232.

124. Ritchie, *Inclusive Populism*, 18.

125. Ritchie, *Inclusive Populism*, 35.

126. Ritchie, *Inclusive Populism*, 97.

127. Francis, "Politics Rooted in People," para. 6, final para.

Pope Francis expresses a desire for every church to connect to people's organizations: "Going out to meet the risen, wounded Christ in our poorest communities allows us to recover our missionary vigour, for it is here that the Church was born, in the margins of the cross."[128] In *Let Us Dream*, he argues that, at the margins, "hidden there are ways of looking at the world that can give us a fresh start,"[129] and highlights that "if the church disowns the poor, she ceases to be the church of Jesus."[130] Ritchie concludes that excluding religious beliefs from politics has the effect of disempowering the poorest communities. He makes the point powerfully that many at the margins in the UK and US are religious—ethnic minorities, recent migrants, and impoverished people.[131]

In this section, we observe how much theological reflection on community organizing starts from the perspective and experience of impoverished and marginalized people and enables people at the margins to play central roles. Thus, this theological reflection relates closely to the option for the poor, another key principle in CST.[132]

Thus, considering all the voices we have engaged so far, henceforth centering the margins will be understood in this book in the following way: *Centering the margins means starting from the perspective of those currently impoverished and on the margins. It then means enabling these people to increase their power and sense of dignity and for their priorities to be the basis for action together on these priorities, rooted in their experience and values.*

3.8 Missing Elements in the Current Theological Reflection on Community Organizing

So far in this chapter we have focused on the main sources of theological reflection on community organizing in the current literature. There appears to be very little theologizing around Black churches' involvement in community organizing in the literature, by Black theologians or any others. Thus, I argue that there is an absence in the current literature.

In this section I will explore sources that people allude to and should do more with but do not in the current literature, such as James Cone, Howard Thurman, Willie James Jennings, and nonwhite, non-male, voices in general. The influence of Latin American liberation theology on community organizing

128. Francis, "Politics Rooted in People," para. 10.

129. Francis, *Let Us Dream*, 119.

130. Francis, *Let Us Dream*, 120.

131. Ritchie, *Inclusive Populism*, 12–15.

132. Ivereigh, *Faithful Citizens*, 170.

appears prominently in the literature. It appears, though, that community organizing is not really engaging the Black liberation theology of James Cone or others. There is only a brief mention in one source of James Cone being involved in the 1970s in theological reflection on community organizing.[133] A Baptist theological ethic for the practice of social justice needs to do better here and I am going to try to address this in chapter 6.

In the US, James Cone, as a Black liberation theologian, was particularly important among Black-majority churches in areas where the IAF was building alliances. Freedman notes that James Cone's Black theology had much influenced Youngblood, a Black Baptist church minister with a leading role in community organizing in New York, during his studies in a seminary.[134] James Cone argues that when Black and white people are speaking about God and Jesus they are not referring to the same reality as they are experiencing life and the world differently.[135] Cone claims that "after being told six days of the week that they were nothings by the rulers of white society, on the Sabbath, the first day of the week, black people went to church in order to experience another definition of their humanity."[136] The Black experience and the Bible together are therefore seen as the point of departure for Black theology. Therefore, this is also helpful in how Black people relate to their local church as an institution and community, and what they see as life within churches and life in broader society.

Cone's conviction is that "the God of biblical faith and black religion is best known as the Liberator of the oppressed from bondage."[137] Cone goes on to argue that "this Jesus of the biblical and black traditions is not a theological concept but a liberating presence in the lives of the poor in their fight for dignity and worth."[138]

Cone notes in the preface to the 1997 edition of *God of the Oppressed* that most white theologians ignored Black liberation theology, preferring instead to dialogue with Latin American liberation theology. This also seems to be true for much of the theological reflection on community organizing. This may reflect, in part at least, that Cortes spent far more time organizing with Mexican and other Latino/a migrant communities in the south and west of the US, rather than with Black Baptist churches in the northeast of the US.

133. Bretherton, *Resurrecting Democracy*, 42.
134. Freedman, *Upon This Rock*, 184.
135. Cone, *God of the Oppressed*, 10.
136. Cone, *God of the Oppressed*, 12.
137. Cone, *God of the Oppressed*, ix.
138. Cone, *God of the Oppressed*, xiii.

Cone argues that "liberation as the fight for justice in this world has always been an important ingredient in black religion. Indeed, black religion's existence as another reality, completely different from white religion, is partly related to its grounding of black faith in the historical struggle of freedom."[139] So, how Black churches understand community organizing may be different. We can ask what this means for how we construct a strengthened Baptist theological ethic, using community organizing to do this.

Freedman highlights that Howard Thurman's *Jesus and the Disinherited*, with its focus on Jesus as part of a poor oppressed minority under imperial domination, also had a big influence on Youngblood.[140] However, Thurman is not referenced in any of the theological reflections on community organizing. Thurman, in highlighting the political, social and cultural context of Jesus' ministry, understands that "Jesus was born and raised in a context of multiple overlapping oppressions, and that he is best understood as a 'man from below,' who led a popular movement of others in the same social location."[141] I argue that Thurman is very helpful in considering power in relation to justice and love, how we can understand this from the margins, and what it looks like in practice. I understand that drawing on Thurman is very helpful in considering whose reality of injustice counts. Therefore, we need to move to recenter our actions that seek justice on what are prioritized as issues and solutions by those who have direct and daily experience of injustices.

In *Jesus and the Disinherited*, Howard Thurman highlights that Jesus spent his time with the people on the margins, the oppressed people. So, it is important to follow Jesus to where he spent time—with the oppressed and marginalized—thus moving more towards Jesus in the world, and overcoming the temptation to seek to remain in control with dominant power over others. Thurman brings a welcome reading of ethics and Jesus from the perspective on those at the margins and on the underside of both history and in the present.

In a very helpful chapter on Black Power, Bretherton reveals that this movement, alongside the experience of the Black churches, was the catalyst for the work of James Cone and the emergence of Black liberation theology. However, Bretherton notes that Black Power as a social movement has received less attention in Christian ethics and political theology than the civil rights movement.[142] One reason for this, according to Bretherton, is that the civil rights movement is seen to validate and exemplify core Christian claims whereas Black Power challenges churches and their approach. Bretherton

139. Cone, *God of the Oppressed*, 141.

140. Freedman, *Upon This Rock*, 184.

141. Gushee, *Introducing Christian Ethics*, 126.

142. Bretherton, *Christ and the Common Life*, 85–86.

then goes on to argue that community organizing is a good example of an approach for Black Power. However, this is the only reference I have found in the literature.

As Bretherton understands, CST is also a vital interlocutor for Anglican political theology.[143] Anglican political theology is described by Bretherton as less institutionalized and more eclectic than CST. However, Anglican political theology "tends to avoid any explicit discussions of power as, in contrast to Black Power and Pentecostalism, it assumes the possession of power." It therefore does not invite questions about who has power and why.[144]

Bretherton highlights the mujerista theology of Ada María Isasi-Díaz. This theology starts from and focuses on *lo cotidiano* or the daily experience of Hispanas and Latinas. This theology "represents both an extension of and a break with prior forms of liberation theology and illustrates a constructive example of the contemporary advocacy of ecclesial and democratic populism."[145]

In the last chapter of *Towards a Politics of Communion*, Rowlands highlights the parallels between covenant and communion advocated by CST and the work of US Baptist theologian Willie James Jennings. This is the only mention of Baptists or Baptist theologians in her important book. Rowlands observes that Jennings connects the way we have thought about land and place to the ways we have thought about race, and how we shape freedom inside ideas of possession. For Rowlands, "Jennings suggests that an understanding of being a covenantal community of the commons offers a way forward," where a covenantal modality imagines already a world of reciprocal exchanges and speech acts.[146] In chapter 6, we will examine how covenantal relationships can strengthen both community organizing and a Baptist theological ethic for the practice of social justice.

In this chapter we have observed, as we also did in the previous two chapters, that much of the current published literature on community organizing is written by white men, whether they are organizers or academics. Broad-based community organizing has enabled women and men from nonwhite backgrounds to play more public and leadership roles in their institutions and communities. Community organizing is about building relational power to be able to tackle injustices. However, the perspectives of Black, feminist, and migrant theologians—those who are critically engaging with power and powerlessness—are currently not being engaged with to any extent by those involved in broad-based community organizing. This seems very ironic given

143. Bretherton, *Christ and the Common Life*, 175.

144. Bretherton, *Christ and the Common Life*, 177.

145. Bretherton, *Christ and the Common Life*, 421.

146. Rowlands, *Towards a Politics of Communion*, 289–90.

that Black churches have been central to community organizing in the US and have much direct experience of the misuse of power as well as the experience of too often feeling powerless.

Finally, despite theological reflection on enabling those currently marginalized to play more central roles in churches, there is very little theological reflection on leadership and leadership development by these theologians and organizers. There is little reflection on how community organizing changes traditional understandings of leadership in churches, nor on people from the margins taking leadership positions in churches. This would be one way of centering the margins in practice, not just in theory. This is despite many examples of people of faith from the margins learning to be leaders within their communities as a result of their experience of community organizing.

3.9 Summary

This chapter reveals a number of themes in current theological reflection on community organizing. I have highlighted the focus on key principles of CST such as solidarity, subsidiarity, and the common good. I have explored and critiqued how a range of theologians have understood these principles in the context of community organizing, and through this I have produced a synthesis working definition of each. This chapter has also revealed some differences in emphasis between Bretherton, Ivereigh, Rowlands, and Ritchie on how they reflect theologically on community organizing.

Current British theologians of community organizing have at least in part been influenced by sources that organizers in the US have previously drawn on, in particular CST. In addition, theological reflections on community organizing are mostly from an Anglican or Catholic perspective. There is much less theological reflection in the literature on organizing with other church traditions, such as Black Baptist churches, despite them being central to community organizing, particularly in many US alliances. I understand these churches to have been more influenced by Black liberation theology and the US civil rights movement than by CST. There does not appear to be any significant theological reflection on community organizing by Baptists in the current literature. In addition, theologians of community organizing are not currently diverse and are not adequately talking about race and power. This shows the limits of the literature and the blind spots of the current theologians of community organizing.

Therefore, the current theological reflection is not going to give us everything we need in developing a strengthened Baptist ethic of social justice. Power, the relations between communal and public language and action, and the mutual sharing and influence between different traditions, are among the themes which will need more work. In addition, a strengthened Baptist theological ethic will need to be sourced from more diverse and currently marginalized voices.

A nonnegotiable in theological reflection on community organizing is that you cannot theologically reflect on community organizing without being involved in the practice. In other words, first you have do community organizing and then reflect theologically on it. This is exactly the same methodological commitment as Black and Latin American liberation theology. However, the difference is that community organizing seems to be more practical, as I have suggested in this chapter. There are examples of liberation theology being incarnated through community organizing. However, community organizing seems much more widely practiced by a range of churches than the on-the-ground practice of liberation theology. In addition, community organizing is not just being done and reflected on by specialist church communities, but by lots of faith institutions and other groups.

So, rather than community organizing being seen as a "safer" alternative to liberation theology, in many ways it is taking a liberationist approach but without the structural change of moving to base communities as the form of church. The reality of theology emerging from the experience, practice and stories of community organizing is a hallmark of theological reflection on community organizing. I believe this is also methodologically significant for the argument in this book. In the next three chapters I will build on this approach and link this to what other theologians have offered, including Baptist and baptistic theologians influenced by theologies of liberation.

So far, we have mainly drawn on Catholic and Anglican theological reflections on community organizing. We will now make the turn in this research to consider the Baptist response, and what Baptists can learn from Catholic and Anglican involvement and theological reflection on community organizing. In addition, we will consider what Baptists can contribute to community organizing thinking and practice. As Rowlands highlights, the post–Vatican II authors of the CST tradition sought to produce a body of work addressed not just to the Roman Catholic Church but to "all people of goodwill."[147]

So, where to start? The following chapters will explore the influence of the past in the present in relation to Baptist engagement in social justice. They will examine a Baptist way of describing and implementing the principles extrapolated from theological reflection on community organizing. These chapters will also examine how these principles can help inform a strengthened Baptist theological ethic of social justice.

147. Rowlands, *Towards a Politics of Communion*, 11.

Chapter 4

The Development of a Theological Ethic for the Practice of Social Justice and Baptist Churches in Wales and England

Part I

4.1 Introduction

In the previous chapter, I extrapolated six principles that represent current theological reflections on community organizing. To recap, these principles are solidarity, subsidiarity, the common good, neighboring, listening, and centering the margins. I produced definitions for each of these principles to be used in this book, considering all the voices engaged in chapter 3.

Solidarity is the rediscovery of the radical shared interest held between people in fraternal relationships, as a key part of being human. Solidarity especially means radical shared interest with impoverished and marginalized people. We were made in God for fraternal relationships. Anything which disrupts solidarity should be resisted. So, part of the work of solidarity is countering the disruption of solidarity.

Subsidiarity brings together the importance of action together by people and institutions on issues facing people, with the principle that decisions should be taken and carried out as close as possible to the people they affect.

In addition, those who are impoverished and marginalized should become active citizens in decisions on issues which affect them.

The common good advances towards the well-being of the community measured by such things as justice, peace, and flourishing. It is best achieved through a communicative process involving all stakeholders in the community.

Neighborliness brings together a communal commitment to a particular people and place and encourages public relationships to be formed and strengthened between people. This neighborliness is motivated by seeking to love our neighbor and incorporates love of the stranger, the enemy, and the friendless. Neighborliness thus recognizes the power dynamics that exist in a neighborhood and seeks to change how this power is distributed.

Listening is where we should always start as churches, with attentiveness to those in the church and to neighbors in community, alongside attentiveness to our tradition and Scripture. Then, who we are listening to matters. Listening well will involve listening to impoverished and powerless people and those at the margins of churches and communities, and so listening for the prophetic minority.

Centering the margins means starting from the perspective of those currently impoverished and on the margins. It then means enabling these people to increase their power and sense of dignity and for their priorities to be the basis for action together on these priorities, rooted in their experience and values.

These six principles were mainly drawn from theological reflections by Anglicans and Catholics. We have observed how reflection on their engagement in community organizing in the UK has strengthened Anglican and Catholic theological ethics for the practice of social justice. Throughout this chapter and the next chapter, I will dialogue with these principles in exploring how Baptists have engaged with them in developing a Baptist ethic for the practice of social justice. As we observed in chapter 1, Baptist churches, particularly Black Baptist churches, have been very much involved in community organizing in the US. However, in contrast, there has been only limited engagement by Baptist churches in Wales and England.

Baptist churches in Wales have a choice of two unions to belong to—the BUGB, and the Undeb Beddyddwyr Cymru (UBC, translated in English as the Baptist Union of Wales or BUW). In contrast, Baptist churches in England have one union, the BUGB. Overall, there are currently more than one hundred thousand Baptists in the UK and nearly two thousand churches in membership of BUGB. BUGB now describes itself as a movement of Baptists Together rather than a union of churches.

There are thirteen regional associations across Wales and England as part of the BUGB, and five Baptist colleges across England, Scotland, and Wales which prepare women and men for church ministry as well as providing other aspects of training. Both BUGB and BUW have a general secretary, which is a permanent position, and a small central staff. There is one BUW general secretary for both the Welsh- and English-language wings of this union.

Both unions also have presidents elected annually for a yearly term. Currently and historically, the two wings of the BUW have usually had separate presidents. There is also a separate Baptist Union of Scotland and an Association of Baptist Churches in Ireland. In addition to this, there are some independent Baptist churches across the nations which are not part of associations or these broader unions, for example the much smaller and separate group, the Association of Grace Baptist Churches.

The focus of this chapter is on the assemblies of the BUGB and the Welsh- and English-language wings of the BUW from 1988 to 2010. This covers the period from the launch of the first community organizing alliances in the UK to the formation of Citizens UK. During this period, the BUW and BUGB held annual assemblies, with separate assemblies for the BUW Welsh- and English-language wings.[1] The public resolutions passed at the assemblies, the presidents' addresses, and the general secretaries' reports are employed as a proxy for exploring the themes and issues which were being raised at the level of the unions during this period.[2]

At the national level in both unions, there was no direct focus on community organizing as understood and practiced by Citizens UK during this period. Therefore, this chapter explores the focus of how the two unions engaged with social justice issues, and how such engagement relates to the six principles I have identified.[3] This chapter then briefly explores the wider

1. The BUW had three general secretaries during this period: D. Islwyn Davies until 1991; Peter Dewi Richards, 1992–2003; and Peter Thomas from 2004 onwards. In this period the BUGB also had three general secretaries: Bernard Green (1982–91), David Coffey (1991–2006), and Jonathan Edwards (2006–13).

2. Copies of the full BUGB presidential address could be located in the union archives only for 1986, 1991, 1992, and 1993 for the period researched. For other years I have relied on how these addresses were recorded in the *Baptist Times* newspaper and also in the BUGB annual reports where these could be located. The pattern at this time appears to be that in the English-language wing, the president made an address to the assembly. However, the text of these could not be located for most years during this period in the union archives. In the Welsh-language wing, the president generally chaired sessions but did not make an address to the assembly.

3. Baptists in Wales and England were engaging in social justice during this period—notably, Steve Chalke and the development of the Oasis Trust. This was focused on work with marginalized young people rather than community engagement and community organizing. Pete Brierley, involved in organizing with Citizens UK for more than fifteen years and now an assistant director, came to community organizing from working with Steve Chalke at the Oasis Trust. Community organizing was just one of many approaches

Baptist context to gain insight into the engagement of Baptists in Wales and England with these six principles during this period.[4] The following chapter will then observe, analyze, and critique the writings of major UK Baptist theologians during this period. In addition, we will examine the ways in which more recent Baptist studies have engaged with these principles and the development of a Baptist theological ethic for the practice of social justice.

4.2 The BUW and BUGB Assemblies Between 1988 and 2010

4.2.1 The Late 1980s

In 1988 the BUW Welsh wing discussed resolutions brought by its Dinasyddiaeth Cristnogol (the Christian Citizenship Committee) on welcoming the agreement to eliminate medium range nuclear weapons, on Northern Ireland, on the Israel/Palestine conflict, the injustice of the proposed UK government poll tax, on the UK government budget, on Breathalyzing motorists for alcohol, and on welcoming a leaflet on HIV and AIDS produced by the union.[5] The

---

that were being used during this period. It appears that other approaches that were seen as more developed from the local UK context got more traction among Baptists.

4. As noted earlier in ch. 1, the Church of England *Faith in the City* report in 1985 focused on the decline of the inner cities, partly as a result of the policies of the UK government, and led to an increased focus on urban mission. An additional piece of context for the discussions on social justice is the miners' strike 1984–85. This was a defining event in the UK in the mid-1980s and has had a lasting impact on UK communities, particularly those in coal-mining areas in Wales and England. This miners' strike was not a success. It was very damaging to the power of the trade unions and to groups that were holding communities together in coal-mining areas. The slogan used in the strike of "Close a pit, kill a community" seemed to be the result in many places. In addition, the UK prime minister in the 1980s, Margaret Thatcher, was pushing against the idea of the common good and ideas of community and society. Both relate to what it means to act from what is seen as the margins and as marginalized communities. Thus, engaging in an approach, community organizing, that seeks to strengthen communities and work for the common good, and involving those being marginalized could be seen as a response to both the decline of inner cities and the impact of the closure of the coal industry on communities. However, I have not focused on Baptist engagement in, or responses to, the development of urban mission nor the miners' strike in this book as both are outside the parameters set for the research in terms of time period and the focus on the BUW and BUGB assemblies between 1988 and 2010.

5. The pattern established was that this BUW committee would meet between assemblies to form and agree public resolutions which were then presented to, and agreed at, the assembly. Most of the resolutions called for the union to send a letter to government or council leaders on social justice issues. BUW Welsh wing resolutions and other assembly reports and documents are not available in English until the same resolutions were brought to both the Welsh and English wings from 2003 onwards.

resolution on the UK government budget states: "We express our dissatisfaction that the recent budget is a sign of a lack of compassion and indifference to social justice."[6] There is a strong link here to the general secretary's report to both assemblies on the theme of "the culture of indifference." In highlighting the welfare state and the threats to it from the UK government, Islwyn Davies, BUW general secretary, argues that "it is a humanitarian as well as a Christian standpoint that we are all bound up in the parcel of life and that demands a strong sense of mutual responsibility."[7] Davies links this to Jesus' command to love God and to love your neighbor as yourself, so calling for people to look out for each other's interests, not just their own. No public resolutions were agreed by the BUW English wing and there was a discussion on the process for bringing resolutions to the assembly.[8]

Colin Marchant was BUGB president for 1988–89. Marchant was the leader of West Ham Central Mission in Plaistow in East London at the time. Thus, it is possible that Marchant had had some contact with community organizing or at least with other faith and community organizations which formed in East London one of the first community organizing alliances in the UK in 1989 and then TELCO in 1996. "Shalom" was Marchant's presidential theme, where he focused on urban mission. Marchant highlights that "to work for peace, to minister God's peace to those in need of body, mind and spirit, and to direct all our Christian endeavour towards the goal of God's kingdom of shalom is the raison d'être of the church."[9] Marchant argues,

> In a black church you can't just sing hymns and forget that some of some of your congregation got roughed up last night and your kids are unemployed. The point is this, the gospel has no cutting edge unless you are addressing the issues that are bugging your people daily.[10]

So, Marchant urges delegates at the assembly to "go into the city, the market place, the divided homes, the racially antagonistic neighbourhoods—and bring 'shalom,' the wholeness and peace of God."[11] During the assembly, delegates also visited various areas, "to encounter for themselves the places where God is working in the inner city."[12] Marchant spoke to the assembly

6. BUW, *Cyfarfodydd yr Undeb 1988*, 15; my translation.

7. BUW, "Appendix 1 [1988]," 22–24.

8. BUW, "Appendix 1 [1988]," 38.

9. BUGB, *Annual Report 1988*, 8.

10. *Baptist Times* (Apr. 28, 1988), 15.

11. *Baptist Times* (Apr. 28, 1988), 1.

12. *Baptist Times* (Apr. 28, 1988), 1.

about living through a revolution in inner-city London where the Christian churches were now in a minority. Marchant emphasized that inner-city mission involved issues of justice. He was passionate about the engagement of churches with working-class people and wrote his PhD thesis on the interaction of church and society in East London.[13]

The public resolutions that were passed focused on racial justice (a call to endorse "a Christian manifesto on race"), alcohol abuse, the National Health Service, and a resolution on South Africa, which it was noted linked to the assembly theme as "it recognised the efforts of those who struggle for shalom in South Africa."[14] A denomination-wide Action in Mission program was also launched at this assembly. The program focused on "concentrating the minds of church members on the realities of their congregations and neighbourhoods." The program signalled "the start of . . . a self-conscious, deliberate approach to localised mission and service."[15]

In writing about his year as president, Marchant makes several important points on which we will reflect further in this chapter. Marchant notes that Baptist assembly resolutions cover a wide spectrum of issues, from personal life and relationships to national and international issues.[16] He underlines the importance of joining hands in common tasks. Marchant notes that there is a question around the extent to which the presidents' themes represented and reflected what was going on around BUGB at the time. As we will discover, a number of these themes did lead to further action by the union.

Marchant argues that his theme of "Shalom" was widened and deepened by John Biggs as the BUGB president the following year.[17] Biggs was a lay person rather than a Baptist church minister. Biggs highlights that in taking the theme "For Such a Time as This," he was keen to bring a focus on the environment and on a wider understanding of mission, including working with others ecumenically.[18] He highlights that his "primary purpose is to encourage the churches in all their activities, both in evangelism and in social

13. *Baptist Times* (Apr. 28, 1988), 14.

14. *Baptist Times* (Apr. 28, 1988), 16.

15. *Baptist Times* (Apr. 28, 1988), 1.

16. Marchant, "My Presidential Year," 24. Between 1989 and 2010 the most popular issues for public resolutions at BUGB Assemblies were: international issues (fourteen resolutions), asylum (eight), peace and disarmament (four), poverty (three), human rights (three), violence (three), employment (two), education (two), and environment (two). There was only one resolution passed on racism in this time period. However, it had been the subject of many resolutions prior to 1989.

17. Marchant, "My Presidential Year," 24.

18. Biggs, "My Presidential Year," 12.

outreach."[19] In his presidential address, Biggs, "in positive hope spoke of the Christian Church's calling to express gospel concern for the whole of creation, *to speak both to and on behalf of rich and poor alike—but more especially on behalf of the poor.*"[20] Biggs underlines,

> We must recognise that the Kingdom of God is more than a lot of individual churches. We need each other. . . . We now have Action in Mission which is another manifestation of the number of churches doing things together which they couldn't do on their own. . . . We are learning that we are much more effective in taking a political stance when we come together across denominational differences.[21]

This connects with a vote at the BUGB Assembly in 1989 to join the new ecumenical bodies formed through the "Inter-Church Process" with 74 percent of votes in favor.[22] Biggs notes that through his role as president in 1989–90 he was able to bring more focus to addressing environmental issues, including lobbying and campaigning in the UK Parliament and with the UK government secretary of state for the environment.[23] The BUGB Assembly in 1989 passed public resolutions on the United Nations Convention on the Rights of Children and on housing and homelessness.[24]

In 1989, BUW Welsh wing public resolutions supported the anti-apartheid movement and action to protect the ozone layer, opposed the Sunday opening of shops, welcomed the banning of public drinking by several Welsh councils, and opposed the burning of holiday homes as part of Welsh language campaign actions.[25] There was discussion on joining Cytûn, a new proposed Welsh ecumenical body, at both the Welsh and English wing conferences. The Welsh wing voted strongly in favor of membership of Cytûn with 72 percent for membership, whereas the English wing voted against membership by around a two-thirds majority.[26] In his address to the English wing, the general secretary urges churches not to quench the Spirit of God, and thus the spirit of fellowship and of service:

19. *Baptist Times* (Apr. 20, 1989), 14.

20. BUGB, *Annual Report 1989*, 9; emphasis in original.

21. *Baptist Times* (Apr. 20, 1989), 15.

22. *Baptist Times* (Apr. 27, 1989), 8.

23. Biggs, "My Presidential Year," 12–13.

24. However, there are no details of the text of these resolutions in BUGB, *Baptist Union Directory, 1989–1990*.

25. BUW, *Cyfarfodydd yr Undeb 1989*, 16–17.

26. BUW, *Cyfarfodydd yr Undeb 1990*, 31; "Appendix 1 [1989]," 57.

> Do not quench the Spirit of Fellowship. "Christianity is a Christ-centred religion and a Spirit dominated religion." The Holy Spirit creates fellowship. The Church is not a company of like-minded people who share the same beliefs and practices. It is the Family of God created by the Holy Spirit who unites believers to Christ and to one another. . . .
>
> Quench not the Spirit of Service. We are called to share in the redemption of Christ and in the service of Christ to the world. Ours is a world of hunger, disease and illiteracy. There are so many who are victims of unjust individuals and iniquitous systems; victims of apartheid and alcoholism and unbridled passions. But Christ has identified himself with the needs of the world.[27]

So, here we have strong endorsements for strengthening relationships with other churches and linking this to tackling issues of social injustice and thus the principles of neighborliness and solidarity. However, while the BUW Welsh wing embraced this, the English wing did not.

4.2.2 The 1990s

BUW Welsh wing resolutions in 1990 focused on Sunday opening of shops and pubs, the violence of the Chinese government towards those calling for democracy, and European support for nuclear disarmament efforts.[28] In contrast, BUW English wing resolutions in 1990 focused on concerns around the UK government's Education Reform Act, changes to the National Health Service, and abortion.[29] After further discussion within and between the two wings of the union through a Joint Council meeting, the BUW became a full member of Cytûn in 1990.[30] In the discussions around public resolutions and around membership of an ecumenical body in Wales, there appear to be some differences between the emphasis and thinking of churches in the two wings of the BUW, with stronger support for action on social justice by the Welsh-language wing. As with the BUGB, the BUW English-language wing developed a strong focus on resourcing evangelism as demonstrated by the evangelism report in the annual reports.[31]

27. BUW, "Appendix 1 [1989]," 41–42.

28. BUW, *Cyfarfodydd yr Undeb 1990*, 48.

29. BUW, *Baptist Union: English Assembly, 1990*, 28–29.

30. BUW, "Appendix 1 [1990]," 19–20.

31. BUW, "Appendix 1 [1990]," 17. It was not possible to locate the BUW general secretary's address to the either wing's assembly in 1990.

In 1990, Derek Tidball took as his BUGB presidential theme "The People of the Future." In his presidential address he posed a number of questions, including: "Have we allowed this present age to shape our thinking too much?" and "What are the immediate prospects for other churches, and for our society that should be fashioning the shape of our mission and evangelism?"[32] He argues that "God's call is much wider than growth, but God's concern is also church growth. Any church should grow: If it is bold enough to preach the Word; if it dares to challenge the cultural status quo; if it refuses to accept present political arrangements as eternally given; and if it is convinced of the truth of its message, and if it is willing to suffer for the truth."[33] Tidball notes,

> We do not want to return to a gospel which is unconcerned about the real world. . . . Evangelicals have acknowledged again the importance of social action. Others, who already had a well-developed social conscience, have also affirmed the importance of evangelism.
>
> It is time to be obedient to our Lord who told us "to go and make disciples" and "to love our neighbour as ourselves." That means working for justice, healing the wounded, challenging the demonic and preaching the gospel, looking outward to a needy world, and abandoning the endless discussions of in-house issues.[34]

So, justice and social action formed part of the address. However, despite his call, internal discussions were not abandoned by Baptist churches and the BUGB in the following years. Tidball focused on, and was enthusiastic for, evangelism during his year as president.[35] Tidball became secretary for mission and evangelism for the BUGB and was head of the Mission Department until 1995. At the 1990 assembly, a resolution on peace, related to the arms trade, was passed, along with one on child pornography. There was also a presentation on the environment.[36]

32. BUGB, *Annual Report 1990*, 7.

33. *Baptist Times* (May 3, 1990), 1.

34. *Baptist Times* (May 3, 1990), 6.

35. Tidball, "My Presidential Year." However, after this series of articles by the BUGB presidents on their presidential years, it appears the series was discontinued as there are no further articles of this nature in the *Baptist Ministers' Journal*, the new name for *The Fraternal*, after 1991. Therefore, in this chapter we are only able to observe what the presidents said in their address to assembly, rather than a fuller picture of other issues and themes the presidents highlighted during their presidential years.

36. BUGB, *Baptist Union Directory, 1990–1991*.

In 1991, the BUW Welsh wing Christian Citizenship Committee focused on reconciliation in Northern Ireland, opposition to the construction of a military radar station near St. David's, the need for a new language act to ensure equal status for Welsh and English, and opposition to the promotion of gambling on Welsh language television.[37]

Roy Jenkins, a Welsh newspaper journalist and BBC broadcaster, founder of Christians Against Torture as well as Baptist minister, took on the role of BUGB president in 1991 with his theme as "Cry Freedom!" Jenkins, in his presidential address, notes that his presidency was in the context of apartheid coming to an end in South Africa, moves away from communist government in Eastern Europe and the (now former) Soviet Union, and ongoing struggles for democratic government in Central and South America, including civil war in El Salvador.[38] In the address, Jenkins argues:

> The only freedom we are in the business of declaring is that which God gives, and which he acts to make possible. The God who leads his people out of captivity in Egypt, who raises up prophets to denounce corrupt rulers, who places himself firmly on the side of the victim, is the God who intends freedom—"life in all its fullness"—for every individual and every community.[39]

Here we have some resonance with the principle of centering the margins. Jenkins continues with this when he goes on to underline that:

> Many [churches supported by BUGB grants] are in the poorest areas of our country. Their members maintain a constant and wearying struggle against indifference, vandalism and the despair bred by generations of deprivation. They witness to a God who sets value on the people of such communities when so many of the structures of society render them worthless. By faithful proclamation and caring action, they point to the Christ who can set them free in the middle of their need.[40]

Jenkins then argues passionately that "if we are to cry freedom for the world with any credibility, we dare not fail to notice what is on our own doorsteps."[41] Then Jenkins gives several examples, including:

37. BUW, *Cyfarfodydd yr Undeb 1991*, 22. Resolutions proposed by the English wing in 1991 could not be located in the union's archives.

38. Jenkins, *Cry Freedom!*, 1.

39. Jenkins, *Cry Freedom!*, 2.

40. Jenkins, *Cry Freedom!*, 7.

41. Jenkins, *Cry Freedom!*, 11.

- The injustice of families being forced to survive in real poverty in a rich society
- The injustice of men and women feeling threatened or diminished by the institutionalizing of racial prejudice
- The injustice of men and women fleeing persecution turned away by immigration controls from a country once proud to be a haven[42]

Jenkins highlights a quote from John Clifford in 1911 to demonstrate what he argues it should mean for Baptists to cry freedom: "Poverty must be dealt with in its causes. Charity must not be accepted as a substitute for justice."[43] Given this theme, it is surprising that there were no public resolutions passed at the assembly. Instead, in this part of the assembly minutes, there is this note:

> The Rev David Clark of Birmingham chaired an hour which commenced with a panel of speakers highlighting contemporary issues of social concern. Delegates were then invited to form small groups to discuss the current social scene, each group to submit by one of its number any comments it wished to make to the Mission Office of the Union.[44]

This is intriguing and raises several questions. It is not clear if there was a decision not to have any public resolutions at this assembly or if there were none proposed. The description of the session resonates with a community organizing approach of a bottom-up listening process on issues from people gathered at the assembly from Baptist churches across Wales and England. The small groups could be seen as equivalent to the practice of house meetings in community organizing. So, had there been any influence of community organizing on the approach taken? We do not know. In addition, it is not recorded what issues were raised from this session, nor whether the Mission Office took up any of the issues raised. Finally, this also implies that, in addition to considering the content of assembly addresses and public resolutions for their focus on social action and social justice, it is also important to analyze the process being used to form the resolutions that came to the assembly and to decide on priorities for mission, and particularly for social justice.[45]

42. Jenkins, *Cry Freedom!*, 11.

43. Jenkins, *Cry Freedom!*, 11. John Clifford was a Baptist leader in the late nineteenth and early twentieth centuries. Jenkins's focus on freedom in this presidential address is very different to Nigel Wright's focus on freedom of worship as a significant Baptist contribution to society in the UK and globally.

44. BUGB, *Baptist Union Directory, 1991–1992*, 38.

45. The minutes of the assembly also record that Jim Wallis from Sojourners in Washington, DC, addressed the whole of the assembly. Wallis became an influential voice on

In 1992, the BUW Welsh wing Christian Citizenship Committee highlighted its support for the European Union ban on tobacco advertising, called for the UK government to increase its spending on the health service, welcomed efforts to bring peace to (now former) Yugoslavia and to free hostages in the Middle East, and urged progress towards a new Languages Act for Wales.[46] In contrast, the BUW English wing Citizenship Committee did not propose any resolutions.[47] Instead, on the theme of citizenship there was a presentation on "Religious Education in Schools."[48] Despite the opposition of the English wing to membership, it appears that the leadership of both language wings of the BUW saw Cytûn as a key vehicle for Welsh Baptist engagement with others on social justice.[49]

In 1992, BUGB public resolutions were passed on Europe, and on environment and development. Eric Westwood's presidential theme was "That the World May Believe." This year was also the bicentenary of the BMS and so the theme of world mission was chosen. Westwood had also worked with the BMS in Brazil.[50] In his address, Westwood challenges the churches to listen to Christ afresh and to listen to Christians in other countries.[51] He quotes John Stott, who argued that "to see need and possess the remedy compels love to act, and whether the action will be evangelistic or social, or indeed political, will depend on what we 'see' and what we 'have.'"[52] However, the overall focus of Westwood's understanding of mission was on evangelism.[53]

In this same assembly, the theme of the new Broad Alliance of Radical Baptists' meeting was "discovering the real meaning of ecumenism in identifying with the desperate plight of the poor in Central America."[54] David Quinney-Mee, who worked with BMS in El Salvador, highlights that in this context "cooperation between Baptists, Anglicans, Roman Catholics and others was . . . a matter of practical solidarity with, and active listening to, the poor." Quinney-Mee argues,

---

social justice for Baptists and other Christians in the UK as well as the US. However, the minutes of the assembly do not record what he said about justice.

46. BUW, *Cyfarfodydd yr Undeb 1992*, 18–19.

47. BUW, *Baptist Union: English Assembly, 1992*, 21.

48. BUW, "Appendix 1 [1992]," 32.

49. BUW, *Baptist Union: English Assembly, 1992*, 29–30. The general secretary's addresses to the assembly of either wing could not be located in the union's archives.

50. BUGB, *Annual Report 1992*, 8.

51. BUGB, *Annual Report 1992*, 9.

52. *Baptist Times* (Apr. 30, 1992), 7.

53. *Baptist Times* (May 7, 1992), 12.

54. *Baptist Times* (May 7, 1992), 3.

> The critical issue between different churches and theological traditions was not resolving the differences, which had to be respected, but how we respond to the poor. It is better to do that together, if we are committed, in the name of Christ, to ending their suffering.[55]

He argues that Christians in Britain could learn from the experience of the church in Latin America what it means to be "alongside the poor," and that this "has radical implications for church style and witness among the poor and marginalised in our own society."[56] Here we have strong connections to the principles of solidarity and centering the margins. So, we observe that there were very different understandings of mission and emphases between Westwood and Quinney-Mee, both BMS missionaries with long experience in different Latin American countries.[57] I understand that Broad Alliance of Radical Baptists was formed because social justice was not being heard in the BUGB. Members of this alliance recognized that they were out of step with most Baptist churches in the union. For this alliance, radical meant being politically engaged and seeking to change the world.[58]

The theme of the BUW English Assembly in 1993 was "God's Mission with Us Creating Faith in the World." Derek Tidball led the Bible studies at this assembly and focused on the mission of the Church. In his presentation as general secretary, Peter Dewi Richards emphasized the need for change and that this change needs to be nurtured in the local church.[59] However, there was no explicit mention of engaging in social justice as part of this. Instead, more of his focus was on evangelism.[60]

Brian Haymes (in 1993) and Nigel Wright (in 2002) were the only two of the Baptist theologians we will focus on in chapter 5 who were presidents of the BUGB during this period. "The Fullness of Christ" was Haymes's presidential theme in 1993. Haymes urges delegates at the assembly to "be more effective Christian disciples at their places of work and to confront the social injustices which disfigure society."[61] He argues for radical discipleship which

55. *Baptist Times* (May 7, 1992), 3.

56. *Baptist Times* (May 7, 1992), 3.

57. The 1992 assembly was also addressed by Steve Chalke, a Baptist minister, and director of Oasis Trust. Chalke became an influential voice on Christian engagement in social justice in the UK.

58. Ruth Gouldbourne, in-person meeting, Jan. 23, 2024.

59. BUW, "Appendix 1 [1993]," 33.

60. BUW, *Cyfarfodydd yr Undeb 1993*; "Appendix 1 [1993]." Public resolutions for 1993 for the BUW Welsh- and English-language wings could not be located in the union's archives.

61. *Baptist Times* (Apr. 22, 1993), 1. Haymes had recently returned from El Salvador

values Baptist tradition and identity.[62] In Haymes's presidential address, he argues that "God has been about the work of reconciliation, peacemaking, taking down dividing walls of hostility, uniting those near and far, in fact, gathering up all things in Christ."[63] For Haymes, these should find expression in the church. The church is to be truly countercultural:

> When Christ's people are true to their calling, where they understand that their task is neither to escape from the world, nor to dominate or to find power or status within it, but to live out in word and deed the life of Christ, the life of the alternative society, the new humanity, then they are a key factor in God's missionary ministry of reconciliation and peace.[64]

Haymes goes on to highlight that this "is something that we can only do together."[65] So, along with the strong focus on community in this address, we also see the importance of acting for justice with others, and so we hear echoes of the principles of subsidiarity, the common good, and neighborliness that we identified from theological reflection on community organizing. He also notes,

> As the churches in Europe continue to weaken in their status and impact, we have so much to learn from partners in the world church. We who are rich and secure in our established churches need to learn again the joy, vitality and sacrifice that goes with following Jesus. Our sisters and brothers in the so-called third world have much to give us here, especially in those situations where the cause of liberation is being lived and died for. It simply will not do to write off liberation theology as Marxist. Such a judgement is in fact part intellectually wrong but more importantly is a slur against those who are living out a great loyalty to Jesus among the lives of the poor.[66]

Through this, Haymes is also making the link to the principle of centering the margins through starting from the perspective of those currently impoverished and on the margins. Later in the address he argues, "I do not see that there can come a greater liberation for the poor of the world unless somehow they can help liberate us from the limited concerns of exploitations that mark

---

when he delivered his address to the assembly and highlighted the hope and courage of Christians there (*Baptist Times* [Apr. 22, 1993], 2).

62. *Baptist Times* (Apr. 22, 1993), 7.

63. Haymes, *Fullness of Christ*, 1.

64. Haymes, *Fullness of Christ*, 3.

65. Haymes, *Fullness of Christ*, 6.

66. Haymes, *Fullness of Christ*, 6–7.

our culture."[67] Haymes describes hearing the perspectives of people from sub-Saharan Africa at the first full assembly of the Council of Churches in Britain and Ireland: "They spoke of the devastation resulting from wars, famines and droughts. Much of their word to us was harrowing. They told us the truth. They had seen it with their own eyes. . . . Theirs was a disturbing story but told with hope [in God]."[68] Here, and later in his address bringing examples from churches engaging in their communities in parts of England, Haymes also makes the case for listening to those directly affected by such issues and the need for solidarity with them. From these examples, Haymes seems to indicate he does not observe that many poor and marginalized people are already part of these Baptist church congregations.

At the 1993 BUGB Assembly, public resolutions were passed on Africa, including on aid and development, and on the provision of drug and alcohol treatment. Many of the BUGB resolutions up to this point encourage churches to write to their MPs or contact local authorities, and to take practical action on the theme. However, there is no mention of joining together with others locally to act on the issue or theme. In addition, there is encouragement to engage with MPs or local councillors but without a methodology or approach to get them to do anything or hold them accountable publicly for their commitments (as community organizing would seek to do).

A third public resolution was proposed by Colin Marchant. This resolution on UK poverty includes agreement to:

> Express the commitment to alleviate poverty locally by
> i. learning more about the experience and causes of poverty, and committing more resources to initiatives designed to combat poverty.[69]

There was also agreement in this resolution to give serious consideration to "establishing a national 'Against the Stream' Fund that would be used to help churches in their desire to relieve poverty."[70] Marchant proposed that this fund be "akin to the Church of England's Church Urban Fund."[71] This funding stream would become a significant Baptist initiative to support churches in BUGB to act on issues of social injustice.

67. Haymes, *Fullness of Christ*, 13.

68. Haymes, *Fullness of Christ*, 13.

69. BUGB, *Baptist Union Directory, 1993–1994*, 37.

70. BUGB, *Baptist Union Directory, 1993–1994*, 37.

71. *Baptist Times* (Apr. 29, 1993), 3. Significantly, the Church of England Church Urban Fund provided initial funding to community organizing alliances in England.

Paul Fiddes, in his only address so far to a BUGB Assembly, focuses on the Great Commission. Fiddes highlights that "we do not make mission: God calls us to join him in the mission he is already carrying out." Fiddes argues for people to be radical disciples of Jesus Christ, and so, echoing Haymes's theme, make mission incarnational:

> As we share the journey of the Son of God, we must also travel out of ourselves, die to the familiar, and open ourselves to what is foreign and strange, if we are to be any use to God in his desire to bring reconciliation to a broken world.[72]

He continues by underlining that "holistic mission must mean getting deeply involved within the world God has made, and being identified with those on the margins."[73] Rene Padilla, a Latin American theologian who introduced an understanding of mission as holistic, or "integral mission," bringing together both evangelism and social justice, also addressed the 1993 BUGB Assembly.[74] Fiddes appears to have picked up on Padilla's address in his own address to the assembly. In addition, Fiddes picks up the themes of the public resolutions passed at the assembly:

> Mission must mean the touching and the transformation of the whole of life. The mission of God means justice for the oppressed, healing for the sick, education for the illiterate, liberation for the captives.
>
> I have heard the voices of witness from our churches this week telling us what this will mean, urging us to share the experience of those who are poor or powerless or on the margins of society.
>
> In the public resolutions debate these voices have called us to feel as others feel; to make a first step on the journey of painful love.[75]

As with Haymes in 1993, Stephen Gaukroger uses being "radical" in his BUGB presidential theme. However, instead of focusing on radical discipleship, he called for radical change. Gaukroger's presidential theme, in the assembly the following year, of "Out with the Church—the World in the World" focuses on mission as evangelism. "Local churches should take a radical look at themselves and consider what changes they should make to their programmes and methods in order to be relevant to the society in which they are set."[76]

72. *Baptist Times* (Apr. 29, 1993), 5.
73. *Baptist Times* (Apr. 29, 1993), 5.
74. *Baptist Times* (Apr. 29, 1993), 9.
75. *Baptist Times* (Apr. 29, 1993), 5.
76. *Baptist Times* (May 5, 1994), 2.

Gaukroger recognizes that "people want to be participants in a cause and not members of an institution," such as churches. He argues that the church should be calling people to follow Christ as part of a community and a cause, rather than just individually.[77] He concludes his address "with an invitation to a new commitment—confidence in the word of God and the Christ who inspired it."[78] In contrast, the public resolutions session included resolutions on lone parent families in churches, higher education, unemployment, South Africa and Bulgaria. The resolution on unemployment includes the following paragraphs:

> 2. If changes of patterns in employment are inevitable, churches, communities and Government must work together to maintain the dignity of each person and to affirm their value to society whether in or out of paid work. . . .
> 5. Churches should debate these issues, seek to cooperate with others who are active in helping unemployed people in their area and keep the local MP informed of their concerns.[79]

Here, as in Haymes's presidential address the previous year, there are echoes of the six principles outlined above, in this case subsidiarity and solidarity. However, in this resolution there is again no mention, crucially, of how churches should work together with others. The resolution on lone parents calls on:

> Churches to lobby their MPs about the inadequacy of Government policy towards lone parents, to make representations to local authorities about housing policy for lone parents, and examine their own approach to lone parents in their fellowships.[80]

As before, there is no mention of how churches should work together with others. There is again a link to solidarity and subsidiarity in what the local church can do to respond to issues around housing and other issues affecting lone parents in churches and in local communities. The resolution on Bulgaria, as with many other resolutions on individual countries at other assemblies, includes an expression of solidarity with Baptists and other Christians in that country.[81]

In 1994, the BUW Welsh wing's Christian Citizenship Committee focused its resolutions on the countryside, religious education in Wales, and in

77. *Baptist Times* (May 12, 1994), 7.

78. BUGB, *Annual Report 1994*, 8.

79. BUGB, *Baptist Union Directory, 1994–1995*, 37.

80. *Baptist Times* (May 5, 1994), 4.

81. BUGB, *Baptist Union Directory, 1994–1995*, 37.

support of Christian Aid's campaign to ban the use of land mines.[82] The resolution on the countryside recognizes the importance of agricultural society to Welsh history and identity, the Welsh language, and the environment.[83]

The BUW Welsh wing passed resolutions on several international justice issues in 1995, including on the World Bank and International Monetary Fund and on Christians Against Torture as well as on the national lottery and religious programming on BBC Radio Cymru. The minutes note that there were comments on several decisions made by the Citizenship Committee, and particularly on the national lottery.[84] The general secretary's report in 1995 "emphasised the need for the Union through the churches to be actively involved in all spheres of ministry and mission, and to grasp the opportunities for service."[85] Again, no BUW English wing resolutions could be located in the documents for 1995. So, despite the focus on mission and service, the English wing did not appear to see engaging in passing public resolutions together as a priority.

Pete Tongeman's presidential theme in 1995 was "To Comfort and Disturb." Tongeman begins his address "by contrasting the truth that comforts with the truth that disturbs and quoted the saying: *Jesus not only came to comfort those who are afflicted, but to afflict the comfortable*."[86] He highlights homelessness as "a task for the prophetic people of God. To disturb the status quo in the name of Christ, exposing what is unholy and unjust, degrading and dehumanising, and to combine the prophetic word with actions that demonstrate we live by what we believe."[87] Tongeman urges churches to "share the comforts of the Gospel" to the UK and a world full of injustice, as well as to "disturb the world with the truth of God's word."[88] As the annual report notes, "The public resolutions session of the Assembly would reveal further disturbing truths about British society today."[89] The public resolutions focused on land mines, fair trade, and education.[90]

82. BUW, *Cyfarfodydd yr Undeb 1994*, 33.

83. BUW, "Appendix 1 [1994]."

84. BUW, *Cyfarfodydd yr Undeb 1995*, 36. Public resolutions for 1994 for the BUW English-language wing could not be located in the union's archives.

85. BUW, "Appendix 1 [1995]," 29.

86. BUGB, *Annual Report 1995*, 7.

87. *Baptist Times* (May 11, 1995),13.

88. BUGB, *Annual Report 1995*, 8.

89. BUGB, *Annual Report 1995*, 7. BUGB annual reports for subsequent years could not be located apart from 2005 and then short annual review documents for 2010 and 2011.

90. BUGB, *Baptist Union Directory, 1995–1996*. It is interesting to note that the text of

The 1995 BUGB Assembly confirmed the union's full membership of the Council of Churches for Britain and Ireland and Churches Together in England with increased majorities compared to the vote in favor of the membership of these ecumenical bodies in 1989.[91]

In 1996 the BUW Welsh wing passed resolutions on protecting the interests of refugees, racism in Britain, homelessness among young people, and safeguarding the peace process in Northern Ireland.[92] The general secretary in his address to the English-language wing "appealed for more involvement within schools as governors and stressed the need for Christians to be involved in education committees. . . . The General Secretary also noted the importance of being involved within hospital trusts and Local Health Authorities. *Social concern* is an integral part of evangelism."[93] The BUW English wing Citizenship Committee focused on a discussion around care for elderly people in the community.[94]

John James followed as BUGB president in 1996 with "Make It Count!" as his theme and public resolutions focused on gambling and the national lottery and on the peace process in Ireland.[95] So, we observe that both BUW and BUGB are picking up similar issues for public resolutions in 1995 and 1996. David Coffey focused on the BUGB Denominational Consultation in his address to a "Focus on Mission" session at the assembly.[96]

In 1997 the BUW Welsh wing passed resolutions on the death penalty, to support Christian Aid's fair trade campaign targeting supermarkets, for greater UK government funding for the health service, and in favor of forming an assembly in Wales as part of greater devolution of the UK government.[97] On the death penalty and health service, the union is encouraged to write to the relevant secretaries of state in the UK government. The general secretary's address focused on the theme of the conference, "The Body of Christ." In his address, Peter Dewi Richards highlighted the importance of coordination within

---

the BUGB resolution in 1995 on banning antipersonnel land mines comes one year after a similar resolution by the BUW Welsh wing on land mines but, unlike the BUW resolution, it makes no mention of the Christian Aid campaign. Christian Aid was, and is still, seen as the international development agency most closely associated with the ecumenical movement and the main ecumenical bodies in the UK.

91. *Baptist Times* (May 11, 1995), 1.

92. BUW, *Cyfarfodydd yr Undeb 1996*, 44.

93. BUW, "Appendix 1 [1996]," 37; emphasis in original.

94. BUW, "Appendix 1 [1996]," 40.

95. BUGB, *Baptist Union Directory, 1996–1997*, 35–38.

96. *Baptist Times* (May 9, 1996), page number unavailable.

97. BUW, *Cyfarfodydd yr Undeb 1997*, 53.

the union to meet their objective "to be a mission-oriented denomination."[98] He then, while acknowledging the English wing's continued objection to BUW participation in Cytûn, noted the importance of Cytûn's work on justice issues in Wales.[99]

V. Frederick George's theme in 1997 was "Take the Risk."[100] As the first nonwhite president of the BUGB, he urges "Baptists to recognise the institutionalised racism which exists within many churches and to be willing to take the risk to combat it."[101] He argues,

> We have to face the painful truth that many of our Black and Asian sisters and brothers are excluded and marginalised by the institutionalised racism present in many of our churches.[102]

While focusing on racial injustice, George argues that Baptists should not ignore the need to combat injustice in relation to women, disabled people, refugees, those in the Global South, "and all who are abandoned to a life of powerlessness and poverty by the political and economic structures of our day."[103] In this we therefore have a strong link to the principles of centering the margins, solidarity, and neighborliness.

With this theme, George promoted racial justice and the work of the BUGB Racial Justice Task Group to tackle racism outside and inside churches. There were five public resolutions agreed, including one on Jubilee 2000, the international campaign to cancel the unpayable debts of the world's poorest countries ahead of the new millennium. This resolution included a request for

> the Mission Department of the Baptist Union of Great Britain to bring to the attention of the churches and associations material to help us engage constructively in the campaign and to provide regular briefings on the impact of the campaign.[104]

Significantly, this resolution asked BUGB to share ways and approaches to engage in campaigning on this issue. The Church and Social Responsibility

98. BUW, "Appendix 1 [1997]," 45.

99. This included the production of a Cytûn report *Wales—a Moral Society* that year, which was debated by both wings of the BUW and its implications for the churches' involvement in all spheres of public life and in thinking through values in society.

100. BUGB, *Baptist Union Directory, 1997–1998*, 34.

101. *Baptist Times* (May 1, 1997), 1.

102. *Baptist Times* (May 1, 1997), 1.

103. *Baptist Times* (May 1, 1997), 1.

104. BUGB, *Baptist Union Directory, 1997–1998*, 36.

Committee of the BUW English wing picked up Jubilee 2000 in 1998.[105] This committee, which was formed in this year, had the primary role "to encourage Association initiatives and to be the catalyst in developing a strategy which will support such initiatives."[106] The resolution on Jubilee 2000 states,

> BUW declares its support for the Christian Aid Jubilee 2000 and calls upon the members of all churches to sign the petition during the year 1998. We as a Union believe we need to pressure the G7 countries to eradicate the debts of the past and to act on the Biblical principle of forgetting all debts in the Jubilee year. . . . The Anglicans have already planned the distribution of the petition and are enthusiastically engaged.[107]

The inclusion of this final sentence in the resolution is encouraging and suggests a change in attitude and a sense of healthy competition; the Anglicans are involved in a justice issue, and it is also one that Baptists in Wales should be involved in. This contrasts with earlier discussions in the BUW English wing where there was much opposition to being involved in Cytûn, where Anglicans were also involved.

"In Step with the Spirit" was Douglas McBain's theme as BUGB president in 1998.[108] Public resolutions were passed on detention centers for asylum seekers and on human rights. For the first time, there was a deliberation session, "encouraging members of the Assembly to reflect on important issues of contemporary living and take insights from the session back to their home churches." The session focused on the following three themes: living in a minority, living in a global village, and genetic engineering. In addition, there was a presentation on violence against women.[109] This focus on living in a minority could have led to discussion around the principles of solidarity, the common good, and particularly neighborliness as these all would connect well with considering what it means to be church as a minority.[110] However, there is no record that it did.

105. Other areas raised this year by the Church and Social Responsibility Committee were on housing and homelessness, schools and communal worship, an integrated transport system in Wales, and the drugs crisis.

106. BUW, *Baptist Union English Assembly 1998*, 23.

107. BUW, *Baptist Union English Assembly 1998*, 23.

108. *Baptist Times* notes that Douglas McBain's presidential address was "impassioned" and "departed substantially from his prepared script" ([May 1, 1997], 1). However, no written record of the address could be located in the *Baptist Times* or elsewhere.

109. BUGB, *Baptist Union Directory, 1998–1999*, 37.

110. This is explored further in Murray, *Vast Minority*.

Public resolutions for the BUW Welsh wing in 1999 focused on nuclear waste, the arms trade, the Welsh language in the assembly, and Kosovo.[111] These resolutions were also presented to, and passed by, the BUW English wing that year.[112] The report of the Church and Social Responsibility Committee of the English wing continued to include a focus on the union's relationships with other denominations and organizations, as the Welsh wing had also been doing for all of the years studied so far. In presenting a paper on ministry in the future, the general secretary again highlighted mission and said that ministry to enable mission was key to the future of the denomination.[113]

Michael Bochenski took as his presidential theme "Sent—into All the World" in 1999. He identifies four "signs of the risen Lord at work": renewal, ecumenism, community action, and spiritual warfare.[114] There was a focus on mission and looking forward to the next century. There was again a public resolution on refugees and asylum seekers. This "encourages Baptist churches to welcome and assist clusters of refugee and asylum seekers who may come to live in their neighbourhood following our Government's new Immigration and Asylum Act."[115] It is not clear that there was a separate approach to enable churches to do this, nor was there a call to meet with MPs or to seek to change this new act. A public resolution on racism, also overwhelmingly approved, focused on internal action by churches in the BUGB.[116]

4.2.3 The 2000s

In 2000, the BUW Welsh wing passed public resolutions on Jubilee 2000, the crisis in the countryside, the powers of the Welsh Assembly, religious broadcasting, and on the Trident nuclear weapons system.[117] The general secretary's address on the theme of "A New Opportunity" notes that "the situation within our churches and society called for a radical change in our conception of ministry and mission. In many churches 'autonomous' has come to mean independence and isolation."[118] However, this related not to joint action together with others for social justice, but to what became a long-running

111. BUW, "Atodiad 1 [1999]," 63.
112. BUW, "Appendix 1 [1991]," 51.
113. BUW, "Appendix 1 [1999]," 48.
114. *Baptist Times* (Apr. 29, 1999), 1.
115. BUGB, *Baptist Union Directory, 1999–2000*, 37.
116. BUGB, *Baptist Union Directory, 1999–2000*, 38.
117. BUW, "Atodiad 1 [2000]," 52.
118. BUW, "Appendix 1 [2000]," 37.

debate about having one council between the two wings of the BUW rather than two separate ones, and the proposal to have one nonconformist denomination in Wales. The order in which the reports are presented in the annual report in the English wing perhaps also gives a sense of the priority given to social justice at that time. The order of the reports was Ministerial Board, Ministerial Fund Committee, Finance, Evangelism Committee, and only then Church and Social Responsibility Committee.

"Christ at Work in the World" was the BUGB presidential theme of Graham Ashworth in 2000. Ashworth challenged churches on rural deprivation, workplace mission, and the environment. In the same week a report had been published highlighting the problems facing rural communities. Ashworth encourages churches in rural areas to be "an agent of concern and practical help' in these communities, and so be 'champions of the deprived.'"[119]

David Coffey's general secretary address to the assembly focused on future perspectives for mission in the twenty-first century. At this assembly the public resolutions again followed a familiar pattern: a country in the news (this time Serbia and sanctions), something related to Baptist churches in the union (in 2000 this focused on churches in rural areas), and a big issue.

In 2000 refugee and asylum issues were again a focus. However, instead of a public resolution, this was a discussion around "Welcoming the Stranger." This form was introduced "because this [a discussion and debate without a formal resolution] could be more conducive to learning and discernment than is sometimes the case in propositional style debates."[120] It appears that BUGB was struggling with how to have assembly discussions and decisions on issues of social justice where there was not an overwhelming majority for one response or another. This situation also reflects the growing polarization of views around immigration in broader UK society.

The 2001 BUW English wing Church and Social Responsibility Committee discussed "contemporary challenges," including racial justice, changes in the Welsh economy and their impact on communities, and "increasing alcohol consumption among young people."[121] One resolution was discussed and passed on the crisis facing rural communities in Wales. The resolution noted that this crisis was "similar in many ways to that faced by the mining communities some years previously."[122] So, here we observe links with the principles of solidarity and centering the margins.

119. *Baptist Times* (May 4, 2000), 1, 11.

120. BUGB, *Baptist Union Directory, 2000–2001–2002*, 41.

121. BUW, *Baptist Union English Assembly 2001*, 23.

122. BUW, "Appendix 1 [2001]," 47–48. No records of the general secretary's address could be located in the union's archives. From the reports, it appears that both the Welsh

In 2001, Peter Wortley took as his BUGB presidential theme "Disciples at Dawn: Sharing Christ with the Rising Generation." This again focused on mission, mainly understood as evangelism.[123] In the public resolutions session, "the Assembly debated two motions, both concerned with the escalation of violence in the world and the consequent threats to peace and stability which this brings."[124] The resolution passed on Congo by a substantial majority contained no explicit recommendation for churches to meet with MPs, only to request the UK government to act. In contrast, a resolution on the ballistic missile defence system, proposed by the Baptist Peace Fellowship, was agreed but only with 295 votes in favor and 195 against. For comparison, most resolutions are recorded as being passed at assembly by a substantial or overwhelming majority. This may indicate a decreasing interest in political action for peace by Baptists in BUGB.

In 2002, the BUW general secretary's report focuses on mission with the theme of "Wells of New Opportunities," highlighting "our responsibility to use the resources we have, both personal and corporate in ensuring that we reach those in need of the gospel."[125] In the same assembly, Denzil John, the chair of the Church and Social Responsibility Committee, expressed disappointment that no resolutions were presented for discussion at this assembly and stressed "the importance of the committee in highlighting the needs of society and the responsibility placed upon Christians to be involved in the world." He went on to underline "the importance for the voice of Christians to be heard and to respond positively when issues are raised."[126]

Nigel Wright was BUGB president in 2002 with a theme and a book both entitled *New Baptists, New Agenda*.[127] He challenged Baptists to "be converted to Christ, to the Church, to the world and to the future."[128] Wright argues,

> We are converted from the world to Christ in order that by him—and through our conversion to the Church—the "world" in this

---

and English wings were seeing social justice as something being worked on by broader groups including the European Baptist Federation and Cytûn, and not just something for the BUW to work on as a union.

123. The headline of the *Baptist Times* reflecting on the assembly was "Re-Imagining Mission" ([May 17, 2001], 1). However, the text of the presidential address could not be located.

124. BUGB, *Baptist Union Directory, 2000–2001–2002*, 46.

125. BUW, "Appendix 1 [2002]," 53.

126. BUW, "Appendix 1 [2002]," 51.

127. The next chapter will include a detailed exploration of this, and other books, by Nigel Wright.

128. *Baptist Times* (May 9, 2002), 1.

> God-resistant sense might be taken out of us, and so that we might be again converted to the world. But this time the world is seen as God's own creation, the theatre of God's glory and the arena of God's saving activity. By ourselves being incarnate in this world, its physicality, its communities, its commerce, its search for a better way, we work towards the better day already made known in Christ.[129]

A public resolution on fair trade was passed unanimously. There was also a debate without resolution on Israel/Palestine.

The BUW Church and Social Responsibility Committee report in 2003 notes that the union had decided to join Churches Together in Britain and Ireland. The report also highlights the importance of communication between denominations on social justice issues. The report also reveals that the resolutions passed on health and on peace in Iraq have been formed together between the two wings of BUW, noting that with the resolutions on Iraq, "minor modifications were made because of the differing positions of the English and Welsh wings of the Union on pacifism."[130] There was also agreement for this committee to focus on issues of "public concern" and for a separate Ecumenical Panel to consider issues brought by other denominations. So, it appears that there is still a sense that Baptists can have a voice in public discussions in Wales and the UK as a union, as well as acting together with others through Cytûn and other ecumenical bodies. The president of the BUW English wing addressed the assembly on the theme of "Being Church," highlighting that church is community and being the community.[131]

In 2003 the BUGB Assembly was held in Cardiff, the capital of Wales, with John Rackley as president. His theme was "Easter People in a Good Friday World." In this Rackley argues,

> We have many fellow travellers beyond the Church. There is much seeking of God beyond our numbers.
>
> There is much anguish over our Good Friday world among people who do not count themselves as among the Easter people. So, our calling to explore God must take us beyond our walls, and groups and fellowships.
>
> Our missionary task is to accompany others in their search. . . .

129. *Baptist Times* (May 9, 2002), 5, 12.

130. BUW, "Programme 2003," 40.

131. BUW, "Appendix 1 [2003]."

> A missionary Church explores the paths of God beyond itself. Easter people travel with the Good Friday world in its tormented search for life.[132]

Rackley argues for the need for Baptists to listen to others, to pursue shalom, to choose for peace instead of war and violence. So, here we observe strong links to the principles of solidarity, the common good, listening, and centering the margins.

Bernadette Farrell, a Roman Catholic, led worship at the conference. Farrell at that time was also an experienced community organizer in London Citizens. This might have been another moment when there could have been exploration by Baptists on how community organizing could assist them on a "new agenda."

As in 2002, there was discussion without a public resolution being passed. This time, "the Assembly debated without Resolution the crisis in Iraq."[133] Perhaps this is again an indication that there were strong opinions both for and against an issue, this time around UK involvement in conflict in this nation. Perhaps this also reveals a lack of confidence in how to discern together what the Baptist "view" should be on this conflict and on other contentious issues.

Public resolutions were passed by the BUW in 2004 on better protection for the environment through improving public transport in Wales, and a second resolution in response to the collapse of World Trade Organization talks in Mexico.[134]

The 2004 BUGB Assembly was again held in Cardiff. Peter Manson's presidential theme was "Jesus." His concern was that Baptist churches should return to focus on Jesus.[135] However, there were no connections made to the six principles. The assembly minutes note that the two-hundredth Against the Stream grant had been awarded to the Ark-T Centre in Oxford, a church meeting in a community space in an economically impoverished area of the city. David Coffey gave a keynote address "focusing on major changes in our culture which constitute a call from God."[136]

Later in the assembly, three public resolutions were discussed and passed, on domestic violence, on personal debt in the UK, and again on refugees and asylum seekers. Refugees and asylum had been growing as a political issue

132. *Baptist Times* (May 8, 2003), 13.

133. BUGB, *Baptist Union Directory, 2003–2004*, 37.

134. BUW, *Baptist Union English Assembly 2004*, 25. The text for Denzil John's presidential address for the BUW Welsh wing could not be located in the union's archives.

135. *Baptist Times* (May 6, 2004),12–13.

136. BUGB, *Baptist Union Directory, 2004–2005*, 38. The full text of David Coffey's address could not be located in the union's archives.

in the UK and reflected what some saw had led to "a major change" in UK culture. However, there was no explicit link made between this address by the general secretary and the public resolutions. One resolution "calls upon the UK government to remove measures from the 2004 Asylum and Immigration Bill" and then lists several measures.[137] However, it does this without indicating an approach to work with others to compel the government to make these changes. The opportunity was thus missed to reflect on the principles of neighborliness and centering the margins. The definition of this in the previous chapter highlighted that this neighborliness is motivated by seeking to love our neighbor which incorporates love of the stranger, the enemy, and the friendless—in other words, people such as asylum seekers and refugees, who are often marginalized within communities.

All three public resolutions passed by the BUW in 2005 were targeted at government ministers in the Welsh Assembly, including one on rural education, focusing on letters to be written to the relevant ministers.[138] The new BUW general secretary, Peter Thomas, focused on "The Baptist Union of Wales in the 21st Century" in his assembly address, highlighting the importance of a focus on mission rather than on maintenance.[139] However, his address was focused on doing this as Baptist churches but without explicit mention of being involved in mission with other churches and organizations.

The 2005 BUGB Assembly was a one-day conference in Birmingham as the Baptist World Centenary Congress was meeting also in Birmingham later that year. Roy Searle was president, with the theme "Celebrating Diversity." Due to the shortened nature of the assembly, there was no public resolutions session. However, there was a "Question Time" event, "exploring topical and social issues."[140] International debt relief and immigration were the main topics discussed in this session.[141]

There was also no presidential address. However, there was a plenary session where Roy Searle and others each examined a Bible passage (John 4:1–42), "giving Assembly the opportunity to experience how different traditions within the Baptist family approach the explanation of one paragraph of scripture."[142] Linking to the assembly theme, this can be seen as an attempt for churches to recognize that there was a diversity of views among churches in membership of BUGB, and in addition, for churches to recognize the

137. BUGB, *Baptist Union Directory, 2004–2005*, 39.

138. BUW, *Annual Report 2005–2006*, 26–27.

139. BUW, *Annual Report 2005–2006*, 30.

140. *Baptist Times* (Apr. 21, 2005), 1.

141. *Baptist Times* (Apr. 28, 2005), 3.

142. BUGB, *Baptist Union Directory, 2005–2006*, 38.

importance of listening to the minority voice and centering the margins, and thus pick up two principles from theological reflection on community organizing. Searle outlines his priorities ahead of the assembly, describing mission not as an activity, but reflecting "the heart of God," and "giving away what is not ours to own or control."[143] Searle goes on to describe church as being about "building communities" with "an unswerving commitment to the kind of social justice exhibited in the Make Poverty History Campaign." On this commitment he argues:

> I'd love us to take up this cause and be known as the denomination that stands up and makes a difference. I wish we were, in Councils and Associations, talking about bigger issues. We can be quite parochial, but some churches are engaged . . . so let's bring this to the table.[144]

On Baptist churches and their commitment to mission, Searle underlines:

> What I also see is a right spirit of non-conformity, which is prepared for the sake of the Gospel to take risks. And I see energy and commitment and desire, which is very heartening—and a growing diversity and willingness to embrace difference. . . .
>
> [There is] an independent streak in Baptist life which is sad. Baptists prefer the default mode of independence—not just ecumenically, but within the denomination as well. If only we would share together for the Kingdom, a lot of troubles would be minimised.[145]

In 2006 the BUW passed three public resolutions, on health and the closure of local hospitals, on prostitution, and on the modern slave trade.[146] Two new BUW departments were established, the Department of Ministry and Mission and the Department of Education and Resource. The latter would include the Church and Social Responsibility Committee.[147] Thus, structurally the union separated mission from engagement with others on social justice issues. The general secretary's report focused on "Reaching Out, Gaining Ground." However, the focus in this was mainly on structural changes in the union to enable mission.[148]

143. *Baptist Times* (Apr. 21, 2005), 13.
144. *Baptist Times* (Apr. 21, 2005), 13.
145. *Baptist Times* (Apr. 21, 2005), 13.
146. BUW, *Annual Report 2005–2006*, 18.
147. BUW, *Annual Report 2005–2006*, 7–8.
148. BUW, *Annual Report 2006–2007*, 38.

Searle's focus was developed further by Kate Coleman's 2006 BUGB Assembly theme of "Centring the Margins." Coleman was the first Black Baptist woman to be president. In her address she challenges the assembly to "stay focused" in a time of transition as society and as churches.[149] Coleman argues,

> Staying focused is about recognising that the great paradox of the Christian faith is that the centre of God's activity usually lies in the margins of human activity. And that the centre of God's concern usually lies somewhere in the margins of our own concerns. . . . If you want to find out what God is doing, look to what is sidelined and marginalised. Somewhere right there you will find God powerfully at work.[150]

She goes on to argue that staying focused will mean engaging with others who Baptists have not engaged with before and standing up and speaking out on issues where Baptists have not done this before. This, Coleman argues, is where new ways of thinking and acting are needed.[151] Coleman continues that for this to take place listening is important:

> When you look to the margins you will find faith in the strangest places. We all need to develop positive presumptions, but we can only do that if we have as wide an understanding as possible. We can only do that if we listen to what other people are saying rather than listening to what we're saying.[152]

Thus, Coleman's presidential address also connects strongly with the importance of the principle of listening to those at the margins. Jonathan Edwards was elected as the new general secretary of the BUGB at this assembly.[153] He pledged to put prayer at the heart of his ministry and encourage the denomination in prayer.[154] A public resolution on Human Trafficking was agreed unanimously. It included the call to churches "to carry out active and political lobbying" on several calls to the UK government.[155] The minutes note that assembly had "an interactive debate on mission which included one Public Resolution [on human trafficking] and discussion of the replacement of Trident, the conflict in Israel and Palestine, and issues centring on Nepal and

149. BUGB, *Baptist Union Directory, 2007*, 40; *Baptist Times* (May 4, 2006), 12.

150. *Baptist Times* (May 4, 2006), 12.

151. *Baptist Times* (May 4, 2006),12.

152. *Baptist Times* (May 4, 2006), 13.

153. Edwards was BUGB general secretary from 2006 to 2013.

154. *Baptist Times* (May 4, 2006), 1.

155. BUGB, *Baptist Union Directory, 2007*, 39.

Zimbabwe."[156] Thus, apart from a local and national focus to the resolution on human trafficking, the others do not call for churches to act locally on justice issues.

BUW resolutions were passed in 2007 on the Trident nuclear weapons system, on supporting the better treatment of asylum seekers by the UK government, on the environment and investing in "non-carbon fuels," on racist language on television, and against the closure of hospitals in mid-Wales.[157]

The 2007 BUGB Assembly theme was "In Search of Freedom." There was no president and there was a "deliberation session" rather than a public resolutions session.[158] A resolution on migrant workers was agreed unanimously.[159] The resolution "calls upon churches to provide essential care and support for migrant workers and their families, and to speak out against instances of injustice and exploitation."[160] In proposing the resolution, David Doonan argues, "In an Assembly where we have the central theme of freedom, we are calling for an end to this modern form of slavery."[161] Both Doonan and Hilary Willmer, in proposing the resolution, highlight the poor pay and cramped living conditions of migrant workers. This resolution provided the front-page story of the *Baptist Times*, with the headline "Assembly Backs Call to End Exploitation of Migrant Workers."[162] There are connections here in particular to solidarity and centering the margins.

The resolution thus joined the assembly with thousands marching in London calling for an end to this exploitation in the UK. The march followed a special mass for migrants at Westminster Cathedral led by the archbishop of Westminster.[163] London Citizens was very involved in the organization of this mass for migrants and what became the Strangers into Citizens campaign. Austen Ivereigh highlights that this radical call of Strangers into Citizens came directly from CST and started with a migrants' mass in 2006, "when the Cardinal Archbishop of Westminster made the first call by a UK religious leader for a pathway into citizenship for immigrants without status."[164]

The Baptist assembly resolution in 2007 was less radical than this call. However, even from those proposing the resolution and its text, it appears that

156. BUGB, *Baptist Union Directory, 2007*, 39.

157. BUW, *Annual Report 2006–2007*, 20–23.

158. BUGB, *Baptist Union Directory, 2008*, 394–96.

159. BUGB, *Baptist Union Directory, 2008*, 396.

160. BUGB, *Baptist Union Directory, 2008*, 396.

161. *Baptist Times* (May 10, 2007), 1.

162. *Baptist Times* (May 10, 2007), 1.

163. *Baptist Times* (May 10, 2007), 1.

164. Ivereigh, *Faithful Citizens*, 130.

this is another time when Baptists and community organizing "touched" or at least came into close contact—unfortunately, without any significant discussion of community organizing and without this leading to significant numbers of Baptist churches in membership of Citizens alliances in Wales and England.

The 2007 assembly also marked the bicentenary of the UK government Act to abolish the transatlantic slave trade.[165] Les Isaac, a Street Pastors pioneer, underlines that churches need to go beyond condemning the slave trade and become risk-takers, to help people enslaved now, noting that "this would require churches to change their concept of mission, and start to see it as an ongoing and integral part of being a Christian."[166] In addition, Isaac argues that congregations "need to look outside the four walls of our churches" and not leave inner-city mission to Black Christians.[167]

Jonathan Edwards led a lament about the slave trade. However, the focus of Edwards's address to assembly was to find God's vision for his church amidst the challenge for Baptists "when the world is pushing us in different directions."[168] Edwards stresses the priority of worship and concludes by "urging the congregation to widen their understanding of the scope of the Gospel."[169]

2008 saw renewed thinking about the role and function of the BUW Church and Social Responsibility Committee with the new union structures. The committee report states,

> It would appear that at present this committee is not fulfilling its potential. Other organisations like Cytûn, BMS and Christian Aid have become the corporate voice of the denomination on many social issues. . . . In order for our voice to be heard, we need to ensure that the churches we serve are in touch with society at large and see their role in serving Christ within their communities, embracing both the call to witness as well as the call to serve.[170]

The Church and Social Responsibility Committee then became the Faith and Social Responsibility Forum.[171] Public resolutions were passed on Burma, against the siting of a military training academy in Wales, and in support of

165. BUGB, *Baptist Union Directory, 2008*, 394.

166. *Baptist Times* (May 10, 2007), 3.

167. *Baptist Times* (May 10, 2007), 3.

168. *Baptist Times* (May 10, 2007), 4.

169. *Baptist Times* (May 10, 2007), 4.

170. BUW, *Annual Report 2007–2008*, 13.

171. BUW, *Annual Report 2008–2009*, 8–10. However, the name has now reverted to Church and Social Responsibility Committee.

Welsh government action to support Welsh farming.[172] Peter Dewi Richards, the former BUW general secretary, was president of the English wing in 2008. In his presidential address entitled "A Letter from London," with the theme of the assembly on "Hopeful Imagination," Richards focuses on remembering our roots as Baptists, focusing on unity of purpose between Welsh and English language Baptist churches, and the importance of a vision.[173] The BUW annual report on this address highlights that

> the importance of cooperation and unity should also be reflected in our relationship with other faiths as well as within our relationships with churches, Associations and Union. We should strive to rise above the constraints and the restrictions that so often inhibit and endeavour to find that common ground that will bring about a sense of belonging and instil in us a vision for the future.[174]

Here we observe a strong encouragement to work together with others who are different to seek common ground, as well as to do this with other Baptist churches in Wales.

Edwards recognized at the 2008 BUGB Assembly that the previous eighteen months had been a period of much reflection for Baptists, particularly on the theme of the apology for the historic injustice of the transatlantic slave trade. However, in his address to the assembly, Edwards stresses the need for the denomination to recommit itself to evangelism: "We are called to build up communities of encouragement and shape our lives so that we are encouraging missionary disciples. We need to pray and worship better."[175] The deliberation session "hosted a debate on issues of public concern, including creation care and one formal resolution on care for church employees."[176] The agreed resolution states:

> The Assembly recognises and affirms the work done by 'Church Action on Poverty' to overcome poverty in the UK, and in particular to highlight the need for churches to work for social justice within their own communities.
>
> In order to give authenticity and credibility to this commitment, Assembly calls upon the churches, associations and colleges in membership with the Baptist Union of Great Britain to:

172. BUW, *Annual Report 2007–2008*, 14–15.
173. Richards, "Llythyr o Lundain."
174. BUW, *Annual Report 2008–2009*, 18.
175. *Baptist Times* (May 8, 2008), 4.
176. BUGB, *Baptist Union Directory, 2009*, 397.

> Give careful consideration to CAP's call for churches to ensure that all their employees receive a "living wage." . . .
>
> This Assembly believes that it is our duty as Christians to follow good employment practices, ensuring that all our employees are treated fairly and justly, and so enabling us to be a credible voice in campaigning for an end to poverty in the UK.[177]

So, there was a resolution in favor of a living wage for church employees. In the debate, "concern was expressed . . . over the fact that many members of congregations themselves have to live only on a minimum wage."[178] This is a strong link to the principles of solidarity and the common good as defined in the previous chapter.

However, we observe that no link was made here to churches campaigning with Citizens on the living wage at a time when many church denominations and other faith groups were active in living wage campaigns to increase wages for people employed in many different public and private organizations. The absence of a direct link to these campaigns in both the resolution and in the debate appears to demonstrate that few Baptists were engaged with community organizing then or, alternatively, that those who were involved were not present at the assembly.

The BUGB president for 2008–2009 was John Weaver, then principal of South Wales Baptist College.[179] In his presidential address on "Living Faith in a Complex World," Weaver argues that "bringing faith and daily living together is the main task facing the Church as we seek to be involved in the mission of Christ."[180] Weaver highlights,

> Many of us have a surprising ability to live in two worlds; the private world of faith and the public world of work and daily life. For example, we are happy to pray for the families of young people tragically and pointlessly murdered in violent incidences in our cities, but we may be ill-prepared and some even unconcerned about the fundamental underlying issues of racism, unemployment, boredom, alcohol abuse and other ills of society.
>
> The massive cultural boundaries which we cross each time we move into or out of the worship service are largely ignored. Once we honestly face this cultural divide, it becomes painfully obvious that as churches we are often lacking in the help we need as we

177. BUGB, *Baptist Union Directory, 2009*, 397.

178. *Baptist Times* (May 8, 2008), 4.

179. South Wales Baptist College is now called Cardiff Baptist College or Coleg y Bedyddwyr Caerdydd.

180. *Baptist Times* (May 8, 2008), 12.

> wrestle with the ever-increasing complexities of living as disciples of Christ.[181]

Weaver later asks how we make connections with people outside church, recognizing that churches are increasingly visible and involved in mission. He argues that "we too can engage individually and as congregations in such mission—the Gospel lived through community building and community transforming activities."[182]

We observe a link here to the principles of solidarity, the common good and neighborliness although Weaver does not use these terms. In addition, there is no link made between this theme and the resolution on the living wage nor with previous resolutions on providing a better welcome for asylum seekers or migrant workers.[183] As we have observed from previous assemblies and addresses, Weaver, in this address, mostly does not provide examples as to how churches can build or transform communities. Again, the opportunity is missed to connect with community organizing as practiced by churches in Citizens UK alliances.

In 2009 the BUW proposed no resolutions. There was discussion as to whether the Faith and Social Responsibility Forum could speak for the union as a whole. As a result:

> It was agreed that if a matter had been discussed and decided by the meeting it should be communicated in the minutes of that committee, but it would not necessarily reflect the voice of the entire Union on that matter.[184]

It is important to note here that the pattern in the BUW is that resolutions were agreed by the committee and then presented to the assembly. This is in contrast to the pattern in the BUGB where resolutions were discussed and agreed at the assembly in the public resolutions session. The general secretary's report to the English wing focused on mission, but almost entirely understood as evangelism.[185]

The theme of the 2009 BUGB Assembly was "Who Do We Think We Are?"[186] In his address to assembly, Jonathan Edwards focuses on serving God

181. *Baptist Times* (May 8, 2008), 12.

182. *Baptist Times* (May 8, 2008), 14.

183. This emphasizes the lack of discussion and integration of speakers and themes in the assembly planning. John Weaver complained about this throughout his involvement as BUGB president and vice-president (phone call, July 28, 2023).

184. BUW, *Annual Report 2009–2010*, 19.

185. BUW, "Appendix 1 [2009]."

186. BUGB, *Baptist Union Directory, 2010*, 353.

with the mind of Christ. Edwards argues that "moving forward as a denomination will require a renewed openness. As we're open, so he [God] opens our lives to other people. Crucial to this is careful listening."[187]

Kingsley Appiagyei focuses, in his presidential theme of "New Hope: An Expectant Community," on encouraging delegates at the assembly to be an expectant community.[188] Two public resolutions were passed in the deliberation session: on mosquito alarms and young people, and on asylum seekers. This resolution calls on the government to:

- Confer a right to work on an asylum seeker waiting longer than six months for final resolution of their case
- Bring an end to the detention of children, whose best interests should be paramount in the decision-making process

Furthermore, the assembly asks that the BUGB

- Share in campaigning and resourcing churches in support of these proposals[189]

Connections are thus made to the principles of solidarity and centering the margins. There was already a Citizens UK campaign to end the detention of children in 2009. However, there is no reference to this in the assembly resolution. This campaign would subsequently be won by Citizens UK through commitments made by MP candidates and party leaders ahead of the 2010 UK general election. So, again we see Baptists picking up on issues which are also the focus of Citizens UK community organizing campaigns but without any indication that Baptists were active in community organizing.

In 2010 the BUW Welsh wing passed a resolution at their assembly calling on the Welsh government to abandon its plan to expand a military base in South Wales as well as to stop using another base for training on military drones.[190] The general secretary's report included a focus on mission and on discussions between the BUGB, BUW, and the colleges on forming one union of Baptists in Wales.[191]

187. *Baptist Times* (May 7, 2009), 2.

188. BUGB, *Baptist Union Directory, 2010*, 353; *Baptist Times* (May 7, 2009), 2, 10–12.

189. BUGB, *Baptist Union Directory, 2010*, 356–57.

190. BUW, *Annual Report 2010–2011*, 22.

191. BUW, *Annual Report 2010–2011*, 33–35. There is currently still the presence of BUW Welsh- and English-language wings plus two regional associations of BUGB in Wales.

The 2010 BUGB assembly's theme was "One World, One Mission."[192] There was no BUGB president. Public resolutions were agreed on nuclear weapons and on violence and human trafficking.[193] Craig Gardiner, a Baptist minister in Cardiff, proposed the resolution on nuclear weapons, arguing, "Security is not the same as peace and it is peace that Christians are called to pursue. The command of God to the church is clear—a command of peacemaking."[194] The resolution on violence and human trafficking was proposed by Rachel Haig, highlighting "the heart of the gospel is to reject violence and bless peacemakers." Haig quotes Pope John Paul II, who said, "Solidarity is a firm and persevering determination to commit oneself to the common good."[195] So, here in this discussion on a Baptist assembly resolution we have brief references to both solidarity and the common good.

Jonathan Edwards as general secretary again focused on listening in his address to the 2010 assembly as he had also done the previous year. Edwards notes:

> Listening sounds so simple. You just sit there! No manual labour involved! And yet anyone who has given themselves to concerted listening will know that it is one of the most totally demanding things that one could ever do.
>
> As Baptists we firmly believe that God speaks through every member of the church, and when we gather together, we deliberately seek to hear what God is saying to us. But, in all truth, we often struggle and fail at this.[196]

From this, it appears that the assembly explored new ways of listening to God. Edwards proposes breaking down church meetings into smaller groups of six to eight people "so that the voices of the weak and shy are heard."[197] So, there is a good connection to how listening is understood as a principle from theological reflection on community organizing. However, Edwards then proposes that churches use this form of listening to focus on listening around the subject of evangelism in the church's area.[198] It is not clear what happened to this initiative. However, at the 2011 assembly the deliberation session was renamed as a "Plenary Session—Listening to God." This session debated and

192. *Baptist Times* (May 7, 2010), 1.
193. BUGB, *Baptist Union Directory, 2011.*
194. *Baptist Times* (May 7, 2010), 7.
195. *Baptist Times* (May 7, 2010), 7.
196. *Baptist Times* (May 7, 2010), 4.
197. *Baptist Times* (May 7, 2010), 4.
198. *Baptist Times* (May 7, 2010), 4.

agreed a public resolution on taxation and then created an open time of listening to God on the assembly theme of "Your Kingdom Come."[199]

4.3 Exploring the Engagement of Baptists in Wales and England with These Six Principles During This Period

So far in this chapter we have examined what BUGB and BUW focused on during the period 1988 to 2010 and how the resolutions and addresses at the assemblies relate to the six principles drawn from theological reflection on community organizing. We have observed where and how connections were made with these principles, and where they were absent. Having examined all these sources, I identify three main themes that I will detail below: the composition and context of Baptist churches in the two unions; the focus on, and understanding of, mission; and ecumenical engagement. These three themes provide some ways to help explore and/or explain the engagement, and at times nonengagement, with these principles.

4.3.1 Composition and Context of Baptist Churches

Let us consider the local Baptist churches in the two unions, their composition and context, and the implications for engagement in social justice. Paul Fiddes, UK Baptist theologian, suggests that Baptists in Wales and England are a group of people who until the twentieth century for the most part were from the working class and self-educated and "for much of their history were oppressed or excluded from positions in society."[200] But by the late twentieth century in the UK, Baptist churches had become a church largely of the middle class. Baptists went from being marginalized and choosing to dissent to seeking acceptance and largely conforming and co-opted within broader church and society.[201]

In addition to this, marginalized and oppressed people were not generally developing the public resolutions and speaking at the assemblies.[202] Ian Randall, UK Baptist historian, notes that Black-majority Baptist churches were

199. BUGB, *Baptist Union Directory, 2012.*

200. Fiddes, *Tracks and Traces*, 7.

201. Bebbington, *Baptists Through the Centuries.*

202. Kate Coleman's focus on centering margins and listening to those oppressed and at the margins is helpful in this regard. Nigel Wright describes an ideal church as one that understands the perspective of people at the margins of communities (*Challenge to Change*).

growing in the 1980s, but many had little contact with white Baptist churches, including in East London.[203] We note that Black Baptist churches, which could have recognized in community organizing a link back to earlier struggles for justice against the slave trade and for civil rights, were not associating closely with white Baptist churches which formed the majority of churches in BUW and BUGB. Marchant understands shalom to include centering the margins through starting with the perspectives of those currently impoverished and on the margins, and for their priorities to be the basis for action together. He, a white man, had a voice through the presidency of BUGB for a year. However, the voices and experiences of Black-majority Baptist churches were mostly not heard directly in the assemblies. If they had been heard more strongly in the late 1980s onwards, this could have shaped Baptist understanding of social justice during this period.

Biggs gives an insight into the state of Baptist churches in Wales and England in 1989. He states, "I would judge that, within England but not within South Wales, there is good ground for hope, many churches are in good heart, expanding in their membership and/or in their vision for mission in their community." But Biggs goes on to state, "We still struggle in council estates, in some inner-city areas, in isolated rural villages and in multi-racial areas."[204]

So, it appears that Biggs recognizes here that Baptists were still wrestling with the influential Church of England's *Faith in the City* report from 1985 which as we observed in chapter 1 led to the formation of the Church Urban Fund.[205] This then provided Anglican funding for community organizing and the COF. It can be argued that community organizing would also have helped Baptist churches in their response.

Randall recognizes that much of the thinking of individual Baptist churches will be recorded in the notes of church member meetings. So, to understand how Black Baptist churches, mainly meeting in inner-city areas, were relating to the principles of solidarity, centering the margins, and so on, we would need to study the church meeting minutes and other sources of these churches during this period. We would also need to do this for other Baptist churches which were engaging actively in social justice during this period.

Randall notes that most Baptist sociopolitical action in England was at local level rather than national.[206] This contrasts with Wales where from my investigation I would argue that much of this action in Wales was at the

203. Randall, *English Baptists*, 458.

204. Biggs, "My Presidential Year," 14.

205. Commission on Urban Priority Areas, *Faith in the City*.

206. Randall, *English Baptists*, 420.

national level.[207] Randall's conclusion for England raises the question of the importance of the public resolutions passed on national and international issues for local Baptist churches. Many of the BUGB public resolutions were proposed by individual associations or Baptist churches who were already seeking to do something locally on an issue, such as homelessness or asylum seekers and refugees. So, these public resolutions reflected seeking further action on a social justice issue where action was already happening at a local level. However, groups passionate about social justice were generally on the margins of the union, such as the Baptist Peace Fellowship, and largely were not at the center of Baptist discussions on priorities for the union.

In Wales, an individual church's membership of a union is usually historically determined. The BUW "has been shaped by Welsh non-conformist history, practices, and heritage."[208] Hunt highlights that there is not homogeneity of culture across the two wings of this union because the English-language wing has been more influenced by the culture of the majority, and dominant, English language Christian culture. However, as Hunt underlines, "there is still a noticeable difference of culture between churches in BUW and those in the BUGB."[209] This may also help explain the relative influence of those focused on social justice in the BUW Welsh wing as well as the recurrent struggle to form resolutions on justice issues in the English wing of this union.

David Bebbington, a UK Baptist historian, argues that "repeatedly the Baptists, in wanting to spread the Christian message, have been moulded by the contexts in which they have operated."[210] Densil Morgan, a Welsh theologian and church historian, focuses on Baptists and other Christian denominations in Wales in the twentieth century.[211] Morgan notes the decline of traditional Welsh denominations and what is seen as the marginalization of religion in contemporary Wales. Membership of churches in the BUW dropped from 47,900 in 1980 to 9,800 in 2020.[212] In the BUGB, membership dropped from 170,338 (in 2058 churches) in 1980 to 138,089 members (in 2028 churches) in 2002.[213]

207. The records of the assemblies during this time period give little indication of any local involvement of Baptist churches in Wales in social justice. Despite the lack of information on this located in the BUW and BUGB archives, this does not mean that no Welsh Baptist churches were involved at a local level during this time period.

208. Hunt, "Unity in Translation," 12.

209. Hunt, "Unity in Translation," 13.

210. Bebbington, *Baptists Through the Centuries*, 283.

211. Morgan, *Span of the Cross*.

212. Lewis et al., *Christianity in Wales*, 307.

213. Goodliff, *Renewing a Modern Denomination*, 213–14.

4.3.2 Focus on and Understanding of Mission

From this context we can understand why there would be a focus on mission, and on institutional changes in the unions to enable such mission, during this period. However, mission was generally understood as evangelism, rather than a holistic understanding which combines evangelism and social justice. Andy Goodliff, a UK Baptist historian, argues that "during the 1980s mission was not something reflected on by Baptists in any significant manner." He argues that where Baptists did talk about mission, the use of the term mission was used interchangeably with evangelism.[214] However, in light of my investigation, I would disagree with Goodliff on this. Marchant, Biggs, and Tidball all reflected on social justice as being part of mission in their presidencies, and this reflected broader discussions in both the BUGB and BUW in the late 1980s.

Bernard Green, who was general secretary of the BUGB from 1982 to 1991, wrote an article in 1980 entitled 'What Baptists Ought to Be Thinking About in the Next Ten Years." In this essay, Green urged "creative involvement in the *struggles of humanity*," and in 1982 he "expressed hope for a revitalised *non-conformist conscience* in public affairs."[215]

From 1970, Don Black was the BUGB director of social responsibility, as part of his role as head of the Department for Mission, and from 1995 as the secretary for social affairs. Randall notes that "Black's view was that when responsibility for social affairs was separated from responsibility for mission, there was a greater opportunity to bring social issues to the attention of the Baptist constituency."[216] However, this then separates engagement in social justice out from an understanding of mission. Social affairs and evangelism were separate headings under mission in the BUGB annual reports in the late 1980s and into the 1990s. In addition, "Mission" and "Partnership with Others" were separate sections in the reports.[217]

Goodliff understands that the 1990s were a period of great change and indeed transformation in BUGB in response to a decline in church attendance, growing evangelical movements and a changing ecumenical movement.[218] In 1991, David Coffey and Keith Jones became general secretary and deputy general secretary of the BUGB respectively. Through these roles they were both influential on the involvement in mission of Baptist churches in Wales and England. Coffey had been BUGB secretary for evangelism since 1988. Coffey

214. Goodliff, *Renewing a Modern Denomination*, 97.

215. Randall, *English Baptists*, 424–25; emphasis in original.

216. Randall, *English Baptists*, 419.

217. BUGB, *Annual Report 1988*, 26–29, 33–39. This pattern continues in later reports.

218. Goodliff, *Renewing a Modern Denomination*, 2.

constantly spoke of mission and in 1991 he outlined a broad vision of mission; "I understand mission to mean church planting and evangelism, social action and prophetic protest, a world mission commitment and a Kingdom of God awareness of international affairs and environmental concerns."[219]

However, as Goodliff notes, "arguably it was evangelism that drove Coffey and especially as churchgoing was declining."[220] Goodliff underlines that Coffey was an Evangelical, and "many of the presidents of the Baptist Union during those years [the 1990s and into the 2000s] were also identifiable evangelicals—Tidball, Gaukroger, James, McBain, Bochenski, and Wright."[221] However, in light of my investigation of their assembly addresses, this did not mean that they did not mention social justice. Randall notes that Jones had a strong awareness of issues of peace and justice. In his role Jones also had responsibility for ecumenical issues.[222] Keith Jones and Myra Blyth, in their roles as deputy general secretaries of BUGB, were able to influence how the assembly included a focus on social justice and engagement with others, including through the public resolutions' sessions.[223]

A listening process in 1991 led to a document entitled *Towards 2000* focused on four areas that would shape the agenda of the BUGB in the 1990s: "To encourage, support and initiate imaginative and effective strategies in evangelism and other aspects of God's mission; to develop our distinctive Baptist identity; to strengthen our associating by mutual commitment at every level; and to promote the greater sharing of people, money and other resources."[224]

So, the focus of the BUGB will be on mission although evangelism will be prioritized over other areas of mission. There is a sense that these strategies will be Baptist strategies rather than joining in with initiatives developed by others. The focus will be on a distinctive Baptist identity rather than identifying with others. Much of the focus of Baptists would be on the denomination, and on the union, rather than on new alliances or partnerships with others. The focus was thus more inward looking rather than outward looking to working with other denominations and other organizations.

219. Randall, *English Baptists*, 472.

220. Goodliff, *Renewing a Modern Denomination*, 23.

221. Goodliff, *Renewing a Modern Denomination*, 75.

222. Randall, *English Baptists*, 471.

223. Myra Blyth was deputy general secretary of BUGB 1999–2004, following a position as director of programs for the Churches' Response to Humanitarian Disasters and Refugee Concerns at the World Council of Churches in Geneva (1988–99). However, the influence of Myra Blyth and Keith Jones was in the background organization of the assemblies rather than in addresses to the assemblies.

224. Goodliff, *Renewing a Modern Denomination*, 8.

In 1995 there was a second series of Listening Days across BUGB. As in 1991, it is not clear if the listening process extended beyond listening to people already in Baptist churches in the union.[225] One area of concern was around mission and the appropriate resources needed.[226] This led to a denominational consultation in 1996. Randall highlights that, in this consultation, "groups looked at issues like associating, justice, leadership, ministry and mission, and finance." Goodliff understands that a key factor was around mission—"Coffey and Jones wanted the whole consultation to be a *missiological prism* that was not about doing more evangelism or church planting, but to begin with a *fresh vision of the Missionary God*."[227] However, as Goodliff notes, the focus of this consultation was on how using a missiological prism offers insights into how the union might be transformed, rather than about how individual churches engage in mission.[228] Randall notes that "the need for new ways of associating emerged as a priority issue."[229] However, it seems that this was mainly about associating together as Baptists rather than with other denominations.

Five Core Values for a Gospel People was produced by the BUGB, in 1998, by a group including Bernard Green and Anne Wilkinson-Hayes. The five core values "arise out of the person of Jesus Christ that should be visible among Baptists in community."[230] It sought to offer a description of what it was to be a gospel people, a people, "determined by the life of Jesus" and "living in radical commitment to him."[231] It calls for a prophetic, inclusive, sacrificial, missionary, and worshipping community. As part of being an inclusive community, an obligation in the local church is "to listen to, value and address the particular needs of people who are often under-represented or absent from leadership and decision-making, and to develop effective strategies to ensure full participation." Alongside this there is an obligation for the denomination "to reflect Christ's bias to the poor."[232]

So here there is an indication of the importance of listening and also on precisely who Baptists should be listening to. This then connects well with the principle of listening to those at the margins. Randall highlights that many

225. The same could be said of the focus on listening instigated by Jonathan Edwards as BUGB general secretary.

226. Goodliff, *Renewing a Modern Denomination*, 8–9.

227. Goodliff, *Renewing a Modern Denomination*, 9; emphasis in original.

228. Goodliff, *Renewing a Modern Denomination*, 101.

229. Randall, *English Baptists*, 488–89.

230. Goodliff, *Renewing a Modern Denomination*, 71.

231. Goodliff, *Renewing a Modern Denomination*, 71; quoting BUGB, *Five Core Values*, 4.

232. BUGB, *Five Core Values*, 8.

Baptist churches studied *Five Core Values* together.[233] Coffey highlighted that these core values were a means of "call[ing] us back to that biblical non-conformity and prophetic dissent which lies at the heart of our calling as God's people."[234] However, Goodliff highlights that there is little or no mention or engagement with *Five Core Values* in any Baptist work post-2000.[235] So, a resource which could have helped churches understand their engagement in social justice as core to being a Baptist church did not continue to be prioritized by the BUGB as a union.

4.3.3 Ecumenical Engagement

As we have already noted, Baptist discussions on ecumenical engagement were largely separated out from discussions on mission. Randall notes that the ecumenical and evangelical visions have seemed to some Baptists in the twentieth century to be in opposition to one another, and so to be ecumenical means not to be evangelical. However, as Randall understands, others saw that it is possible to be both.[236] Randall argues that, in the 1980s, "in many respects Baptists provided a bridge between ecumenical and evangelical movements."[237] In the 1980s and into the 1990s, the church growth movement gained influence and as we have noted there was a growing evangelical identity among Baptists.[238]

David Coffey, as BUGB president in 1986 and five years ahead of becoming general secretary, focused on "Build That Bridge." Randall highlights that through this theme Coffey argues for "bridges of acceptance within local churches, of understanding in the denomination, of toleration between Baptists and other Christians, and of compassion into the world."[239] For Coffey, this will involve both evangelism and social action, and a faith lived out in public.[240] In 1989 the BUGB Assembly voted in favor of Baptist membership of both Churches Together in England and Churches Together in Britain and Ireland. However, crucially this did not commit any local Baptist church to ecumenical involvement. The involvement of Roman Catholic churches in

233. Randall, *English Baptists*, 502.
234. Goodliff, *Renewing a Modern Denomination*, 71.
235. Goodliff, *Renewing a Modern Denomination*, 134.
236. Randall, *English Baptists*, 6.
237. Randall, *English Baptists*, 440.
238. Randall, *English Baptists*, 430–39.
239. Randall, *English Baptists*, 471.
240. Coffey, *Build That Bridge*, 14–15.

these ecumenical bodies was a key worry for some Baptist churches.[241] So, in the same year that early community organizing alliances were forming in Wales and England with strong Roman Catholic involvement, Baptists were conflicted about joining ecumenical bodies which also had Roman Catholic churches in membership. We also noted earlier the tensions in the English wing of the BUW on their involvement in Cytûn in Wales which also had Roman Catholic Church involvement.

All of this meant that, in addition to concerns about working ecumenically, Baptist churches in BUGB and the BUW English wing often did not have a strong understanding that social justice—as a key component of mission—could be practiced through working with other church denominations and organizations locally or nationally. In contrast, the BUW Welsh wing understood that ecumenical bodies played a key role in working for social justice at a national and international level. This to some extent can help explain the lack of reference to the principles of neighborliness and subsidiarity. This lack of understanding was also built on a diminishing understanding of both how Baptists should relate to wider society and the world, and how they should associate together with other Baptists.

4.4 Summary

This chapter has focused on how the six principles central to community organizing relate to the public resolutions and themes chosen by the BUGB and BUW presidents and general secretaries from the late 1980s to 2010. This chapter has also examined these sources to understand how and to what extent Baptists were relating to each other and to other church denominations, to other institutions in civil society, and to government. From these sources, this chapter has examined how all this contributed to a Baptist theological ethic for the practice of social justice.

The period 1988 to 2010 was a period of great change politically, economically, and culturally in the UK and globally. For many Baptists in Wales and England, there is a sense that social justice is something Baptists should be involved in. However, the focus on social justice in resolutions is largely not reflected in the addresses and themes of general secretaries and presidents of the two unions. There was a lack of synchronization between the public resolutions passed and the themes for president and general secretaries.

The themes selected by the presidents reflect an issue that was being discussed in the union or a theme that the president thought should be taken up.

241. Randall, *English Baptists*, 446.

So, where the president was passionate about social justice, they raised it and occasionally the principles came to the fore in their addresses.

The focus on social justice in the public resolutions was generally, with some notable exceptions, tangential to the focus and themes of these presidential addresses. Public resolutions were in some ways a hangover from an earlier time (in the late nineteenth and early twentieth centuries) when Baptists were confident that they could have influence and a strong voice on national political issues.[242] This appears to have lasted longer in the BUW Welsh wing than elsewhere in the two unions. This could be understood as the result of these churches identifying with others on the margins in relation to dominant power structures or, conversely, about continuing a chapel culture that continued to be understood as influential in the Welsh context.

Baptists were focused on mission during this period. Overall, it appears that the BUGB and BUW Assemblies had a focus on mission every year. However, during this period, they did not generally understand social justice as a key part of mission. So, although mission was high on the agenda, social justice was not.

At the same time, several attempts were made to find new approaches for discussion and debate at the assembly on social justice issues with people gathered from churches. Baptists were being encouraged, notably through the public resolutions, and in BUGB through the Against the Stream Fund and *Five Core Values* document, to engage in social justice. However, this was without an approach for practical action.

Through this period Baptists appear to have found it harder to associate together and to find a united Baptist voice on issues of injustice or other areas, while at the same time engaging actively with both other evangelical churches and ecumenically at a local level. Baptists were often "outsourcing" action on social justice to Christian Aid for international issues and to ecumenical bodies, notably Cytûn in Wales and Churches Together in England and the Council of Churches for Britain and Ireland in England.

Examining this period does lead me to question the degree to which Baptist churches are interested in associating with one another, and to what degree they are interested in engaging with the wider community on issues of social justice. The concern and focus for most of the themes for the general secretaries and presidents of the BUGB was thus much more on what they saw would help in keeping the union together through an understanding of mission, which emphasized evangelism and church growth. Baptist discussions

242. Bebbington, *Baptists Through the Centuries*; Briggs, *English Baptists*; Morgan, *Span of the Cross*; and Randall, *English Baptists* all provide detailed accounts of Baptist engagement in UK politics during this period.

on ecumenical engagement were largely separated out from discussions on mission. If they had been brought together, it is possible that this would have led to more engagement with and theological reflection on community organizing by Baptists in Wales and England.

Overall, examining these sources has not provided us with a sense that there is a strong shared Baptist theological ethic for the practice of social justice. The principles which come through most strongly from these BUGB Assembly resolutions and themes, but still only in a limited way, are solidarity, centering the margins, listening and to a lesser extent the common good.

Connections are made with solidarity particularly in relation to resolutions which express solidarity with people in situations of injustice both internationally and domestically.

The theme of listening is regularly raised but there is often the question of who these processes of listening are listening to.

The common good underpins many of the resolutions and some presidential themes although the term itself is not used.

Finally, on centering the margins, we need to consider the impact of whose voices are being heard in the assemblies. The context and location of the majority of Baptist congregations often meant they were facing different issues to Roman Catholic and Anglican churches in inner cities. Related to this, as we have observed, the perspectives and voices of Black Baptist churches were largely not heard by the wider union. Listening closely to these and working from their perspective may have led to an increased priority on social justice and a stronger Baptist theological ethic of social justice.

There is very little in the material from the assemblies that relates to the principle of subsidiarity. We could see this as due to the focus in this chapter on discussions and addresses to national assemblies of the unions rather than on the discussions and decisions of church meetings of local Baptist churches. Baptist ecclesiology should lend itself well to picking up the principle of subsidiarity through engaging with those who are directly affected by issues of social injustice and enabling them to play a central role in decisions on these issues.

The next chapter should be understood as a part 2 to this chapter. It will explore how the writings of major UK Baptist theologians during this period from the late 1980s to 2010, and more recent writing by Baptists, have engaged with these six principles from current theological reflection on community organizing. The chapter will also examine how these writings have contributed to developing a Baptist theological ethic for the practice of social justice.

Chapter 5

The Development of a Theological Ethic for the Practice of Social Justice and Baptist Churches in Wales and England

Part II

5.1 Introduction

The previous chapter critiqued the state of the Baptist social justice conversation in Wales and England in the period that community organizing was developing in the UK, from the late 1980s to 2010. The prominent UK Baptist theologians writing during this period were Paul Fiddes, Brian Haymes, Richard Kidd, and Nigel Wright. All four were also principals of Baptist colleges in England in membership with the BUGB during this period. This chapter, following on from the previous chapter, will describe, critique, and analyze the strengths and weaknesses of these major UK Baptist theologians in what they write in relation to a Baptist theological ethic of social justice. I will explore the main themes in their writing and how these also engage with the six principles we have observed from current theological reflection on community organizing. I will explore the interweaving between their writings and how this develops, and consider the extent to which they engage with each other's thinking. I am primarily concerned with how their focus and arguments can help in strengthening a Baptist theological ethic for the practice of social justice.

As in the previous chapter, I will explore how these figures' thinking and writing developed between 1988 and 2010 by examining their work in publication order. As with the assembly discussions we considered in chapter 4, the UK Baptist context, and particularly the nature of discussions within the BUGB during this time influenced the focus of their writing. This is the case particularly where the UK Baptist churches appear to be the primary intended audience for several of their published works. I will also explore the extent to which their writing reacted to and then influenced and shaped the agenda of the BUGB during this period.

I focus in this chapter on these authors' books, chapters, and booklets which contain the most, or the closest, references to the six principles. The key interests and themes for these theologians appear in several or all of their published works. Where this is the case, I draw on the most in-depth or clearest exploration in this chapter. Given the focus on Baptist identity during the 1990s and into the 2000s, I will explore their focus on Baptist identity and the place of social justice within this. None of these theologians are explicitly writing and reflecting on their direct experience of, and engagement in, community organizing. However, I will argue that their writing is helpful in thinking about community organizing from a Baptist perspective, and how organizing can strengthen a Baptist theological ethic for the practice of social justice.

5.2 The Late 1980s

Fiddes, Haymes, and Kidd were among a group who wrote *Bound to Love* in 1985. This book considered how the concept of covenant provides a theological basis for Baptist life and mission. In this they sought to recover an image which "used to play such a luminous part within the Baptist tradition," but which by the later twentieth century had been lost or was at best "barely appreciated in its richness and depth."[1] For Fiddes, in *Bound to Love*, the covenant relationship is prior to how the covenant might be expressed.[2] So, to speak of covenant is not to speak of something static, but dynamic.

In 1986, in *A Question of Identity*, Haymes argues for a renewed sense of Baptist identity. One aspect of this is pushing for the importance of interdependency as a central part of being Baptist rather than a focus on independent Baptist churches. Haymes states that "associational life is marginal to most

1. Fiddes et al., *Bound to Love*, 4–5.
2. Fiddes et al., *Bound to Love*, 5.

congregations," and argues that "associating with other congregations should not be *marginal* to the life of Baptist churches."[3]

In his 1986 book *The Radical Kingdom*, Wright argues for the church to "rediscover the ethic of Jesus who presented the Kingdom of God not as a programme of social conservatism but as a force which confronted and contradicted the powers of his day."[4] Thus, in this book, Wright appears to be drawing on Anabaptist thinking that is rooted in following Jesus' teaching, and passionate in its conviction that the kingdom of God is radically distinct from the kingdom of the world. Anabaptists, and then Evangelicals drawing on this tradition, have—like Saul Alinsky, Ed Chambers, and others in community organizing—been comfortable in using the term "radical" to describe themselves.

Unlike his later books, Wright is not just writing this book for a Baptist audience. He argues that to be radical "will cause us to take a radical stance over against the structures of our society" in a context where, Wright highlights, "the church, even the radical church [including Baptists] has hugely accommodated itself to the forms of this world in her social attitudes."[5] Referencing Anabaptists and Martin Luther King, Wright describes the church as a community that is called to follow Jesus and that is the agent of social change.[6] However, he gives no indication of an approach, such as community organizing, for the church to use to be this agent of social change.

In 1988, in *The Creative Suffering of God*, Paul Fiddes "develops an idea of divine suffering, affirming that God freely chooses to limit himself, to suffer change, to journey on the path of time, and even to experience death, while remaining the living God."[7] Fiddes is "well aware of the cautious warnings often uttered against theological speculation in our pragmatic age," but he goes on to write, "I hope we may all learn to take the risk of talking about God."[8] Fiddes realizes that Baptists and others are keener to be pragmatic rather than engage theologically, and so perhaps senses what will happen in the 1990s and beyond in the BUGB and the BUW.

Fiddes's 1989 book *Past Event and Present Salvation* asks how our salvation in the present can depend on an event in the past. He understands atonement as a creative act of God, enabling response and thus transforming personality, overcoming evil and healing relationships. A book on doctrine

3. Haymes, *Question of Identity*, 11.
4. Wright, *Radical Kingdom*, 10.
5. Wright, *Radical Kingdom*, 119.
6. Wright, *Radical Kingdom*, 127–28.
7. Fiddes, *Creative Suffering of God*, back cover.
8. Fiddes, *Creative Suffering of God*, vii.

may not at first seem the most promising place to engage in ethics. However, as with much of Fiddes's writing, there is much here that relates to ethics and its practice by churches. As he notes early on in his book, "The many strands of human experience run through the cross-roads of the cross."[9]

For Fiddes, the idea of atonement "insists that salvation depends upon the restoring of a relationship between human beings and God, who are estranged from each other."[10] Later, he notes that the atoning work of Christ helps in "meeting the questions of our day, which are directed to the fragmenting of personality and loss of social relationships."[11] Thus, here we observe something of Fiddes making connections between salvation, atonement and the principle of solidarity as defined earlier.

"When God reconciles persons [in salvation] he brings them into community in a new way," through sharing in the body of Christ. Fiddes argues that atonement should be about "the healing not only of individuals but of groups and structures in our society."[12] The restoring of relationships between individuals is a continuous process and "must be created anew through the meeting of persons."[13] This appears to be equivalent to the understanding of one-to-one conversations in community organizing. He understands that "God's nature is fully relational; he is ecstatic love, love that goes beyond the self to another . . . to be a person is not to be a self-contained individual but to live in relationships."[14] Thus, here we observe links to both the principles of solidarity and neighborliness. Fiddes, drawing on Dietrich Bonhoeffer, understands that

> we are to look in all the life of the world, in the secular world that lives as if there were no God, to discover where Christ is . . . God is . . . in the centre, not on the boundaries. Christ is present in the midst of what people can do, not simply the one who steps in to what they cannot do.[15]

Therefore, God is on the side of those on the margins, and there is a link here to the principle of centering the margins. However, it is not just in the margins of communities that we look for where God is present and for what God is doing. We should also look in the center of the life of communities and in what is

9. Fiddes, *Past Event and Present Salvation*, 3.
10. Fiddes, *Past Event and Present Salvation*, 3.
11. Fiddes, *Past Event and Present Salvation*, 12.
12. Fiddes, *Past Event and Present Salvation*, 13.
13. Fiddes, *Past Event and Present Salvation*, 14–15.
14. Fiddes, *Past Event and Present Salvation*, 163.
15. Fiddes, *Past Event and Present Salvation*, 164.

seen by many Christians as the secular world. Fiddes argues that the presence of Christ can be met in the community of the church or the community of the wider world.[16] Later in his book he explores the relevance of this for political engagement. He highlights the power of future salvation in the present, through offering a theology of hope, "in a future which is radically different from the present, rather than merely being an extension of it."[17] Thus, we find

> a stimulus to change the present. For if we hope in a God who can do something altogether new and unpredictable in future salvation, we shall be alert to the new possibilities he offers here and now. Future salvation "contradicts" the present, liberating us into new attitudes and actions. Those who have hope refuse to regard any structures as final or sacrosanct, in church or society. They have a holy discontent that is always breaking open old structures and institutions to find new life.[18]

Fiddes goes on to argue that "by promising a future liberation of the whole of creation, God contradicts the powers which sustain themselves by oppressing others."[19] It follows therefore that teaching on atonement leads to engagement in movements for liberation of the oppressed and involves political engagement. He explores this in more detail later in this book.

The last three chapters of *Past Event and Present Salvation* are about working out atonement in everyday life through "experiences." This is a good reminder that, in community organizing, theological reflection is on experiences, rather than on the theory of organizing. In a chapter on political engagement, Fiddes asks "how the past event of the cross of Christ . . . is related to the experience of engaging in politics today."[20] He picks up the importance of understanding power structures within our own society. Then, drawing on the El Salvadorean liberation theologian Jon Sobrino, Fiddes understands that

> we shall only find the meaning of the cross by entering into its experience, which means engaging ourselves with the cause of those who are poor and who suffer injustice. The cross . . . invites us to participate in a process within which we can actually experience history as salvation.[21]

16. Fiddes, *Past Event and Present Salvation*, 165.
17. Fiddes, *Past Event and Present Salvation*, 30–31.
18. Fiddes, *Past Event and Present Salvation*, 31.
19. Fiddes, *Past Event and Present Salvation*, 32.
20. Fiddes, *Past Event and Present Salvation*, 190.
21. Fiddes, *Past Event and Present Salvation*, 195. See also Sobrino, *Principle of Mercy*.

Liberation theology begins from the social, economic, and political situation and then reflects theologically on it. Fiddes argues that "the church begins to engage in politics when the humiliated and crucified Christ is *recognised* among groups and classes who are discriminated against and unjustly treated." Here, we can again observe a link to the principle of centering the margins, where we see God at work. Fiddes notes the images of a black or female Christ in Black theology and feminist theology, and understands "it is not that Christ is identical with any one group but that he identifies with them, so that we can find Christ with them."[22]

Fiddes asks whether the atoning death of Christ provides any clues as to the *way* we might engage in resisting and breaking the powers. He argues,

> God's process of atonement is one of forgiveness and reconciliation, and in social terms this means seeking a consensus and common consent to what is right and just. We have to go on living together. When our own political ideal is not worked out fully by a government, though the substance of it has been taken account of, we must learn to forgive what has been left undone. Such a compromise is not a betrayal of political vision, as long as it is held in the context of continued action and protest.[23]

There are several points to note from this. There is a link to the principles of the common good and neighborliness, and what it means to live as neighbors. This also relates to the focus in community organizing on compromise and on continuing to live in and build relationships with those with power to help make change on an issue. Here, and elsewhere in this book, Fiddes highlights the importance of relationships. The focus on relationships relates to all of the six principles drawn from current theological reflection on community organizing. All these principles involve thinking about relationships. Solidarity is the rediscovery of the radical shared interest held between people in fraternal relationships. Subsidiarity and the common good require strong relationships between people and organizations in communities. Neighborliness encourages public relationships to be formed and strengthened between people. Good listening requires people to be in relationship to listen to others. Finally, centering the margins focuses on relationships between people currently on the margins with those people in the center whose priorities currently often dominate in communities and in wider society.

In a final chapter on suffering, Fiddes underlines that "God is out ahead of the world, [as well as being present in the current suffering] protesting

22. Fiddes, *Past Event and Present Salvation*, 199; emphasis in original.

23. Fiddes, *Past Event and Present Salvation*, 205.

against what is imperfect and incomplete in its present state."[24] He argues that sharing in the cross "has meaning only because of the movement of protest and action that surrounds it, we can say yes to the whole of life and, loving it, want to change it."[25] Throughout this book, there is the outward-facing call to take action on issues of injustice and suffering. Likewise, in Fiddes's work on covenant theology, this is about the church connecting with where God is already at work in the world. Fiddes concludes,

> If we are to learn how to protest against suffering and to change the conditions that cause it, we must first simply be present (as God is present) to those who are the victims. Either by listening to their stories or by actually sitting in fellowship—probably without speaking—with those who are suffering now.[26]

Thus, here again this links to the principles of listening and solidarity.

5.3 The 1990s

Wright's 1991 book *Challenge to Change*, "is written . . . in the expectation of change and as a conscious and unembarrassed attempt to influence the course of discussion and the flow of events" and as "a book written by a Baptist for Baptists."[27] Wright summarizes what he is arguing in this book:

> Baptists need to undergo a theological renewal to re-appropriate and re-express the Baptist values which are at the basis of their life. This ought then to lead to a renewal of local churches and of wider denominational relationships.[28]

He argues that with increasing respectability and prosperity, once-radical Baptist thinking has "accommodated itself to the establishment, adopting its attitudes and style, betraying its heritage."[29] However, Wright's focus on change is largely in the way Baptists and Baptist churches act and associate rather than on how they engage with others in the community. For example, he argues for a church to be "more concerned about reality of relationship," but his focus is mostly on relationships between people already in the church.[30] In contrast, as

24. Fiddes, *Past Event and Present Salvation*, 210–11.
25. Fiddes, *Past Event and Present Salvation*, 215.
26. Fiddes, *Past Event and Present Salvation*, 218.
27. Wright, *Challenge to Change*, 12–13.
28. Wright, *Challenge to Change*, 21–22.
29. Wright, *Challenge to Change*, 38.
30. Wright, *Challenge to Change*, 67.

we have already observed, Fiddes is concerned with relationships with others beyond Baptist churches.

Wright sets out a picture of what he sees as an "ideal Baptist church." This section is particularly interesting for how he sees Baptist engagement in political action and social justice. Wright notes this "ideal Baptist church" thinks of local mission in three ways, "evangelism, social action and political action," and has connections with the local community.[31] He describes that

> in its political action the church had understood that the social conditions of the neighbourhood were directly affected by the politics of local and national government. It had also understood that most issues are complex in nature and need a lot of thinking through. Politically-minded and involved church members were invited to form a think-tank to address specific issues and come to a common mind.
>
> Faced with this task, a consensus emerged as to how the needs of the area might be tackled. Local councillors and MPs had been invited on different occasions to visit the church and answer questions. Faced with a community of well-informed and thoughtful people they had found the experience a gruelling one. They had gained a new respect for the church, and the pastoral staff were now frequently consulted on local matters.[32]

This appears to be a vision, rather than a reference to a specific example of a Baptist church engaging in this way. However, the picture that is presented by Wright is still of a church in the center, deciding on needs, having the power to act and addressing justice issues on its own, rather than joining in with others, and especially with non-church and non-Christian organizations. Politicians are brought to the church building rather than church members going out and joining in with the initiatives of others in order to engage on the priorities of the local community. Wright does note that this "ideal Baptist church" is involved ecumenically and is associating with other Baptist churches but there is no mention of this involvement being on the social action and social justice work outlined above.[33] So, here we have strong endorsements of the principles of neighborliness and the common good, but not of the principles of listening nor of centering the margins as defined earlier.

In a chapter focused on associating, Wright underlines that "the location of the local church needs to be balanced by the catholicity of a wider grouping and of the whole, so that the local may be enriched by the whole . . . such

31. Wright, *Challenge to Change*, 82.

32. Wright, *Challenge to Change*, 84–85.

33. Wright, *Challenge to Change*, 86–87.

solidarity is biblical, helpful and necessary."[34] We observed in the previous chapter with assembly resolutions, and also observe here with Wright, they tend to use the term solidarity in relation to other Baptists or other Christians rather than with everyone, and especially with impoverished and marginalized people as understood in the definition used earlier. Therefore, Wright's focus on association does not go beyond associating with other churches.

Wright, in a chapter on being "Called to Nonconform," argues that in the nineteenth century nonconformists were good at being against things but not at proposing solutions to problems; "the nonconformist is thus reduced to reacting to an agenda someone else has set, while creative political progress is left to others."[35] He goes on to argue it is crucial that Baptists "engage legitimately in the attempt to make the State serve the moral welfare of the people, they should be seen to be acting for the good of all . . . the Dissenting approach enables us to do this."[36] Here, we observe a link to the principle of the common good. We will observe how Wright develops his thinking in this area over the decade later in this chapter.

We can also compare Wright's argument here with the Baptist assembly public resolutions in the previous chapter, and to consider to what extent these were reacting to the political agenda in the UK and internationally, and to what extent they were proposing positive solutions to problems. In addition, as we observed in the previous chapter, Baptists in Wales and England became very internally focused on finding "solutions" to "problems" in Baptist institutional life and so were less externally focused on justice issues. Only in the last few pages of Wright's chapter "Called to Nonconform" do we come to what Wright understands nonconformity to mean in engaging on social justice issues. He argues,

> Working from this centre [focusing on Jesus Christ and his teaching], much thinking has to be done about how believers live in today's society and engage with it socially and politically. The positive political philosophy which Baptist Christians need, to make them actors rather than reactors in the political realm, can be found by a renewed reflection on the meaning of Christ for the complexities of our world.[37]

Wright concludes, "This is the kind of nonconformity that we should enter into; radical, Jesus-centred living, assisted by the community of God's people

34. Wright, *Challenge to Change*, 135.
35. Wright, *Challenge to Change*, 201.
36. Wright, *Challenge to Change*, 207.
37. Wright, *Challenge to Change*, 209–10.

committed to the same pilgrimage."[38] Wright underlines that the "ecumenical process is about giving and receiving. If Baptists have a distinctive witness, it is not for themselves alone but for all the church."[39] Wright concludes that Baptist churches should be relevant to society:

> For the sake of the well-being of society, it is vital that the church learn how to be the church in the way which accords most fully with Jesus Christ. . . .
>
> God's way of social transformation is to use a social structure to change other social structures. That social structure is the church, the community of men and women who are learning Christ together and introducing into society a new power which liberates and humanizes.[40]

Thus, he appears to be arguing for Baptists to engage ecumenically in partnership with others, and to engage politically, but without spelling out an approach to do this, such as community organizing. Writing in 2002, he highlights that *Challenge to Change* was written in the context of a debate among Baptists in Wales and England on "the health, shape and future of their particular way of being church."[41] He recognizes that it had some impact. However, there is no evidence that either Wright's or Fiddes's writing had much influence at this point in terms of increasing Baptist engagement with others on social justice issues.

In 1994 Fiddes, Haymes, and Wright were all involved in a report called *The Nature of the Assembly and the Council of the Baptist Union of Great Britain.*[42] The concept of covenant is a particular thread throughout this report. Fiddes notes that covenant "expresses the mutual commitment of church members to each other as covenant partners with God, so that early Baptist churches wrote church covenants in which they promised to *walk together and to watch over one another in love.*"[43] Covenant is described as "a mutual and binding relation, and at its centre is the activity of God."[44] In writing about assemblies of churches, Fiddes suggests that "perhaps we should distinguish

38. Wright, *Challenge to Change*, 210.

39. Wright, *Challenge to Change*, 241.

40. Wright, *Challenge to Change*, 243–44.

41. Wright, *New Baptists, New Agenda*, 1.

42. BUGB, *Nature of the Assembly.* Fiddes chaired the BUGB's Doctrine and Worship Committee which prepared the report. Haymes and Wright were also members of this committee.

43. BUGB, *Nature of the Assembly*, 7; emphasis in original. These were English Baptist churches in the seventeenth century.

44. BUGB, *Nature of the Assembly*, 7.

between *a church* (the local congregation), *the church* (universal) and *being church* when we are together in wider union."[45] Fiddes appears to be here thinking of assemblies at local, regional, and national level and highlights the importance of seeking to find the mind of Christ together at all these levels.[46] Fiddes highlights several times "the importance of listening to one another in Assembly" and argues for more time and space for public resolutions sessions, "for the covenant relationship of the Union to be actualized."[47] Fiddes understands that in these sessions, "those gathered seek to speak a prophetic word to the principalities and powers of our society."[48] Thus, although this report is focused on assembly and council, it does highlight theological principles and develops them in ways that can be applied to Baptist engagement in broader alliances, and in discussions with other churches and institutions.

For publications by Fiddes, Haymes, Kidd, and Wright, 1996 was a bumper year.[49] Haymes chaired the BUGB General Superintendency Review Group which produced the *Transforming Superintendency* report. The report recognizes that in many places there are associations of churches but only weak associational life. The view of the report group is "that to be a Baptist church is to be in active association with others,"[50] understanding associating, "as a means of better answering God's call to mission, the God who exists only in relationship."[51] So, although this report is focused primarily on internal discussions on associating between Baptist churches, this can also be applied to associating with other churches.

There was much discussion and debate among Baptists about the understanding of baptism, a key part of Baptist identity. Fiddes, Haymes, and Kidd all contribute chapters to *Reflections on the Water*. This book focuses on how believers' baptism can help us understand God's creative activity in human society, the political life, the Christian community, and the nature of the triune God who calls people into relationship. Fiddes argues that baptism enables participation in the activity of God that is taking place in human community.[52] Haymes understands believers' baptism as an event with political

45. BUGB, *Nature of the Assembly*, 10; emphasis in original.

46. BUGB, *Nature of the Assembly*, 11.

47. BUGB, *Nature of the Assembly*, 24, 27.

48. BUGB, *Nature of the Assembly*, 27.

49. This was also the year that the first of the Citizens UK community organizing alliances, TELCO, was formed.

50. General Superintendency Review Group, *Transforming Superintendency*, 28.

51. General Superintendency Review Group, *Transforming Superintendency*, 31.

52. Fiddes, *Reflections on the Water*, 3.

significance which confronts the powers.[53] Kidd focuses on the motif of liberation within believers' baptism which enables the church to reach out to the marginalized, and so a "[church] community open to others does not lose its identity but gains it." Fiddes understands that in baptism, "a person becomes involved in a deeper and new way with the web of loving relationships that God weaves with His whole creation."[54] He argues the community that witnesses the baptism, and that the person baptized joins, also become involved in this web of relations and more aware of the presence of God in other situations in wider society.

In this book, Fiddes, Haymes, and Kidd are not making many strong connections to the six principles. However, they are connecting a key Baptist practice, baptism, with society and issues in the wider world, where God is already at work. Writing in 2000, Fiddes, Haymes, and Kidd underline that, in *Reflections on the Water*, they argued that "baptism should open up . . . the meaning of the acts of God not only in the local church, but in society, political decision-making and in the whole of the natural world."[55] In writing this book on baptism, they were writing out of Baptist identity, rather than about Baptist identity.[56]

Baptists are often more concerned about boundaries than Anglicans and Catholics are, as we observed in their reflections on community organizing in chapter 3. For example, Fiddes notes, "Baptists have tended to emphasise the aspect of baptism as a boundary marker for believers; a moment of separation from past life and commitment to new Kingdom values."[57] Fiddes, Haymes, and Kidd in this book and elsewhere seek to encourage Baptists to be more open to wider society and connecting with others. Fiddes also links this to the principle of listening by churches:

> It [a local church] will always be open to listen to the voices of others, aware that it is dependent upon their help in finding the mind of Christ, whether the voices come from wider groupings of churches or from society outside the church.[58]

Haymes understands that baptized people are called to be immersed in their wider communities, "with all the moral and political implications that go with

53. Fiddes, *Reflections on the Water*, 4.
54. Fiddes, *Reflections on the Water*, 59.
55. Fiddes et al., "Doing Theology Together," 10.
56. Fiddes et al., "Doing Theology Together," 11.
57. Fiddes, *Reflections on the Water*, 62.
58. Fiddes, *Reflections on the Water*, 65.

sharing a common life."[59] He makes connections to the principles of solidarity, common good and neighborliness without using these terms. Haymes, at the time of writing this chapter, was principal of the Northern Baptist College in England. He describes that

> in the chapel of the Northern Baptist College, Manchester there is a mural that pictures the life of Manchester through its buildings and institutions. There you can see the banks, the commercial offices, the hospitals, the university, the council flats, the city offices, the churches—all that makes up the life of this modern city. The artist has delicately shot the tapestry through with silver and gold thread so that when the light shines on it it is transformed. In this way, those who come to worship in chapel have the city kept before their eyes. There is no escaping the context of worship and the place where we are called to be disciples in hope that even this all too-human city might know the "shalom" that belongs to the city of God.[60]

Haymes here is making connections with the principle of neighborliness. He highlights the thread that exists between and throughout all these institutions. In addition, I understand that in bringing these threads together into fabric, Christians are joining in with where God is already present and strengthening relationships that God is already making.

Writing in 2000, Haymes along with Fiddes and Kidd underline that Haymes's chapter in *Reflections on the Water* entitled "Baptism as a Political Act" understands that "oppressive powers . . . can only be stripped bare by a community which is really immersed into the reality of the world."[61] This is a different emphasis than that of Wright in his Whitley Lecture, *Power and Discipleship*, also published in 1996. In this, Wright focused on developing a Baptist theology of the state. He argues for the separation of church and state:

> The church of Christ, although profoundly interested for God's sake in the public and political spheres and able to speak prophetically to specific situations, best fulfills its mission when it maintains a critical distance from established political parties and interests.[62]

Wright notes that nonconformity can be a "means of incubating new forms of communal and civic life which have the power to transform the political

59. Haymes, "Baptism as a Political Act," 80.

60. Haymes, "Baptism as a Political Act," 81.

61. Fiddes et al., "Doing Theology Together," 12.

62. Wright, *Power and Discipleship*, 5.

community at large."[63] He highlights that historic Anabaptist thought encouraged separation of church and state but did not have a concept of social justice. In contrast, Wright notes that a "Baptist" approach to government, with the important role of covenant, "has strong commitment to achieving a just civil realm." In this, "government . . . might become the very means of promoting the common good."[64] Wright then argues that a Baptist theology of the state must hold together both Baptist and Anabaptist perspectives.[65] However, he does not articulate how Baptists should work together with others for social justice.

In the lecture, Wright argues for "a community to be gathered [the church] which is sufficiently distinct from the world in the way it goes about its own life to be able to offer to that world an alternative way and a greater hope." Thus, he appears to be arguing for the church to model the justice, love and community that it wants to see in the world. Wright argues that "the state exists for the sake of the church, to provide that framework of order and stability within which the humanity and redeeming work of the gospel can run its course."[66] Thus, there is no acknowledgement of God on mission beyond the church in *missio Dei*. Instead, Wright presents a much more church-centered mission. Wright does distinguish state and society but then he does not develop how God might be working in broader society. It is also not clear if Wright thinks God is working in and through the "secular" state.[67]

Wright notes the importance of covenant that "is embedded in all social and political systems," and argues that "human beings have been made for harmonious relationships with God and with each other." Thus, there is a nod to the principles of solidarity and seeking the common good here, but without using these terms. Wright also appears to have a narrower understanding to Fiddes of covenant relationships and what these mean for mission. Wright concludes that Baptists should not place "excessive dependence upon political action as the principal thrust against social evils."[68] So, Wright seems to be suggesting that Baptist churches should engage in social justice but not to see the state as the main answer to achieving this. This then would relate to the principle of subsidiarity, although Wright does not mention or engage with this principle here.

On Earth as in Heaven: A Theology of Social Action for Baptist Churches was published in the same year as Wright's Whitley Lecture. In his foreword,

63. Wright, *Power and Discipleship*, 9.

64. Wright, *Power and Discipleship*, 15.

65. Wright, *Power and Discipleship*, 16.

66. Wright, *Power and Discipleship*, 27.

67. Wright, *Power and Discipleship*, 28.

68. Wright, *Power and Discipleship*, 37.

Roy Jenkins, a former BUGB president, argues that the chapters in this resource "start with the local congregation . . . [and] encourage churches to think about social action as a natural extension of their community life; indeed to understand their own life as a form of social action."[69] This seems to resonate with Wright's lecture and the Anabaptist view of creating an alternative community. However, Anne Wilkinson-Hayes, then BUGB social action adviser, in her introduction highlights that this resource centers largely on the interaction between a local church and its wider community.[70] Four models of social action are highlighted, including a collective action-based or empowerment model which is markedly different to Wright's focus. This model seeks to

> enable oppressed groups to take greater control of their situation and work for change within it. This model assists people to organise themselves and to have a voice in the public arena. It is a risky model because those we work alongside may be enabled to ask challenging questions of the church as well as of the authorities. We cannot control this model of working and many therefore feel uncomfortable with it. It also demands that the church makes choices about whose side it is on. The side of the poor, or the side of the establishment? For all these reasons, this is not the most popular model in church practice, but it may have the greatest long-term effects, and perhaps have most to offer in terms of enabling people to discover their God-given dignity.[71]

There are strong connections here with solidarity and centering the margins. This description also picks up very well on a number of areas which local Baptist churches may struggle with, such as giving up its control. This also therefore helps explain why Baptists did not engage in community organizing to any great extent during this period.

Andy Bruce, then member of the BUGB Mission Committee, in his chapter in this resource, engages with Fiddes's book *Past Event and Present Salvation*. Bruce highlights Fiddes's description of God making a journey into the far country on the journey of salvation, and that God is found in the "far country" in mission among the people and communities to which the gospel is addressed.[72] Bruce highlights that the church is no longer at the center, although many churches yearn to be, and understands that

69. Roy Jenkins, in Finamore, *On Earth*, 2.

70. Anne Wilkinson-Hayes, in Finamore, *On Earth*, 3.

71. Finamore, *On Earth*, 4–5.

72. Bruce, "Exploring the Far Country," 12–13.

> given the co-existence of the local church with numerous other groups in the community, Christians need to discern where they are distinct from other bodies and how they may form *alliances* with a range of diverse groups and individuals for the sake of *the common good*. There is a crucial need for building bridges.[73]

Without mentioning community organizing, this is a very close description of it. Bruce goes on to highlight the importance of relating to people on the margins, and a commitment to dialogue and collaboration.[74] Thus, we observe competing visions for Baptist engagement in social justice being presented to UK Baptists at this time.

Something to Declare was jointly written by Fiddes, Haymes, Kidd, and Michael Quicke, the principals of the four English colleges in membership with the BUGB at that time. It was written in the context of a "ferment of thinking, talking and doing," all with a focus on Baptist structures and initiatives. They acknowledge that responses to *The Nature of the Assembly* report indicated disagreement on its use of covenant as the primary distinctive of Baptist identity.[75] Kidd underlines that covenant language is important as "we [Baptists] are inter-dependents, not independents, and we locate authority in community, not in hierarchy." Kidd argues that covenant language "is still the best and theologically most consistent focus around which to be gathered, and on which to build our future strategies for mission."[76] Kidd and the others argue,

> In covenant together we are willing to hear what Christ has to say to us through the weakest members of the Body, those who seem in the eyes of the world the most insignificant. In finding the mind of Christ we need to listen to the marginalised, the overlooked, with whom he identifies himself.[77]

Thus there is a clear link to the principles of listening and centering the margins here. They also make an explicit mention of solidarity in arguing that associating allows those seen as strong to learn from the marginalized and weakest, "to allow the weak to give something to the strong . . . this is solidarity in covenant with each other and with Christ."[78]

73. Bruce, "Exploring the Far Country," 21; emphasis added.
74. Bruce, "Exploring the Far Country," 23.
75. Kidd, *Something to Declare*, 12.
76. Kidd, *Something to Declare*, 16.
77. Kidd, *Something to Declare*, 35.
78. Kidd, *Something to Declare*, 35–36.

The following year Fiddes, Kidd, Haymes, and Quicke wrote *On the Way of Trust* in the context of questions about the nature of the union, associations, superintendency, and mission. They also wrote this in response to their earlier publications, *The Nature of the Assembly*, *Transforming Superintendency*, and *Something to Declare*, not being taken up by others. They understand trust as essential for life together as Baptists, as "trust comes to the fore as the irreplaceable condition of being church in a Baptist way," in a culture of community and responsibility communally rather than as individuals.[79]

Trust comes from strong relationships. As we have observed earlier, building relationships is a central focus in community organizing. Kidd et al. again emphasize the importance of covenant making for a life of trust as Baptists. God forms covenants and God gathers people together—"bringing together those who are naturally quite unlike each other," so they see the need for trust through relationships between people.[80] They understand that union (as with covenant) "roots us in a vision of the triune God, as we see our relating to each other as an image of the relationships within God himself."[81] They again pick up the principle of centering the margins in highlighting that trust as a union "can keep us attentive to crucial prophetic voices speaking to us all from the margins."[82]

Wright convened the BUGB Task Group on Associating. Their 1998 report *Relating and Resourcing* argues that action is needed to rediscover the reality of associating. The report explores the importance of associating for mission and sets out the basis for associating in "covenant commitment" to one another. In the BUGB letter which accompanied this report, Wright indicates that the report "was written on the foundation of the theological analysis set out in the report *Transforming Superintendency*."[83] However, the report does not refer directly to *Something to Declare* nor *On the Way of Trust*, despite highlighting and focusing on the importance of relationships between Baptist churches:

> Relating to the broader church of Christ must inevitably reach beyond the boundaries of Baptist churches alone. Relating between churches will include other Baptist congregations but it is inevitable and desirable in the present climate in which denominational boundaries have been blurred that different churches will

79. Kidd, *On the Way of Trust*, 9.

80. Kidd, *On the Way of Trust*, 18–19.

81. Kidd, *On the Way of Trust*, 22. This will be developed further and in much greater depth by Paul Fiddes in his book *Participating in God*.

82. Kidd, *On the Way of Trust*, 38.

83. BUGB letter that accompanied Task Group on Associating, *Relating and Resourcing*.

> relate in different combinations according to the realities of their situation.[84]

Thus, whereas in Kidd, Fiddes, and Haymes's writing, these relationships and associating are about being ecumenical and working as part of the whole church universal and for social justice, here it seems to be more about broadly evangelical churches coming together pragmatically.

Keith Jones's book *A Believing Church*, also published in 1998, describes a "gathering" rather than a "gathered church." In contrast, gathered church is the term most used by Fiddes, Wright, and others to describe a local Baptist congregation. Jones is following an Anabaptist approach, and highlights that he "writes about a *gathering church* in order to emphasise that this is not a complete body of Christ, but a dynamic group of believers, to whom the Triune God continues to add," as a community on a journey of discipleship.[85] On associating with others, Jones understands the importance of this for listening to the testimony of others and for changing society for the better.[86]

5.4 The 2000s

In *Participating in God*, published in 2000, Fiddes is concerned with the social life we lead together. As Fiddes underlines, speaking about himself and the other major Baptist theologians in the 1990s, "we were not directly involved in community building work but we were very concerned to think about doctrine and society."[87] In *Participating in God*, he brings the doctrine of the Trinity into conversation with key issues, such as the relationship between the individual and community, the nature of power and authority, and living a sacramental life. He engages with thinking about the Trinity, the triune communion, in Catholic, Orthodox, and Protestant theology.

Fiddes develops a radical understanding of the persons in God as nothing other than relations, or as movements of divine relationship into which we are drawn. In *Participating in God*, he notes that "when the early church mothers and fathers developed the doctrine of the Trinity . . . they were finding concepts to express an experience."[88] "They found God in a new energy and guidance they experienced within their community, opening up relationships

84. Task Group on Associating, *Relating and Resourcing*, 5.
85. Jones, *Believing Church*, 38; emphasis in original.
86. Jones, *Believing Church*, 54.
87. Paul S. Fiddes, in-person meeting, July 7, 2023.
88. Fiddes, *Participating in God*, 5.

beyond the accepted social boundaries."[89] Fiddes says that "this experience of God is not of three personal realities in isolation from each other, but of persons in relation, always *interweaving* and interpenetrating each other."[90] He understands that "personal language for God has the capacity to be a language of participation, pointing to engagement in God and drawing us into such involvement."[91] As he argues, "This language of participation only makes sense in terms of our involvement in the network of relationships in which God happens."[92]

By being engaged in God's relational life, in what Fiddes describes as "sharing in the currents of the personal relationships of God,"[93] as movements of relationships rather than as individuals who "have" relationships, "we can discover . . . how it needs us to represent the signs of the Christ in order to be a community open to the needs of all, and so participating in the triune life of God."[94] He emphasizes that this thinking and language encourages the value of relationships, community and mutuality between persons. It is about interdependence and not domination by one group, so challenging inequalities and injustices in human society.[95] Drawing on Leonardo Boff,[96] Fiddes notes that "involvement in the movements within God that make space [for God's liberation] will help us perceive where our actions of protest and resistance are truly making space for others."[97] There are echoes of the principles of solidarity and centering the margins as Fiddes explains:

> Engagement in the triune God also means the experience of "participation" in the making of freedom. As we participate in the liberating movements within the communion of God's life, we discover that those who are bound and oppressed must share in the action of their own liberation.[98]

Fiddes concludes, again in linking participating in God with participating in mission as seeking justice, that "whenever we affirm the worth of bodies and give them respect and justice, giving of ourselves to sustain them in being,

89. Fiddes, *Participating in God*, 5.
90. Fiddes, *Participating in God*, 6; emphasis added.
91. Fiddes, *Participating in God*, 33.
92. Fiddes, *Participating in God*, 37.
93. Fiddes, *Participating in God*, 71.
94. Fiddes, *Participating in God*, 52.
95. Fiddes, *Participating in God*, 66.
96. A Brazilian theologian most well known as a Latin American liberation theologian.
97. Fiddes, *Participating in God*, 98.
98. Fiddes, *Participating in God*, 98.

we are sharing in this distinctive movement of God."[99] He summarizes his argument thus:

> We should envisage sacraments drawing us deeper into the heart of the interweaving relationships in God. The key is participation, so that God is always open to make room for the world, while remaining an event of relationship in God's own self. God has a body, in so far as finite bodies are in God, and so movements of love and justice in God are expressed through bodies.[100]

Therefore, this is participation by the gathered community outwards to the world. Fiddes ends this book concluding that

> we should feel through their [our neighbors'] reaction the real pain of facing the particular. This is the kind of cost to be carried by those who are willing to be "living sacraments." The sacramental life is one that is open to the presence of God, and can open a door for others into eternal movements of love and justice that are there ahead of us, and before us, and embracing us. This openness can be felt like the invitation to a dance, but sometimes like the raw edges of a wound. This is participation in God. This is theology.[101]

Fiddes's understanding of what it means to be participating in God links to the principles of neighborliness and solidarity. In this book, Fiddes makes few explicit references to the six principles or to covenantal relationships. However, participating in God, and the participation of God with and in others, is helpful in what can be contributed to community organizing from a Baptist perspective. We will explore this further in chapter 6.

In 2000, the four Baptist college principals produced *Doing Theology in a Baptist Way*, their third and last in the series following *Something to Declare* and *On the Way of Trust*.[102] Haymes highlights a tension of Baptist and ecumenical identity and calling and understands that "certain insights which have been important in the Baptist story remain significant for the whole church of God."[103] Haymes notes that a Baptist way of doing theology will be reflection on practice and will be done together in community, as a gathered church.[104] Fiddes builds on this in highlighting that theology will be shaped from the experience of the community, its stories of dissent, and the relationships

99. Fiddes, *Participating in God*, 300.

100. Fiddes, *Participating in God*, 300.

101. Fiddes, *Participating in God*, 302.

102. Fiddes, *Doing Theology*.

103. Haymes, "Theology and Baptist Identity," 2.

104. Haymes, "Theology and Baptist Identity," 4.

between people. The Baptist way of community will then mean that from a local identity, "we are called into as wide a fellowship as is possible."[105] Fiddes understands that

> commitment to a world communion of churches will bring the surprises and challenges of links with places which were not originally in our horizon of interests, and with people who are different from us and who are to be valued for who they are. We will make covenant with others for fellowship and mission. . . . We will identify with those who we cannot agree with about everything . . . but in whom we catch even an echo of the Baptist story that is ours.[106]

Kidd also focuses on the importance of stories, particularly the stories of those who live at the edge, on the underside of history. He argues that "Baptists . . . should feel very much at home with this. Historically, we have always valued testimony, the stories people tell as they reflect on their experiences of God."[107] The sharing of testimony in citizens' actions and assemblies is a central feature of community organizing. We observe that in this one way a Baptist practice has potentially influenced organizing.[108] Kidd explores connections between Baptists and theologies of liberation. He recognizes that early Baptists in their context also took "a risk with open possibilities which arise when 'church' is allowed to develop more organically, with strong attention to the reality of shifting contexts, fired by energy from the 'roots' below rather than from 'authorities' coming from above."[109]

Liberation is not one of the principles I have picked up from current theological reflection on community organizing by UK theologians. Perhaps we should not be surprised by this given that this reflection has largely been done by Anglicans and Catholics in hierarchical church structures and the lack of influence of liberation theology in UK churches. However, as we noted in sections 1.3 and 2.5 of this book, and as Luke Bretherton, Mary Beth Rogers, and Jeffrey Stout make clear in their books, the way Latin American immigrant Roman Catholic churches in the US understood community organizing was through liberation theology.[110]

105. Fiddes, "Theology and Baptist Way," 30.

106. Fiddes, "Theology and Baptist Way," 30.

107. Kidd, "Baptists and Theologies," 39.

108. Warren, *Dry Bones Rattling*; and Bretherton, *Resurrecting Democracy* both reveal how religious practices of their member organizations have influenced community organizing practices in the US and UK. Alternatively, it may be that Baptists and community organizing are coming to the same place.

109. Kidd, "Baptists and Theologies," 45–46.

110. Bretherton, *Resurrecting Democracy*; Rogers, *Cold Anger*; Stout, *Blessed Are the Organized*.

Kidd puts forward a liberating Baptist agenda. He argues for a Baptist agenda developed through a liberation theology approach. In arguing for this he is taking Baptists back to their dissenting roots. Kidd also argues that early Baptists took a liberation theology approach. Thus, an approach that seems to be at least in part aligned with liberation theology should be one Baptists can use to strengthen their theological ethic for the practice of social justice. Kidd notes pioneering new patterns of community is a theme which has been crucially significant for Baptists and which is also important in theologies of liberation. Kidd highlights that for Baptists this led them toward "embracing broader patterns of inter-dependence. . . . It is responsiveness to context which is crucial and determines at each level . . . the appropriate structure for decision-making and agenda for mission."[111] So, here we observe a link to the principle of subsidiarity without using the term.

Kidd highlights as part of this liberating Baptist agenda the importance of staying in the struggle with a "proper sense of dissent, a non-conformism, which always keeps us living near an edge . . . [as it is] on the edge where the reality of God has been and is most strongly made known."[112] Here again Kidd makes a link to solidarity and centering the margins.

Fiddes, in his introduction to *Bound for Glory?*, notes that this publication builds on the earlier *Bound to Love* which he edited in 1985. Similarly to Kidd's understanding of this liberating Baptist agenda, Fiddes notes that covenant theology provides a way for Baptists to give depth to theological discussions on "the link between relations in God and relations in human community" where this is "often associated with a critique of models of domination."[113] Fiddes highlights that

> covenant theology is at the base of the idea of a "gathered church," demarcated from the world, and yet God's covenantal life provokes us, at the very same time, to break all boundaries down. We may have to think imaginatively of different ways of belonging within the covenant community. While not losing a sense of commitment to each other and to God, we shall always be searching for new ways to make space for others within the capacious love of God.[114]

Covenant relationships formed by God between people in a local church should encourage us in our relationships with others beyond the church. We will explore this further in the next chapter.

111. Kidd, "Baptists and Theologies," 48.
112. Kidd, "Baptists and Theologies," 52.
113. Fiddes, "Introduction," 6.
114. Fiddes, "Introduction," 8.

In *New Baptists, New Agenda*, published in 2002 as part of his presidency of the BUGB, Wright considers the changes that took place among Baptists in the 1990s. Wright reveals that this book "is a bid to define Baptist identity at the beginning of the twenty first century."[115] He argues that the form of evangelical faith expressed by Baptists is now "progressive, ecumenically open (but not particularly enthusiastic about formal ecumenism), holistic in its approach to mission and often profoundly engaged in social action and regeneration projects alongside evangelism."[116] Thus, Wright sees that the focus is on social action, often as a tool of mission, rather than social justice. In addition, Baptist churches are a step away from being actively engaged with others on these initiatives. I understand that this is often because they are looking at the mission of the local Baptist church. He argues later for the contribution of different denominations in which Baptists see "an opportunity for fruitful interaction in which we learn from those of other traditions and wherever possible allow ourselves to be enriched by their insights."[117] Therefore, we observe that Wright in this book is keen on listening, neighborliness, solidarity, and the common good. However, for Wright, this is framed within relations with other churches rather than with the diversity of institutions in civil society. In addition, for Wright, this is also framed in terms of evangelism—drawing others into the church.

Wright goes on to consider what Baptists can contribute and what they can learn from others. He argues that "because radical and dissenting groups have often found themselves on the margins of society they have needed to seek solidarity with those who are like-minded in order to endure."[118] Here Wright is referring to Baptist congregations in the sixteenth and seventeenth centuries which sought to associate with other such congregations. Later, he argues that the Baptist tradition "does not look for any privileged position in society but accords equal freedoms to other voices."[119] We could link this to the principle of centering the margins through the focus here on bringing in marginalized voices. However, Wright does not make this link clearly. He makes a much stronger link to the principle of subsidiarity when discussing self-government by congregations:

> At its best, church government is exercised by the people, closest to their own situation and with maximum ownership of decisions

115. Wright, *New Baptists, New Agenda*, 21.
116. Wright, *New Baptists, New Agenda*, 12.
117. Wright, *New Baptists, New Agenda*, 52.
118. Wright, *New Baptists, New Agenda*, 53.
119. Wright, *New Baptists, New Agenda*, 60.

> made. Such flexibility grants church members a high degree of involvement in their own destinies.[120]

Wright understands that through this and in other ways the Baptist tradition has "pioneered and hatched some of the formative ideas and practices that have come to be part of our standard expectation in democratic societies."[121] In *New Baptists, New Agenda* Wright recognizes that

> congregations are good for communities, providing places where people can be nurtured, supported, empowered and inspired by spiritual and ethical values for the wider well-being of society. They bring people together across the boundaries of age, ethnicity, culture and class in a common concern for each other and for God's world.[122]

In discussing the relationships formed in congregations, Wright does mention covenant membership.[123] However, he does not explore how covenant relationships work beyond the church membership. So, he does not engage with Fiddes and others' work on covenantal relationships here. Later in this book, Wright explores what it means when churches are now in the minority and argues that "accepting the new situation allows the churches to forge new alliances with other faith traditions." Through this, churches will need to "recover [their] understanding of dissent, identity and community."[124] For Wright, mission by local congregations is key. Wright does not comment on mission through broader alliances in which local churches participate.

Fiddes approaches the involvement of Baptists in mission differently. *Tracks and Traces*, published in 2003, could be seen as a response to Wright's *New Baptists, New Agenda*, published in 2002. However, all but one of the chapters in *Tracks and Traces* were written before Wright's book appeared. The origin of most of the chapters in *Tracks and Traces* is in papers presented at ecumenical gatherings during the period when Fiddes was writing *Participating in God*.

However, it is worth exploring whether some of Wright's and Fiddes's writing is, at least partly, in reaction or response to the writing of the other. Wright's quote on the back cover of *Tracks and Traces* notes that "it succeeds in being faithfully Baptist and profoundly Catholic at the same time."[125] Wright

120. Wright, *New Baptists, New Agenda*, 61.

121. Wright, *New Baptists, New Agenda*, 62.

122. Wright, *New Baptists, New Agenda*, 67.

123. Wright, *New Baptists, New Agenda*, 79.

124. Wright, *New Baptists, New Agenda*, 107–8.

125. Nigel G. Wright, in Fiddes, *Tracks and Traces*, back cover.

writes during this period for a Baptist church audience, whereas Fiddes writes for an ecumenical theological audience. Fiddes is an ecumenical theologian among Baptists and this runs throughout *Tracks and Traces*. The focus in this book is on reframing Baptist ecclesiology in an ecumenical perspective. It is possible that Fiddes and Wright were responding to each other's writing on areas such as on baptism and on the authority of ministers in churches. Therefore, this would be on areas that I am not particularly focusing on in this book. If Fiddes uses covenant theology as the basis to understand church action in mission with God in communities or society, Wright uses it as the basis of his understanding of the church modelling the change it wants to see.

Chapter 1 of *Tracks and Traces* focuses on Baptist identity through looking backwards at tracks and looking forwards for traces. This chapter builds on the earlier book edited by Fiddes, *Doing Theology in a Baptist Way*. In this chapter Fiddes argues that Baptist theology builds on the experience of a community responding to the rule of Christ and what Christ is saying to the church. Fiddes argues that covenant rather than stories is the central element of how we do theology as Baptists. However, Fiddes highlights that we need to pay attention to the hidden stories, such as those of women, in how we do church. This then relates to the principle of seeking to center the margins.

Fiddes defines *tracks* as those "made by Baptists in the past that have the potential still to offer guidance for the present day." He also highlights that Baptists share pathways with others who have travelled that way, as part of the church universal. Fiddes notes that "the term *traces* belongs more to our present age . . . it looks at uncertainty, at ambiguity in both knowledge and direction."[126] The emphasis in tracks is on mission. For traces, this means being open to the kingdom of God in community. This means being bound together in covenant in seeking God in community, being open to what God is doing, rather than just seeking to follow tracks. It will also mean looking at other tracks in the world that Baptists have not focused on within covenant life. Fiddes goes on to note that traces, "enable us to participate in God's life and in the context of community."[127] The experience of being part of a Baptist community is "of walking together . . . and . . . of being led by each other into the interweaving life of the triune God."[128] In this understanding of walking together there are echoes of the principles of solidarity and subsidiarity. Importantly, Fiddes understands that

126. Fiddes, *Tracks and Traces*, 1.

127. Fiddes, *Tracks and Traces*, 3.

128. Fiddes, *Tracks and Traces*, 7.

> this is the experience of a group of people who—in Britain—have been for the most part from the working classes, until the last century largely self-educated, for much of their history oppressed or excluded from positions in society, and who have been throughout their history advocates for liberty of religion and conscience for all.[129]

He highlights that Baptist theology will need to take reflection on this experience into account. It follows therefore that Fiddes, more than Wright, argues that Baptist practices come from their social and economic context and experience as much as from their understanding of the Bible. Fiddes underlines that "stories of dissent shape the community, and they need to influence theology too."[130] Despite this, involvement in community organizing in Wales and England is strongest among Catholics and Anglicans, rather than among denominations which have stories of dissent in their tradition. Perhaps, these stories of dissent now have less influence in local Baptist churches than Fiddes hopes.[131]

Fiddes emphasizes a theology of identification, rather than identity: "It is not that we share an already-existing identity through establishing a common list of agreed items, but we willingly *identify* ourselves with others who want to make or keep covenant with us because they catch an echo of their story in us."[132] He argues that these covenant relationships are in the context of "a society at present in which people find commitment difficult," and experience a lack of trust.[133] Thus, this Baptist theology of covenant relationships can contribute to building trust in society and to the community organizing approach of building accountable public relationships between institutions and with decision-makers. So, Baptist churches should be involved in relationships because God is. Churches should be relational because God is relational. Fiddes seeks to show that a "theology of covenant will be fruitful for . . . the tendency of covenant towards openness to others." Related to this, Fiddes highlights what his reflection on *The Nature of the Assembly* takes up, urging,

129. Fiddes, *Tracks and Traces*, 7–8.

130. Fiddes, *Tracks and Traces*, 11.

131. Baptists have sought to become accepted and culturally acceptable, and to hold positions of power and influence. In addition, Baptists have tended to laud those who have reached such positions: MPs and business executives, and even theologians. It is as Weber observed, the sect becoming an institution.

132. Fiddes, *Tracks and Traces*, 16; emphasis in original.

133. Fiddes, *Tracks and Traces*, 20.

> If the local church meeting aims to find the mind of Christ for its life and mission, it should be equally anxious to discover how churches together in assembly find his mind.[134]

Later, he argues that in seeking to find the mind of Christ a local congregation:

> Will seek fellowship, guidance and counsel from as much of "the whole body of Christ" as it can relate to. It will associate and unite with others, not just for the convenience of getting a job done, but because Christ is calling it to covenant with others.[135]

In this he emphasizes that a local church "needs to listen to others to understand its mission." Fiddes mentions listening to poor Christians in a Latin American favela and to Black Christians in a South African township and how they understand mission and justice, and to churches that seem weaker in local associations. Thus, here, he highlights the importance of the principles of listening and of centering the margins. However, Fiddes could do more here to recognize the importance of listening to local communities and their experiences of injustices, which is what he learned from the Latin American and South African experiences.

Fiddes understands that "when Baptists speak of a *gathered church*, they certainly mean that believers have agreed to gather together, but this is only in response to the Christ who has gathered them."[136] He makes this point in several places in *Tracks and Traces*. It is important in the context of how Baptist churches then gather with others, for example in a wider community organizing assembly or alliance. We must consider what it means to assemble together with others. In addition, we should return to the earlier points about seeking the mind of Christ together and participating with and in God together with others in community and wider society. We will develop this further in chapter 6. Later, Fiddes argues that this understanding of gathered church:

> Means that the local church is a community which gathers together a whole range of people, cutting across barriers of age, class, culture and temperament. . . . Its strength comes from being a gathering of the "unlike," people quite different from each other.[137]

This will mean hearing the voice of God through those who are different from us and may not hold the same beliefs or faith perspective as we do. Fiddes here appears to be describing what he sees as an "ideal church." As with Wright's

134. Fiddes, *Tracks and Traces*, 45.

135. Fiddes, *Tracks and Traces*, 54–55.

136. Fiddes, *Tracks and Traces*, 233; emphasis in original.

137. Fiddes, *Tracks and Traces*, 254.

earlier picture of an "ideal Baptist church" in *Challenge to Change*, it only too rarely reflects the reality of local Baptist church congregations.

Fiddes explores the deep connection between a Baptist passion for both mission and liberation, and their context in a Baptist theology of covenant. He argues that mission and liberation "belong to the being of the church because they belong to the being of God."[138] Fiddes reveals that mission and covenant are intertwined. He understands that the missionary God is also the covenant-making God. He argues that this perspective has implications for the character of the mission in which the church is engaged. Thus, mission is "essentially relational, essentially a matter of making communion and community."[139] This, he argues, means,

> Mission should take the form of community; the community of the church "goes out" by opening up its life to draw in the alien, the outcast and the estranged just as God makes room for us in an inner life of communion. The most effective form of mission may be the impact of the community life of the church on its neighbourhood, not enclosed in self-preservation but open in risky welcome. Mission will thus be concerned with making relations at every level of the world, in reflection of the triune God. It will offer prophetic criticism of competitive individualism in society, and seek to encourage political and economic policies that are committed to inter-personal relationships.[140]

I understand this as a key quote in linking up a Baptist passion for mission with engagement in a relational way of working with others in the neighborhood or wider community and in addressing social injustices. Fiddes, in highlighting that "the most effective form of mission may be the impact of the community life of the church on its neighbourhood," makes a similar point to that by Wright in his Whitley Lecture where church models the type of society it wants to see.[141] However, Fiddes then goes much further than Wright in encouraging Baptists, and others, to make relationships beyond the church as part of engaging in mission. Thus, Fiddes concludes,

> Mission is a sharing in the mission of God (*missio Dei*) and so it will also involve partnership with those who are fostering human health and welfare whether or not they are professing Christians. . . . If we are truly to carry through God's "preferential option

138. Fiddes, *Tracks and Traces*, 249.

139. Fiddes, *Tracks and Traces*, 253.

140. Fiddes, *Tracks and Traces*, 253–54.

141. Wright, *Power and Discipleship*, 27.

> for the poor," then we shall have to discern where the grace of God is at work in the world, and seek to cooperate with movements and structures which are in tune with the purpose of God.[142]

This is a very useful quote on Baptist engagement with others in social justice, and in making these points Fiddes is aware that concerns about whether another group is Christian or not is often still a barrier for some Baptists in whether they can engage with and then partner with others. *Tracks and Traces* can be seen as far removed from the reality of local church life but it might shape how Baptists think and act, in seeking to understand tracks and look for traces. In this way, *Tracks and Traces* is also critical of many of the current manifestations of Baptist church life. Covenant is seen by Fiddes as both a track and a trace, and covenant theology can be understood as weaving strands together. *Tracks and Traces* was written in the context of the 1990s when Wright and others were arguing that to be Baptist was to be evangelical. However, in this book, Fiddes does not engage with relationship between Baptists understanding themselves as Baptists or Evangelicals.

In covenantal relationships, God is drawing people together and binding people together. This contrasts with a consumerist model of church of people choosing to gather together as an individual choice. If we are gathered or called into covenant with others in a local church, then we do not pick who we are gathering with. Thus, church becomes a place for the marginalized rather than being a self-selecting group. We are in groups of the "unlike" gathering together and through this participating in God.[143] This participation is about participation in the gathered community and also outwards to the world. So, for a local church this means entering into a movement with a dynamic God and participating with God.

Haymes, Ruth Gouldbourne, and Anthony Cross, in their book *On Being the Church*, pick up the distinction made in *The Nature of the Assembly* in being church both as local congregation and when coming together as a wider group.[144] Both assemblies and local churches are able to seek the mind of Christ for that group.[145] They highlight that "to be manifestation of the church, in whatever form, is to be formed into a particular kind of people, and that has implications for the ways in which the individuals who are part of the community will live in other contexts."[146] The authors here highlight how the prac-

142. Fiddes, *Tracks and Traces*, 265.
143. Karen Smith, UK Baptist theologian, online meeting, Mar. 19, 2023.
144. Haymes et al., *On Being the Church*, 199.
145. Haymes et al., *On Being the Church*, 200.
146. Haymes et al., *On Being the Church*, 202.

tices of the local gathered church, the Baptist way of doing church, making decisions, focusing on mission, can influence how wider gatherings can work and vice versa. Therefore, there is something here about how community organizing can influence Baptist churches but also how Baptist churches can influence community organizing.

In writing about the nature of local church congregations, the authors note that "despite our ideal of broadly based congregations we are, often, fairly self-selecting in the nature of our communities," and therefore not diverse. They go on to highlight that when Baptists do meet with those with different experiences, assumptions and values these "encounters can be deeply enriching, as our horizons are broadened and our assumed ways of looking at things challenged. But these encounters can also be deeply disturbing and significantly hard work as we try to find common ground and some meeting of minds."[147] The authors are writing here about churches coming together but this could also apply to churches and others coming together in a broad-based organizing alliance through community organizing.

Wright's *Free Church, Free State* was published in 2005, two years after Fiddes's *Tracks and Traces*. Thus, we can consider whether and how Wright reacts to Fiddes in this book. Wright highlights that in this book he repeats arguments he made in both *The Radical Kingdom* and *Challenge to Change*.[148] His stated conviction is that "the positive Baptist vision implies a new conception of society arrived at by means of a particular understanding of the church."[149] Then later, "the Christian community must in some way and in some measure display in its social existence a pattern for the rest of humanity. . . . What is being attempted in the church therefore has relevance and transformative potential for the world."[150] He emphasizes the importance of maintaining the distinction between church and state and in this book focuses on "the interaction of the ecclesial or *churchly* and the social and political."[151] Thus, in this book Wright is also building on themes he developed earlier in his 1996 Whitley Lecture. However, he does not reference that lecture in this book.

Wright "takes as his primary community of reference the Baptist churches of England and, in a parallel way, lives within the stable liberal democracy of the United Kingdom."[152] Therefore, his focus is on the English rather than the Welsh context. As we established in chapter 4, the Welsh-language wing of

147. Haymes et al., *On Being the Church*, 205.

148. Wright, *Free Church, Free State*, xvii.

149. Wright, *Free Church, Free State*, xx.

150. Wright, *Free Church, Free State*, xxi.

151. Wright, *Free Church, Free State*, xxii; emphasis in original.

152. Wright, *Free Church, Free State*, xxvi.

the BUW in particular could be seen as quite different in its context, outlook and focus. The BUW Welsh-language wing, shaped by its nonconformist history and practices, had relatively more focus on social justice compared to its English-language wing and to the BUGB.

Wright highlights that the church "must be seen as a community of persons in relationship with God and with each other, participating on an equal basis in the life of God."[153] He references Fiddes's *Participating in God* and *Tracks and Traces* but without engaging with Fiddes's focus on covenant relationships. Wright also indicates the priority of mission for the church—as it "participates in the life of God it is caught up in God's outreach to the world."[154] However, unlike Fiddes, Wright does not emphasize what this then means for ecumenical engagement and for working together with others and beyond the church. Wright's is the evangelical Baptist position.

Wright notes that "Christian disciples are most likely to feel a sense of participation in those local communities which play a large part in their own lives . . . here is one reason why baptist Christians often have a strong local ecclesiology and weaker sense of anything beyond."[155] Here, he is referring to a church community but we could say that this also applies to participation in the local community and wider neighborhood beyond the local church. He argues that the church has been a social pioneer, "incubating within itself a love for humankind and ways of living together inspired by its discipleship of Christ."[156] This relates in part to the principle of neighborliness. However, Wright's view may be limited to those who have, or potentially might share, a Christian faith.

On the separation of church and state, Wright highlights that this "does not mean separation of church and society. The church is fully involved in society, doing its best to serve and shape it."[157] More than engagement with the state on social justice issues, he appears to argue that the church should model what it wants to see in the state, with the church "as a transformational community."[158] Wright understands that

> existence as a freely choosing and disciplined community is the authentic form of the church's life. This requires the reformation of existing ecclesial bodies and the renewal of congregational life in a decentralised direction in which power is commonly owned

153. Wright, *Free Church, Free State*, 5.
154. Wright, *Free Church, Free State*, 16.
155. Wright, *Free Church, Free State*, 196.
156. Wright, *Free Church, Free State*, 204.
157. Wright, *Free Church, Free State*, 213.
158. Wright, *Free Church, Free State*, 234.

> by the church's members. Only so can the church adequately act as an evangelistic, socially transforming community.[159]

There are echoes here of the principles of subsidiarity and neighborliness. In seeking the redemption of the state, churches should, first, faithfully be the institution keeping the state focused on justice, peace and freedom. Second, the church should do this by "participating constructively in the social order and the intermediate structures of society," as "civil society and culture provide space for voluntary human association in ways which enable both government and market to function less coercively."[160] Here again there is a link to the principle of subsidiarity and the common good. However, Wright's approach seems more like modelling than actively trying to change social injustices through direct engagement with decision-makers in the state or market. Third, the church should seek the redemption of the state through "political participation."[161] However, he then focuses on this as the involvement of individuals in political roles rather than as engagement of a local church together as a group. In a concluding chapter sketching out ways for Baptists to engage in the social and political environment, he argues for participation without "religious possession of the organs of government and social control."[162] This participation is "in recognition of their [faith groups] contribution to the moral formation of citizens, [and] their involvement in local communities."[163]

In addition to being president of the BUGB in 2006, Kate Coleman also delivered the Whitley Lecture that year.[164] In her lecture, *Being Human: A Black British Christian Woman's Perspective*, Coleman addresses the relationship between theological values and social location.[165] She highlights that "the consideration of any system of ideas is not complete without an investigation of the social context in which the system arose."[166] Coleman quotes James Cone, who argues, "Theology is not universal language; it is interested language and thus always a reflection of the goals and aspirations of a particular people in a definite social setting."[167] As with Fiddes, Haymes, and Kidd,

159. Wright, *Free Church, Free State*, 234.

160. Wright, *Free Church, Free State*, 243, 244.

161. Wright, *Free Church, Free State*, 244.

162. Wright, *Free Church, Free State*, 277.

163. Wright, *Free Church, Free State*, 278.

164. See sec. 4.2.3.

165. Coleman, *Being Human*, 10. As Coleman highlights in her lecture, the relationship between theological values and social location is a key feature of black, feminist, womanist, and other theologies of liberation.

166. Coleman, *Being Human*, 12.

167. Coleman, *Being Human*, 12; quoting James Cone.

Coleman is engaging with and is influenced by theologies of liberation. She is drawing here on a Black theology of liberation. This contrasts with the others who drew largely on Latin American liberation theology in their writings. Coleman notes that Black people share a common experience of oppression. She goes on to highlight that, for Black women seeking to resist oppressive forces, "partnership, community and togetherness are key."[168] Coleman notes that there has been a failure to acknowledge the knowledge claims emerging from marginalized communities. She argues,

> A theology that fails to call for change in the socio-political realities of the marginalised, such as Black British women, or fails to attend to the issues of freedoms from oppressions, equality and recognition as fully accepted participants in British life, is at best inadequate and at worst demonic.[169]

Thus, in this lecture we can observe resonances with her BUGB presidential address and its theme of "Centring the Margins." As with this address, there are strong links made to the principles of solidarity and centering the margins. Coleman argues for a theology that takes action on these and other injustices that keep people marginalized and oppressed. We will develop this further in chapter 6.

In 2008, Fiddes edited *Under the Rule of Christ*. This book, uniquely during this period, includes chapters by Fiddes, Kidd, and Wright. As the preface makes clear, "the Baptist sense of being under the rule of Christ has been strongly marked by the experience of oppression, especially in the early days of Baptist life." In addition, spirituality under this rule "must be connected . . . with the mission of God in the world to bring about peace and justice for all."[170] Fiddes understands that being under the rule of Christ means "to cultivate the habit of attentiveness to the demand that Christ makes upon us in the encounters of everyday life, so that all experience is *ruled* or measured by the discernment of this demand." Fiddes follows this with noting the importance of attentiveness to what is other than the self, namely attentiveness to the needs and demands of the other person.[171] Thus, there is a link here to the principles of listening and neighborliness in everyday life. Fiddes's critique of hierarchical models of church in *Tracks and Traces* and in this book provides ways to open up Baptist engagement with ecumenical partners and brings

168. Coleman, *Being Human*, 14–17.
169. Coleman, *Being Human*, 55.
170. Fiddes, *Rule of Christ*, ix.
171. Fiddes, *Rule of Christ*, 26; emphasis in original.

Baptist thinking into the thinking of other churches, such as on finding the mind of Christ together.[172]

Anthony Clarke edited *For the Sake of the Church*, a Festschrift for Fiddes, in 2014.[173] As Kidd highlights in his chapter, "Dance has long been recognised as a vital component of the ritual activity that binds communities together, confirming and consolidating their identity."[174] In *Participating in God*, Fiddes affirms "the energetic and subversive power of dance."[175] In this form of progressive dance, "God can be thought to move out, penetrating the circle of dancers, providing their energy and drawing them back into unity of God's own life," and in this, "there is a relational movement enabling our own dynamic participation in God's trinitarian life."[176]

Haymes, in his chapter, acknowledges that Fiddes's writings on the theological concept of covenant, "while still not widely read in the denomination, are an immensely creative resource for those who know we must above all think seriously about God."[177] A reason for the lack of engagement with Fiddes's covenant theology comes later in Haymes's chapter. Haymes notes that "contemporary British Baptists, children of their age and cultures, are nothing if not pragmatic. We have a wariness of 'theology' for we can fear that it is remote, academic, out of touch with the realities of life, not least in the church."[178]

Fiddes, writing in 2014, underlines that "the relations within the triune life of God are irrevocably bound up with the covenant that God makes with human beings."[179] He argues,

> The eternal relationships within the Trinity may themselves be envisaged as a kind of covenant relationship. Then, just as there is a human communion that participates in the "communion" of the Trinity, there would be a human covenant within the "covenant" of the Trinity.[180]

172. However, neither Kidd's nor Wright's chapters in *Rule of Christ* include any links to the six principles. There is also no interaction between Wright's and Fiddes's thinking in their respective chapters.

173. Kidd, Haymes, and Wright all have chapters in this book. However, even in a Festschrift for Fiddes, Wright does not engage with Fiddes's writing in his chapter.

174. Kidd, "On Realising the Dance," 12.

175. Kidd, "On Realising the Dance," 13.

176. Kidd, "On Realising the Dance," 13–14.

177. Haymes, "Still Blessing the Tie," 95.

178. Haymes, "Still Blessing the Tie," 97.

179. Fiddes, "Communion and Covenant," 134.

180. Fiddes, "Communion and Covenant," 134–35.

This then helps link together participating in the relations of God with covenantal relationships formed by God, which are, "a flowing of love, a movement of infinitely generous giving and receiving within God."[181] As Fiddes understands, "In the *perichoresis* of God with the world, human persons also stand between the movement of divine love that we identify as being like a Father, Son and Spirit . . . God relates to God's self through human relations." He goes on to argue that "much of this vision can be expressed in terms of an interweaving 'communion.' The language of 'covenant' makes clear that God's own purposes are being reshaped by the entering of human community into God with its own purposes, aims, and intentions."[182]

In a chapter by Fiddes on participation, in a further book written with Haymes and Kidd, Fiddes argues,

> While the covenantal principle can be seen most clearly in the shape of the Christian church, it is in that context that the doctrine of the communion of saints has its immediate location, the idea of two intersecting vectors can be extended beyond the walls of the church if we understand the relation of God to the world to be generally covenanted.[183]

Fiddes then underlines that while "the church offers the context for a 'particular' covenant . . . others outside the community of the church will . . . be living in another covenant."[184] Fiddes highlights how the idea of covenant makes sense of complicated and challenging relationships in a community. He notes that in his own theological work:

> I have often asked what happens when the trinitarian theology of "participating in God" merges with the ecclesiology of "covenant." One important result is that we can see how there are different kinds of covenant between God and created beings, just as human persons participate in God in different ways and at different depths of commitment. Not all relations are the same, and not all covenants are the same.[185]

Fiddes then offers some reflections on the idea of a "variety" of covenants, where he suggests "we need an inclusive view of a covenantal relation with God, identifying a whole range of covenants that God makes with created

181. Fiddes, "Communion and Covenant," 136.

182. Fiddes, "Communion and Covenant," 137.

183. Fiddes, "Participation," 161.

184. Fiddes, "Participation," 162.

185. Fiddes, preface to *Covenant and Church*, 1–2.

beings."[186] Fiddes, Haymes, and Kidd have all brought concerns for peace and justice in the wider world into a theology of covenant. Fiddes recognizes that Baptists have not usually thought of covenant in this expansive way. Engaging with Fiddes's thinking on covenant allows us to take the covenant theology out from a local church into wider society. One trajectory of this can be found in the writing of Daniel Sutcliffe-Pratt, a Baptist minister in England. Sutcliffe-Pratt makes the proposal that, even within the borders of a local church, "there is room and hospitality for different kinds of covenant."[187] As Fiddes describes it, Sutcliffe-Pratt argues,

> An expansive vision of a church founded on covenant. And because there is a history of covenant between God and others that we do not know, we can expect that listening to their story will deepen our own faith, it will enrich and expand our own understanding of what our story is.[188]

Sutcliffe-Pratt highlights that "this horizontal and vertical perichoretic covenant *is one of movement and action*, where one can become involved in the very life of God."[189] For him, "This horizontal aspect of covenant raises questions relating to the nature of community, as well as the relationship between covenant and community."[190]

Sutcliffe-Pratt explores the implications of perichoresis and covenant for a local church (57 West) with deliberately open boundaries to the wider community.[191] However, this is a church-centered exploration of how groups that engage with the church during the week (through coming to a church-run café, etc.) are involved in covenantal relationships and participating in God rather than how a local church can participate in wider covenantal relationships that God forms in the community without involvement of the local church, or covenantal relationships that God forms in the wider community that the local church is then invited to join in with. Therefore, we could see it as God forming covenantal relationships in a Citizens UK alliance and then a local Baptist church is invited to join in with these. Sutcliffe-Pratt proposes that:

> To join in *perichoresis* through mission, or the pursuit of the common good therefore directly relates to the integrity of self and openness to others. . . . In order to participate in both covenant

186. Fiddes, preface to *Covenant and Church*, 2.
187. Fiddes, preface to *Covenant and Church*, 4.
188. Fiddes, preface to *Covenant and Church*, 4.
189. Sutcliffe-Pratt, *Covenant and Church*, 20; emphasis added.
190. Sutcliffe-Pratt, *Covenant and Church*, 21.
191. Sutcliffe-Pratt, *Covenant and Church*, 27.

> and *perichoresis*, openness to others is essential, particularly as many within the 57 West community have experienced rejection or marginalisation by other parts of society. In participating within an ecclesial community and within the life of God, participants have opportunities of finding hope, healing and liberation.[192]

Taking a sacramental view of church, and of the world, Sutcliffe-Pratt concludes that "if the world is viewed as God's body, then this has implications for humankind as we participate within that body. In relation to entering into a dynamic *perichoretic* relationship with the world, we do not only experience God, but God experiences the world. Indeed, God communicates himself through the world."[193] Thus, he concludes that "as the world is God's body, and God experiences the world, so his body the Church is called to experience that world."[194] This links to Pope Francis's view of the church, outlined in section 3.2, of a church of the poor and marginalized.

Fiddes, Haymes, and Kidd understood that they were "extending concepts of covenant to cover a more catholic understanding of the church as well as the activity of God in society outside the church."[195] They were seeking to retrieve something from the past and develop it for the current context. Fiddes acknowledges that "adoption of covenant language in the denomination has been widespread but covenant theology has had much less impact." However, Fiddes highlights that

> I remain convinced that the idea of covenant has urgent importance, not only for the shape of the church but for cooperating with the activity of God outside the church where God has many covenant relationships of which we are scarcely aware.[196]

Thus, Fiddes is concerned with how we might engage in covenantal relationships formed by God beyond those formed by church communities. Fiddes's understanding of covenantal relationships beyond the local church is something that can be offered to community organizing. We will explore the implications of this for strengthening a Baptist theological ethic in the next chapter.

192. Sutcliffe-Pratt, *Covenant and Church*, 38.

193. Sutcliffe-Pratt, *Covenant and Church*, 50.

194. Sutcliffe-Pratt, *Covenant and Church*, 51.

195. Paul S. Fiddes, response to Goodliff's book, in Goodliff, "*Renewing a Modern Denomination* Launch."

196. Paul S. Fiddes, in Goodliff, "*Renewing a Modern Denomination* Launch."

5.5 Summary

This chapter has explored how the writings of four major UK Baptist theologians during this period from the late 1980s to 2010 have engaged with the six principles from current theological reflection on community organizing. In this chapter we have considered the strengths and weaknesses of the writing of these four major UK Baptist theologians over a nearly thirty-year period in relation to strengthening a Baptist theological ethic of social justice. We have explored the main themes in their writing and how these also engage with the six principles. We were primarily concerned with how their focus and arguments can help in strengthening a Baptist theological ethic for the practice of social justice. We have also explored the interweaving between their writings and how this developed, and considered the extent to which they engaged with each other's thinking in their writing. The context for Baptists in England particularly, and in Wales to some extent, also affected the focus of Fiddes, Haymes, Kidd, and Wright's writing during this period, as it did the focus of the BUW and BUGB Assembly addresses and resolutions that we explored in chapter 4.

For the period of the 1980s we observed how the major themes of these theologians were beginning to emerge in their writing. They were also writing when much Baptist focus in Wales and England was external, to engagement with others. However, much of the rest of the period studied was dominated by discussion and reflection on Baptist life and identity. This crowded out to a large extent discussions on engagement with others and looking outwards, for example through using community organizing.

For the 1990s, we then observed how their writing expressed competing visions for the future of Baptists in the two unions and how much of their writing appears to have an aim to influence internal debates which dominated discussions during this period, particularly in BUGB.

Finally, we observed for the 2000s that while the writing of all four was seeking to set a Baptist agenda, Fiddes, Haymes, and Kidd, perhaps disillusioned by their inability to significantly influence BUGB discussions, increasingly engaged in bringing Baptist identity and principles to ecumenical discussions.

Fiddes and Wright both draw on Baptist roots (or "tracks"). However, they differ in their focus. Fiddes, in contrast to Wright, understands that Baptist identity cannot be reduced to an agreed set of values or beliefs. Instead, Baptist tradition is about an ongoing shared life and is held in community. However, neither Wright nor Fiddes understand Baptist identity as static. Both understand that it is dynamic, able to draw on its past and also on its engagement with other church denominations and the wider community. Wright focuses on an Anabaptist view of separation of Church and State. In contrast, Fiddes focuses on participating in God through relationships formed far beyond the local church. Mission is central to the writing of both Fiddes and Wright. However, importantly, Fiddes focuses on the mission of God, and Wright on the mission of the Baptist church.

Participating in the life of the triune God who forms covenantal relationships is a major theme in much of what Fiddes writes during this period, including in his reports and books written with Haymes and Kidd. Indeed, covenant, Trinity, and participation are a focus of almost everything Fiddes writes during these years. Liberation theology appears to have been a strong influence on each of these three theologians. The theological reflections on community organizing explored in chapter 3 reflect the influence of CST and an understanding of Christian mission that is contextual and liberating. Thus, one sees the basis for a focus on solidarity and relationships, dialogue through listening, and theology emerging from the margins. The writings of Haymes and Kidd demonstrate a degree of convergence with CST.

Wright's writing during this period was less influenced by theologies of liberation or CST. In contrast, Wright is much more focused on reconnecting with an Anabaptist heritage. His focus was thus more on a church-centered approach to mission by a gathered Baptist church. In contrast, Fiddes, Haymes, and Kidd were engaging more with theologies of liberation and CST, and thus their writing engages more with the six principles. Fiddes, Haymes, and Kidd were also much more concerned than Wright with listening to and learning from other church traditions. Wright and Fiddes had different visions of Baptist ecclesiology. There was overlap when it comes to ecumenism. Wright was keen for Baptists to engage with other Evangelicals. In contrast, Fiddes, Haymes, and Kidd were keen on Baptist engagement with all parts of the church.

Fiddes and Wright were writing for different audiences and were essentially writing different sorts of books, although both produced booklets and reports particularly for a BUGB audience and discussions. Fiddes is an ecumenical theologian. Wright is writing as a theologian to Baptist churches, especially those sitting within an evangelical tradition. Despite the influence, or not, of these four theologians on decisions that led to restructuring the BUW and BUGB to ensure a central focus on mission by Baptist churches, their writing did not result in a strong Baptist theological ethic for the practice of social justice during this period. It appears that much of their writing was not widely read in Baptist churches.

This chapter and the previous one have reflected further on the six principles developed from theological reflection on community organizing and considered them in light of how Baptists thought about these during the period when community organizing was being established in England and Wales. From the writings of Fiddes, Haymes, Kidd, and Wright during the period studied, in this chapter we have considered the extent to which there are connections in their writing with the six principles.

Fiddes, Haymes, and Kidd's writing demonstrates the most extensive links, particularly in their writing on participating in God and covenantal relationships and the connections made with solidarity, the common good, neighborliness and centering the margins. Fiddes understands that covenant and participation are held together, a covenant not just with God, but in God. For Fiddes, the Baptist understanding of covenant, centered in the language of walking together, is relational language and implies openness, trust, and being on a journey together. Thus, the focus on covenant theology that is about relationships and journeying together with others can be related to the principles of solidarity, listening, and neighborliness. Fiddes's writing engages with and challenges what is the center and what are the margins. Thus, his writing asks what it then means to center the margins. Wright makes the strongest connections to the principle of subsidiarity. However, it should again be noted that the six principles come from reflection on the practice of churches with an outward focus and engaging with others in wider communities and civil society.

The writings of these four theologians can contribute to strengthening a Baptist theological ethic for the practice of social justice. However, more diverse sources will be needed to strengthen a theological ethic for its practice. In the next chapter we will draw on these and we will also consider what was not picked up in the existing theological reflection on community organizing but that may be revealed through bringing Baptist theology to it. There appear to be promising areas to take forward from the analysis of the writings of these four Baptist theologians for a strengthened community organizing and a strengthened Baptist theological ethic. Fiddes's ecumenical focus brings Baptist theology into that which has been developed in other denominations and vice versa. Therefore, Fiddes's thinking on participating in God and covenantal relationships may also be areas that can help strengthen the practice of broad-based community organizing.

The next chapter will bring this chapter and chapter 4 into dialogue in seeking to propose a way forward in Baptist social justice understanding and practice. It will consider how community organizing can strengthen a Baptist theological ethic for the practice of social justice. It will also consider what

Baptist theology, identity, and practices can offer to community organizing to strengthen its practice in Wales and England.

Chapter 6

A Way Forward for Baptist Social Justice Theology and Ethics

6.1 Introduction

In this chapter we will explore trajectories from the material examined in the previous five chapters and the ethical implications of these trajectories for a Baptist theological ethic for the practice of social justice. I will seek to bring together all that has been learned in the previous five chapters, and how this can be combined to strengthen this ethic. I will thus address the overall research question for this research. This asks how an investigation of the theory and practice of community organizing can help form a more adequate theological ethic for the practice of social justice by Baptist churches in Wales and England. Up to this point the exploration and analysis reveals a theme of disconnection and the development of separate strands between community organizing and Baptist churches in Wales and England. It also reveals a theme of disconnection between Baptist theological writing and practice in these nations.

I have used a metaphor of weaving and reweaving in this book.[1] As we observed in chapter 1, Citizens UK has recently used a metaphor from

1. In *Melodies of a New Monasticism*, Craig Gardiner, a UK Baptist theologian, explores the nature of Christian community and presents a theology of how Christians

weaving to explain how community organizing reweaves the fabric of local communities. Warp and weft are used in weaving to turn thread into fabric. In this metaphor, churches and other local civil society organizations are the warp, and the relationships built between community leaders are the weft.[2]

I will seek to weave together the strands developed through analysis and evaluation in chapters 1–5 to present a way forward for Baptist theological social ethics through an alternative understanding and practice. I will propose a synthesis which challenges the limits both of the community organizing paradigm and what Baptist churches in Wales and England have understood and practiced about mission. I believe that this will challenge the Baptist legacy, where this has not developed a strong theological ethic for the practice of social justice. However, I will seek to draw on some of the strengths that have already been developed. I will then seek to develop a new synthesis through weaving together the best insights from community organizing with the best insights of Baptists in Wales and England during the period studied. This chapter, in dialogue with earlier chapters, considers how community organizing can strengthen a Baptist theological ethic for the practice of social justice; and what Baptist theology, identity, and practices can offer to community organizing, to strengthen its development in Wales and England. I will suggest new directions for Baptist social ethics, which will inform the conversation.

In the first section of this chapter, we will begin by surveying the development of the book so far. Having done this, we will then review the essential purpose of ethical inquiry, and I will then provide an outline of this chapter.

6.1.1 The Development of the Research So Far

In the first half of this book, I examined the development of community organizing first in the United States and then in England and Wales (ch. 1), how churches have understood and used organizing (ch. 2), and then reflected theologically on their practice of it, drawing out six principles from this current theological reflection (ch. 3). These six principles are: solidarity, subsidiarity, the common good, neighborliness, listening, and centering

might seek to live together. He does this by bringing together the life and work of Dietrich Bonhoeffer, German minister and theologian imprisoned and subsequently executed by the Nazi regime, and George MacLeod, founder of the Iona Community in Scotland, two twentieth-century Christians who never met and yet shared a passion for Christian community. Gardiner uses the metaphor of polyphonic music in his book. He explains that polyphonic music permits and encourages individual difference, yet unites them in what might be deemed a community of melodies.

2. See sec. 1.5.

the margins. These principles were extrapolated from theological reflection mainly by Catholic and Anglican theologians. I will now provide some more detail on these three chapters.

The literature review in chapter 1 revealed the key focus of broad-based community organizing in both the US and UK on developing leaders, strengthening institutions, and making change. The roots of community organizing were in specific places and community institutions, and in leadership by local people themselves. We noted how the historical and current context of churches and civil society influenced the development of broad-based community organizing in both the US and in Wales and England.

It may be that context is key. For example, Black Baptist church involvement in the US was specific to their particular context and experience. As we observed in chapter 1, community organizing in the US was influenced at least to some extent by the theology and practices of Latin American and Black liberation theologies, and by the continued influence of the US civil rights movement on Black Baptist churches. Neither theologies of liberation nor the civil rights movement have had such a level of influence on Baptist churches in Wales and England up to now.

The Baptist experience and theological engagement in broad-based community organizing is not dealt with in any depth in the current literature, despite Baptist involvement in the US underpinning and playing a central role in several alliances and key campaigns. Black Baptist churches and Roman Catholic churches, their traditions and practices, had a strong influence on community organizing in the US. However, the involvement of Baptist churches does not get translated into community organizing in Wales and England. There are few written reflections on community organizing in the US from a Baptist perspective, despite the extent of their involvement.

Chapter 2 then focused on how community organizing has been taken up by churches and what it means for their practice of social justice. In community organizing, churches and other institutions are challenged to live up to their values. This review of churches' understanding and use of community organizing revealed the fact that, for many churches, their understanding of community organizing and theological reflection on it has come from their experience and practice of it rather than the other way round.

Exploring this further, and building on the themes emerging from the previous two chapters, chapter 3 focused on extant theological reflection on community organizing. This revealed a number of themes. I highlighted the focus on key principles of CST such as solidarity, subsidiarity, and the common good. I explored and critiqued how a range of theologians have understood these principles in the context of community organizing, and through this I produced a synthesis working definition of each. Theologians of community organizing are not particularly diverse, nor are they adequately writing about race and power. This shows the limits of the literature and the blind spots of the current theologians of community organizing. Therefore, the current theological reflection has not given us everything we need in developing a strengthened Baptist ethic of social justice.

The reality of theology emerging from the experience, practice and stories of community organizing is a hallmark of theological reflection on community organizing. I believe this is also methodologically significant for this investigation. This is the same methodological commitment found in Black and Latin American liberation theology. There are examples of liberation theology being incarnated through community organizing. However, community organizing seems much more widespread in practice by a wide range of churches than the on-the-ground practice of liberation theology.

Up to this point in the research we had mainly drawn on Catholic and Anglican theological reflections on community organizing. We now made the turn to consider the Baptist response to this, what Baptists can learn from Catholic and Anglican involvement and theological reflection on community organizing, and what Baptists can contribute to community organizing thought and practice. As Rowlands highlights, the post–Vatican II authors of the CST tradition sought to produce a body of work addressed not just to the Roman Catholic Church but to "all people of goodwill."[3]

In the second half of the book I proceeded to examine the development of a theological ethic for the practice of social justice through Baptist churches in Wales and England. In dialogue with these six principles, I explored how Baptists have engaged with them in developing a Baptist ethic for the practice of social justice during the period when community organizing was developing in England and Wales. I explored the period from the late 1980s to 2010, so covering the period from the launch of the first community organizing alliances in Wales and England to the formation of Citizens UK (chs. 4–5).

Chapter 4 focused on how the six principles extrapolated from theological reflection on community organizing relate to the public resolutions and themes chosen by the BUW and the BUGB presidents and general secretaries from the late 1980s to 2010. This chapter also examined these sources to understand how and to what extent Baptists were relating to each other and to other church denominations, to other institutions in civil society, and to government. From these sources, this chapter examined how all this contributed to a Baptist theological ethic for the practice of social justice.

3. Rowlands, *Towards a Politics of Communion*, 11.

Chapter 5 explored how the writings of four major UK Baptist theologians during this period from the late 1980s to 2010 engaged with the six principles. The four theologians were Paul Fiddes, Brian Haymes, Richard Kidd, and Nigel Wright. In this chapter we considered the strengths and weaknesses of the writing of these four theologians over a nearly thirty-year period in relation to strengthening a Baptist theological ethic of social justice. We explored the main themes in their writing and how these engage with the six principles. We were primarily concerned with how their focus and arguments can help in strengthening a Baptist theological ethic for the practice of social justice.

Chapters 4–5 reflected further on the six principles developed from theological reflection on community organizing and played them back through a Baptist lens on how Baptists thought about and understood these during the period when community organizing was being established in England and Wales. These chapters thus explored the influence of the past in the present in relation to Baptist engagement in social justice. The intense theological reflection on Baptist identity in the period studied between the late 1980s and 2010 is useful in discovering what Baptists can bring to community organizing and to strengthening a Baptist theological ethic for the practice of social justice for the future.

6.1.2 The Essential Purpose of Ethical Inquiry

Luke Bretherton's approach to Christian ethics is built on three questions: What is going on; what is to be done; and how then shall we live?[4] He notes that Christians must also ask what it means "to pursue the art of living well in the midst of brutal chaos and oppression"[5]—in addition to this, what it means to live well where flourishing and thriving "depends on being embedded in some kind of loving and just form of common life," where right and truthful relationships are important.[6] Similarly, David Gushee highlights that the big questions of ethics are: "How should we live? What are the rules that should govern how we live? What are the goals that we should seek to achieve in

4. Bretherton recognizes an overlap between his approach and the "see, judge, act" approach of Joseph Cardijn, the Roman Catholic co-founder of Young Christian Workers. Cardijn's approach was then adapted into CST as a way to frame relationships between theology and practice. This also influenced Latin American liberation theology and subsequently mujerista theology—"of becoming aware of reality, taking responsibility for reality, and transforming reality" (*Primer in Christian Ethics*, 19n15).

5. Bretherton, *Primer in Christian Ethics*, 1–2.

6. Bretherton, *Primer in Christian Ethics*, 9–10.

life overall? What serves the needs of people and relationships?"[7] This final question makes people and relationships central to ethics, as also highlighted by Bretherton. Ethics therefore considers what course of action cares best for others and strengthens relationships.

It can therefore be argued that ethical inquiry concerns how we should live and recognizes that this should happen in a way that builds relationships and enables all to live well. As we discovered in chapter 1, a key area of understanding in community organizing is that we need to live and act in the tension between the world as it is and the world as it should be.[8] As Gushee posits, "Every time someone draws a contrast between how the world should be and the world as it is . . . we are still being nourished by the biblical vision of the way God intended the world to be. That is, as a sacred world, created and sustained by both divine and human love."[9] Bretherton notes that we aspire to live in the world as it should be, where justice prevails and love rules. However, organizing for power is needed to go from the world as it is to the world as it should be.[10] Hak Joon Lee, a US Christian ethicist, argues that "community organizing . . . is the attempt to bridge the gap between the world as it is and the world as it should be."[11] Therefore, both ethics and community organizing are not just about noticing where injustice exists, but doing something about it, making the world as it is closer to the world as it should be.

Gushee asks, "What kind of community should we seek to develop?"[12] He then observes that from the perspective of marginalized and oppressed people, the question is more focused: "What must we do to demand that this community stops doing injustice to us?" This then leads us to liberation ethics which emerges from below, rather than within a community's power structures, and asks, "What steps of liberation might we undertake to create a just community?"[13]

Howard Thurman's book *Jesus and the Disinherited*, with its focus on Jesus as part of a poor oppressed minority under imperial domination, provides a key foundation piece for Gushee's *Introducing Christian Ethics*. Thurman, in highlighting the political, social, and cultural context of Jesus' ministry, understands that "Jesus was born and raised in a context of multiple overlapping oppressions, and that he is best understood as a 'man from below,'

7. Gushee, *Introducing Christian Ethics*, 6–7.

8. See sec. 1.3.

9. Gushee, *Introducing Christian Ethics*, 115.

10. Bretherton, "Ability to Act."

11. Lee, *God and Community Organizing*, 152.

12. Gushee, *Introducing Christian Ethics*, 9.

13. Gushee, *Introducing Christian Ethics*, 10.

who led a popular movement of others in the same social location."[14] Gushee highlights that Christian ethics should be "in practice and not just in theory . . . part of the resistance tradition that Thurman helped to pioneer rather than the oppressive tradition that Thurman so powerfully critiqued."[15] Thus, this chapter is focused on strengthening an ethic that can be practical in the cause of increasing social justice and enabling all to live together and to flourish.

In proposing a way forward and building on Thurman's resistance tradition, I argue that community organizing enables us to do this from the perspective of marginalized and oppressed people. As I highlighted in the summary of chapter 5, a strengthened Baptist theological ethic will need to be informed by more diverse sources.[16] There are only a few female Baptist theologians to be found in the literature during the period studied. Kate Coleman, Ruth Gouldbourne, and Anne Wilkinson-Hayes were the only Baptist women I have found within the available literature.[17] In addition, there is a lack of Black Baptist church literature reflecting on broad-based community organizing as practiced by the IAF alliances in the US, or by Citizens UK in Wales and England.[18]

In Wales and England, there have been over four hundred years of conversation about what it means to be Baptist. These conversations have explored Baptist identity, theology, and practices, such as a focus on freedom

14. Gushee, *Introducing Christian Ethics*, 126.

15. Gushee, *Introducing Christian Ethics*, 41.

16. See sec. 5.5. I recognize the approach taken by Amy Chilton and Steve Harmon in their book *Sources of Light*. This focuses on listening to more diverse sources and brings a liberational approach to theology. Community organizing is a liberational approach, and they provide a liberational approach to developing Baptist social ethics.

17. It is normal academic practice to include diverse sources. However, the focus here has been on four white male theologians. There is not diverse sourcing here because of the nature of the power structures in these Baptist unions and churches. People on the margins of churches and communities were not central to discussions. If the power structures had been structured differently, it might have been that some of the emphases of churches and the unions would have been different during this time period, for example, with more focus on people on the margins. We can also note that there was Black Pentecostal church involvement in community organizing in East London from early on in the development of organizing in Wales and England. It is important to highlight that many of these churches were formed because Black Jamaican Baptists and others from Caribbean countries who came to the UK were not made to feel welcome in existing white Baptist churches.

18. This is not to say that there is no literature on Black church engagement in organizing. There is much literature on this, highlighting Black church involvement since before the US civil rights movement. The experience of marginalization and oppression of Black people has strongly informed Black liberation theology and Black Baptist church thinking on social justice and their involvement in community organizing in the US.

of religion, the church meeting, associating, and covenanting together, which are all principles and practices initially formed in the context of radical dissent and oppression and Baptists fighting for their right to exist. However, once Baptists gained acceptance and respectability and found themselves in the center of society, my research would lead me to conclude that they ceased to be as concerned for those on the margins. Thus, starting from marginal and dissenting voices will help strengthen a Baptist theological ethic of social justice. So, as highlighted previously, a Baptist way of doing theology will involve starting with experience and developing theology in community.[19]

There have been more than eighty years of thinking about and practicing community organizing in the US, initially influenced by Roman Catholic, Jewish and trade union practices. Subsequently, over the last fifty years, churches have been central to the civil society alliances formed. Community organizing in the US has been influenced in particular by the theology and practices of Latin American immigrant Roman Catholic churches, which themselves have been strongly influenced by liberation theology, and Black Baptist churches. These Black Baptist churches play central roles in many alliances and have been strongly influenced by Martin Luther King Jr., the US civil rights movement, and Black theologies of liberation.

We noted that Saul Alinsky founded the IAF in the US in 1940, and Neil Jameson founded the COF (the precursor to Citizens UK) in 1989.[20] So, in Wales and England there have been fewer than forty years of conversation about what community organizing means for churches. Baptists in the UK have only participated in this conversation in a limited way up to now. In addition, this has not been alongside a Baptist conversation about justice. I suggest and will go on to argue that this should be the next step for Baptists. This chapter proposes a way forward for a Baptist theology of social justice and ethics through engagement with community organizing.

6.1.3 Outline of the Chapter

Section 6.2 considers the state of Baptist social justice theology and ethics in Wales and England, through a synthesis of the analysis of chapters 4–5. This incorporates what people were doing on the ground, what was being discussed at Baptist assemblies in Wales and England, and what Baptist theologians were writing about during this period. In addition, I consider how and where all of

19. See sec. 5.4.

20. See sec. 1.2, 1.4.

this picked up, or did not pick up, on the six principles drawn from current theological reflection on the practice of community organizing.

We then proceed to examine, in section 6.3, how practicing the six principles can strengthen a Baptist theological ethic for social justice. I will weave together the six principles, drawn from theological reflection on community organizing, with the focus on covenantal relationships. This focus has come through a study of the development of a Baptist social ethic during the period when community organizing was developing in Wales and England.

In section 6.4, I will examine how covenantal relationships can strengthen both a Baptist theological ethic and community organizing. I will argue that the concept of covenant and covenantal relationships has the potential to be an organizing framework to bring together community organizing and Baptist social ethics. Through this, people in churches and other institutions can, through their involvement in community organizing alliances, enter into a shared covenant together and contribute to the common good, the kingdom of God, and the flourishing of people and communities.

Section 6.5 considers how covenant and the general Baptist discussion in Wales and England on social justice challenges Baptists as it relates to an understanding of the mission of God in the world that is much broader than one that is church centered. This section therefore seeks to address the conundrum of the church being relevant to wider society, as well as God using the wider society to speak to churches.

Section 6.6 then considers how joining in with the mission of God and walking together in covenantal relationships implies the need for disorganizing and reorganizing relationships. This section seeks to consider the implications for Baptists of disentangling themselves from some practices and thinking about who Baptists associate with, and how they understand covenant and mission. The purpose of disentangling is for Baptists to then be better able to re-entangle themselves with others to act for social justice. It can be argued that this is the key challenge.

6.2 The State of Baptist Social Justice Theology and Ethics

6.2.1 The Lack of a Strong Baptist Theological Ethic for the Practice of Social Justice

From the analysis of what people were doing on the ground, what was being discussed at Baptist assemblies in Wales and England, and what Baptist theologians were writing about during this period, it would appear that the development of a strong Baptist social ethic never became a priority at the national level of either the BUW or BUGB. Overall, examining these sources in chapters 4–5 did not provide us with a sense that there is a strong shared Baptist theological ethic for the practice of social justice in Wales and England. However, that is not to say there was no understanding of social ethics among Baptists in Wales and England during this time.[21] The reasons for this will be explored in this section, drawing on and synthesizing the analysis undertaken in the previous two chapters.

The lack of a strong, shared ethic is evident, despite the production of two BUGB resources during the period studied. First, there was the launch of a union-wide Action in Mission program at the BUGB Assembly in 1988 which focused on "concentrating the minds of church members on the realities of their congregations and neighbourhoods."[22] Second, there was the publication in 1996 of *On Earth as in Heaven: A Theology of Social Action for Baptist Churches*.[23] This was centered on the interaction between a church and its wider community.[24] In the same year, Wright's Whitley Lecture, published as *Power and Discipleship*, focused on developing a Baptist theology of the state, which suggests that Baptist churches should engage in social justice.[25] However, Wright appears to be arguing for the church to model the justice, love and community that it wants to see in the world, and does not articulate how Baptists should act with others outside the church for justice. So, two competing visions for Baptist engagement in social justice were presented to UK Baptists through publications in the same year.

It can be argued that the writings of the four Baptist theologians studied—Paul Fiddes, Brian Haymes, Richard Kidd, and Nigel Wright—can contribute to strengthening a Baptist theological ethic for the practice of social justice.[26] The addresses of several BUGB presidents—Colin Marchant, Roy Jenkins, Brian Haymes, Fred George, John Rackley, Roy Searle, and Kate Coleman—can also all make helpful contributions.

However, they do not appear to have been listened to during this period. In fact, they were largely ignored. Much of the writing of the four theologians was not widely read in Baptist churches and so did not influence their

21. The public resolutions were formed by Baptist churches and associations in different parts of Wales and England. They do enable us to draw on more diverse sources than the available published literature.

22. *Baptist Times* (Apr. 28, 1988), 1. See sec. 4.2.1.

23. See sec. 5.3.

24. Anne Wilkinson-Hayes, in Finamore, *On Earth*, 3.

25. See sec. 5.3.

26. See sec. 5.5.

practice.[27] As Haymes acknowledges, "Contemporary British Baptists . . . are nothing if not pragmatic. We have a wariness of *theology* for we can fear that it is remote, academic, out of touch with the realities of life, not least in the church."[28] In addition, there was little interaction between the themes focused on by the four theologians and the themes and addresses made at BUW and BUGB Assemblies. There was also little interaction between the assembly public resolutions and addresses, apart from a few exceptions. Finally, Fiddes and Wright did not engage to any great extent with each other's writing in their own publications during the period studied.[29]

Separate strands of thinking and focus developed in the public resolutions passed by the BUW in comparison with the BUGB Assemblies. For example, between 1989 and 1991, the BUW Welsh wing resolutions included the following: welcomed the banning of public drinking by several Welsh councils; opposed the burning of holiday homes as part of Welsh language campaign actions; and supported the call for a new language act to ensure equal status for the Welsh and English languages.[30] In the same years, BUGB resolutions focused on housing and homelessness, and the arms trade, among other issues. Although the two unions rarely focused on the same social justice issue for a resolution in the same year, in both unions' resolutions were often based on issues that were dominating the Welsh or UK political agenda at the time.[31]

However, the approach to these resolutions and their focus revealed a lack of a methodology for listening to others in the examination of which social justice issues should be prioritized for resolutions. They also revealed a lack of a shared methodology for acting together with others on these social justice issues. For example, a BUGB resolution in 1993 on the provision of drug and alcohol treatment locally, and BUGB resolutions in 1994 on lone parent families and on unemployment, encourage churches to contact their MPs but with no mention of calling for action or of holding them accountable publicly for their commitments.[32] In 1999 and again in 2004 there were

27. See sec. 5.5.

28. Haymes, "Still Blessing the Tie," 97; emphasis in original. See sec. 5.4.

29. See sec. 5.4.

30. See sec. 4.2.1—4.2.2. The Welsh language and Welsh-speaking rural communities remained a regular focus for BUW Welsh wing resolutions; for example, there were further resolutions on these in 1994 and 2001.

31. However, there appears to be a further disconnect, a disconnect between the BUW and BUGB during the period studied, in that it is unclear what interaction or sharing there was between the two unions beyond mentions of representatives at each other's assemblies, and the rare occurrence when the two unions picked up on the same issue for a public resolution.

32. See sec. 4.2.2.

BUGB public resolutions on refugees and asylum seekers, but again with no accompanying approach to take action on this as a justice issue.[33] In addition to the public resolutions, the presidential addresses and writings of the theologians gave little indication of a proposed methodology.

Regarding the disconnect between the two unions in Wales and England, we can add the disconnection and separate strands in thinking and practice between mainly smaller and economically poorer churches meeting in inner cities and larger and economically wealthier churches in suburban areas, especially in England. This appears to have contributed to the lack of understanding of the reality and experiences of people at the margins in Wales and England. Although Haymes, Kidd, and Fiddes made explicit mention of visiting and being influenced by their time with churches and communities in Africa and Latin America, I contended that much of the writing of these three theologians and that of Wright was out of an English context and for an English context, rather than a Welsh context. In addition, it was largely for Baptist churches in more suburban contexts, rather than inner cities.

I argued that this is particularly true of Wright. His description of an ideal church appears to be that of a large church, meeting in the suburbs, rather than a small inner-city church.[34] In addition, we observed that Wright "takes as his primary community of reference the Baptist churches of England."[35] Therefore, his focus was on the English rather than the Welsh context.

As we established, the Welsh-language wing of the BUW could be seen as quite different in its context, outlook and focus, and more attuned to the social justice issues facing communities where the churches met. These separate strands in thinking and practice between inner-city and suburban churches and the disconnection between them also become important when considering the resolutions brought to the annual assemblies and the overall focus of discussions. I have argued that the BUGB overall was not listening to, nor seeing discussions on mission from, the perspective of impoverished and marginalized people.[36]

Marchant, as BUGB president in 1988–89, focused on urban mission from his experience in inner-city East London. He brought the everyday experiences and perspectives of people at the margins into discussions of mission. Marchant argued,

33. See sec. 4.2.2—4.2.3.

34. See sec. 5.3.

35. Wright, *Free Church, Free State*, xxvi. See sec. 5.4.

36. See sec. 4.3.1.

> In a black church you can't just sing hymns and forget that some of your congregation got roughed up last night and your kids are unemployed. The point is this, the gospel has no cutting edge unless you are addressing the issues that are bugging your people daily.[37]

Marchant's focus is one example of Baptist engagement in social action and social justice during the period, particularly in the context of urban mission. There was real concern about urban collapse in inner-city areas with growing unemployment and poverty, poor housing and racial justice issues.[38] However, there is the question of why this was not taken up by the BUW or the BUGB.[39] Disconnection seems to be part of the answer to this question. The 1980s was a period with a strong sense of separation between the impoverished inner cities and the economically wealthier suburbs and "middle England."[40] In this context churches were struggling with how to respond. I have argued that the perspectives and voices of Black Baptist churches, mainly meeting in inner cities, were largely left unheard by the wider union.[41] Listening closely to these and working from their perspective may have led to an increased priority on social justice and a stronger Baptist theological ethic of social justice.

As we noted in chapter 4, Jenkins, in his presidential address in 1991, underlined that

> many [churches supported by BUGB grants] are in the poorest areas of our country. Their members maintain a constant and wearying struggle against indifference, vandalism and the despair bred by generations of deprivation. They witness to a God who sets value on the people of such communities when so many of the structures of society render them worthless. By faithful

37. *Baptist Times* (Apr. 28, 1988), 15. See sec. 4.2.1.

38. This context is much changed as a result of the ongoing gentrification of inner-city areas in London and elsewhere since the 1980s.

39. Some Baptists were involved in social action and social justice through ecumenical rather than Baptist initiatives, such as Oasis Trust, Community Action Networks, and the Evangelical Coalition for Urban Mission. These local incidental initiatives were neither integrated into policy of the Baptist unions nor discussed by the Baptist theologians we have reviewed.

40. Paul Cloke and Mike Pears explore the importance of considering place and space in urban mission theology in their trilogy of books, *Mission in Marginal Places*. This approach provides another way to explain why there was so much separation and disconnection between suburban and inner-city Baptist churches in their understanding of social issues in urban areas.

41. See sec. 4.2.2—4.2.3, 4.3.1.

> proclamation and caring action, they point to the Christ who can set them free in the middle of their need.[42]

Jenkins then argued passionately that "if we are to cry freedom for the world with any credibility, we dare not fail to notice what is on our own doorsteps."[43] I understand that he was seeking to address the disconnect present in discussions at a national level in the BUGB and to strengthen a Baptist understanding of social justice. It is important to explore how a Baptist theological ethic develops out of the experiences of people often on the margins of communities and churches. We will consider this further in the next section.

We noted that the BUGB and BUW Assemblies had a focus on mission every year, yet generally they did not understand social justice as a key part of mission.[44] So, although mission was high on the agenda, social justice was not. In numerous assemblies, for example in 1992, 1993, 1994, and 2001, the emphasis was on evangelism in discussing mission. Mission was generally understood as evangelism, rather than a holistic understanding combining evangelism and social justice. A further disconnect is that Baptist discussions on ecumenical engagement were largely separated out from discussions on mission. We concluded that Baptist churches in the BUGB and in the BUW English wing did not have a strong understanding that social justice could be practiced through working with other church denominations and other organizations locally or nationally.[45]

Many strands of Baptist thinking continued to be understood as separate during this period. In some cases, these were becoming further apart. The fabric of Baptist church organization was also unravelling, at least to some extent. Haymes understood in 1986 that "associational life is marginal to most congregation," and argued that "associating with other congregations should not be *marginal* to the life of Baptist churches."[46] As we noted from the focus of several publications by the four UK Baptist theologians covered in chapter 5, such as *The Nature of the Assembly*, *Something to Declare*, *On the Way of Trust*, and *Relating and Resourcing*, associating between Baptist churches in associations and at assembly became even more marginal to the life of most Baptist churches over the following years. There are no longer any public resolutions sessions in the BUGB and BUW Assemblies. Thus, the opportunity to listen to the experience of impoverished and marginalized people in associations

42. Jenkins, *Cry Freedom!*, 7. See sec. 4.2.2.

43. Jenkins, *Cry Freedom!*, 11.

44. See sec. 4.3.2.

45. See sec. 4.3.3.

46. Haymes, *Question of Identity*, 11. See sec. 5.2.

and to discuss and agree public resolutions on social justice issues at national Baptist assemblies was lost. It can be argued that this needs to be challenged.

We observed that discussions on mission and covenant were not brought together in BUGB and BUW Assemblies.[47] However, Fiddes revealed that mission and covenant are intertwined. He understood that the missionary God is also the covenant-making God. Fiddes argued that this perspective has implications for the character of the mission in which the church is engaged. Thus, mission is "essentially relational, essentially a matter of making communion and community."[48] In addition, Kidd understood that covenant language "is still the best and theologically most consistent focus around which to be gathered, and on which to build our future strategies for mission."[49] In section 6.4 we will focus on how covenantal relationships can strengthen a Baptist theological ethic of social justice through helping make connections where there have been disconnects.

6.2.2 Where and How the Six Principles Were Picked Up in Baptist Discussions and Writing

The previous section has highlighted a number of separate strands in the thinking and practice of Baptists in Wales and England during the period studied. These separate strands contributed to the lack of a strong shared Baptist theological ethic for the practice of social justice. In this section, I will summarize from the analysis in chapters 4–5 where the writings of the four theologians and Baptist assembly resolutions and presentations picked up on the six principles that I extrapolated in chapter 3. These represent current theological reflections on community organizing and so, at least to some extent, weave together these various Baptist discussions and writings. To recap, these principles are solidarity, subsidiarity, the common good, neighboring, listening, and centering the margins. I produced definitions for each of these principles to be used in this book, considering all the voices engaged in chapter 3.

Solidarity is defined as the rediscovery of the radical shared interest held between people in fraternal relationships, as a key part of being human. Solidarity especially means radical shared interest with impoverished and marginalized people. We were made in God for fraternal relationships. Anything

47. For in-depth analysis of mission and covenant and how these were separate groups of discussion in the BUGB during this period, see Goodliff, *Renewing a Modern Denomination*.

48. Fiddes, *Tracks and Traces*, 253. See sec. 5.4.

49. Kidd, *Something to Declare*, 16. See sec. 5.3.

which disrupts solidarity should be resisted. So, part of the work of solidarity is countering its disruption.

Subsidiarity brings together the importance of action together by people and institutions on issues facing people, with the principle that decisions should be taken and carried out as close as possible to the people they affect. In addition, those who are impoverished and marginalized should become active citizens in decisions on issues which affect them.

The common good advances towards the well-being of the community measured by such things as justice, peace and flourishing. It is best achieved through a communicative process involving all stakeholders in the community.

Neighborliness brings together a communal commitment to a particular people and place and encourages public relationships to be formed and strengthened between people. This neighborliness is motivated by seeking to love our neighbor and incorporates love of the stranger, the enemy and the friendless. Neighborliness thus recognizes the power dynamics that exist in a neighborhood and seeks to change how this power is distributed.

Listening is where we should always start as churches, with attentiveness to those in the church and to neighbors in community, alongside attentiveness to our tradition and Scripture. In this it is to whom we are listening that matters. Listening well will involve listening to impoverished and powerless people and those at the margins of churches and communities, and so listening for the prophetic minority.

Centering the margins means starting from the perspective of those currently impoverished and on the margins. It then means enabling these people to increase their power and sense of dignity and for their priorities to be the basis for action together on these priorities, which is rooted in their experience and values.

From the analysis in chapters 4–5, connections were made most strongly with these six principles in four main areas. First, in relation to understanding and focusing on the context and lived experience of impoverished and marginalized people. Second, in relation to why and how to work together with others. Third, in thinking about the mission of God beyond the actions of local Baptist churches. Fourth, in relation to covenantal relationships. We will now consider each of these in turn.

6.2.2.1 The Context and Lived Experience of Impoverished and Marginalized People

In this section, we will consider the strongest links made in relation to understanding and focusing on the context and lived experience of impoverished and marginalized people. Coleman's theme in 2006 was "Centring the Margins." She highlighted that

> the centre of God's activity usually lies in the margins of human activity. . . . The centre of God's concern usually lies somewhere in the margins of our own concerns. . . If you want to find out what God is doing, look to what is sidelined and marginalised. Somewhere right there you will find God powerfully at work.[50]

In addition to the principle of centering the margins, Coleman also connects strongly with listening to people at the margins.[51] Both Marchant and Jenkins, as we noted earlier, highlighted the lived experience of impoverished and marginalized people in the UK and the importance of bringing their experiences more centrally into discussions about mission as a union. George highlighted the importance of tackling injustice in relation to "all who are abandoned to a life of powerlessness and poverty by the political and economic structures of our day."[52] In this we therefore again have a strong link to the principles of centering the margins and solidarity. Jenkins highlights "the God who leads his people out of captivity in Egypt, who raises up prophets to denounce corrupt rulers, who places himself firmly on the side of the victim, is the God who intends freedom—*life in all its fullness*—for every individual and every community."[53] This resonates with the principle of centering the margins.

David Quinney-Mee, as part of the Broad Alliance of Radical Baptists, highlighted this principle and also that of solidarity when he focused on learning from the experience of the church in Latin America and what it means to be "alongside the poor," and "witness among the poor and marginalised in our own society."[54] Haymes, a year later, again made the link to centering the margins through starting from the perspective of those currently impoverished and on the margins. In also drawing on the experience of churches in Latin America, he highlighted "our sisters and brothers in the so-called third world have much to give us here, especially in those situations where the cause of liberation is being lived and died for."[55] In addition, Haymes highlighted the importance of solidarity with and listening to these churches, as well as to Baptist churches engaging with impoverished communities in England.

50. *Baptist Times* (May 4, 2006), 12.
51. See sec. 4.2.3.
52. *Baptist Times* (May 1, 1997), 1. See sec. 4.2.2.
53. Jenkins, *Cry Freedom!*, 2; emphasis in original. See sec. 4.2.2.
54. *Baptist Times* (May 7, 1992), 3. See sec. 4.2.2.
55. Haymes, *Fullness of Christ*, 6–7. See sec. 4.2.2.

From the analysis in chapter 5, we noted the influence of theologies of liberation, and particularly Latin American liberation theology, on the writings of Haymes and Kidd.[56] Kidd proposed a liberating Baptist agenda developed through a liberation theology approach, which would keep "us living near an edge . . . [as it is] on the edge where the reality of God has been and is most strongly made known."[57] In addition, Fiddes also made the link to solidarity and centering the margins through drawing on the El Salvadorean liberation theologian Jon Sobrino, and noted that "we shall only find the meaning of the cross by entering into its experience, which means engaging ourselves with the cause of those who are poor and who suffer injustice. The cross . . . invites us to participate in a process within which we can actually experience history as salvation."[58] Fiddes argued that "the church begins to engage in politics when the humiliated and crucified Christ is *recognised* among groups and classes who are discriminated against and unjustly treated."[59] Here, we again observed a link to the principle of centering the margins, where we see God at work. Finally, in their writing together, Fiddes, Haymes, and Kidd highlighted that acting as a union of churches "can keep us attentive to crucial prophetic voices speaking to us all from the margins."[60] The importance of listening to impoverished and marginalized people is thus again highlighted.

6.2.2.2 Baptist Churches Working Together with Others

Let us consider the links made in relation to why and how Baptist churches can work together with others. Drawing again on the thoughts of Quinney-Mee, for him, in the context of poverty and injustice, "cooperation between Baptists, Anglicans, Roman Catholics and others was . . . a matter of practical solidarity with, and active listening to, the poor."[61] Quinney-Mee argued,

> The critical issue between different churches and theological traditions was not resolving the differences, which had to be respected, but how we respond to the poor. It is better to do that together, if we are committed, in the name of Christ, to ending their suffering.[62]

56. See sec. 5.5.
57. Kidd, "Baptists and Theologies," 52. See sec. 5.4.
58. Fiddes, *Past Event and Present Salvation*, 195. See sec. 5.2.
59. Fiddes, *Past Event and Present Salvation*, 199; emphasis in original.
60. Kidd, *On the Way of Trust*, 38. See sec. 5.3.
61. See sec. 4.2.2.
62. *Baptist Times* (May 7, 1992), 3.

Thus, as we noted before, strong connections are made to the principles of solidarity and listening. Then, Haymes also makes these connections to these principles and to the common good when he highlighted that being involved in God's mission in the world "is something that we can only do together."[63] Rackley also made strong links to the principles of solidarity, the common good, listening and centering the margins. He highlighted that

> we have many fellow travellers beyond the Church. There is much seeking of God beyond our numbers. . . . So, our calling to explore God must take us beyond our walls, and groups and fellowships. Our missionary task is to accompany others in their search. . . . A missionary Church explores the paths of God beyond itself.[64]

Here Rackley is also thinking about the mission of God beyond the actions of local Baptist churches, the focus of our third area where strong connections are made. Similarly, Fiddes argued that the presence of Christ can be met in the community of the church or the community of the wider world.[65] Fiddes, Haymes, and Kidd encouraged Baptists to be more open to wider society, to connect with others, and in this they highlighted the importance of listening. As Fiddes argued, a local church "will always be open to listen to the voices of others, aware that it is dependent upon their help in finding the mind of Christ, whether the voices come from wider groupings of churches or from society outside the church."[66] Haymes argued that Baptists are called to be immersed in their wider communities, "with all the moral and political implications that go with sharing a common life."[67] He thus makes strong connections to the principles of solidarity, common good and neighborliness without using these terms. It can be concluded that all these writers are offering a clear challenge to Baptists.

6.2.2.3 *The Mission of God Beyond the Actions of Local Baptist Churches*

We can now consider the links made to these principles in thinking about the mission of God beyond the actions of local Baptist churches. Fiddes, in his only address so far to a BUGB Assembly, underlined that "we do not make

63. Haymes, *Fullness of Christ*, 6.

64. *Baptist Times* (May 8, 2003), 13. See sec. 4.2.3.

65. Fiddes, *Past Event and Present Salvation*, 165.

66. Fiddes, *Reflections on the Water*, 65. See sec. 5.3.

67. Haymes, "Baptism as a Political Act," 80. See sec. 5.3.

mission: God calls us to join him in the mission he is already carrying out." Fiddes argued that this means, "as we share the journey of the Son of God, we must also travel out of ourselves, die to the familiar, and open ourselves to what is foreign and strange, if we are to be any use to God in his desire to bring reconciliation to a broken world."[68] He continued by underlining that this "mission must mean getting deeply involved in the world God has made, and being identified with those on the margins."[69] So, here again we see connections to the principles of solidarity and centering the margins. Bruce highlighted Fiddes's description of God making a journey into the far country on the journey of salvation, and that God is found in the "far country" in mission among the people and communities to which the gospel is addressed.[70] Thus, we again observe connections with solidarity and centering the margins. Bruce then went on to connect this with seeking the common good.[71] Roy Searle also picked up on these principles, describing mission not as an activity, but reflecting "the heart of God" and "giving away what is not ours to own or control."[72]

6.2.2.4 *Covenantal Relationships*

Finally, let us briefly consider the links made to the six principles in relation to covenantal relationships. Importantly, these connections were made in the writings of Fiddes, Haymes, and Kidd and not in the assembly resolutions and addresses. They argued,

> In covenant together we are willing to hear what Christ has to say to us through the weakest members of the Body, those who seem in the eyes of the world the most insignificant. In finding the mind of Christ we need to listen to the marginalised, the overlooked, with whom he identifies himself.[73]

Thus, there is a strong connection made to the principles of listening and centering the margins. Fiddes, Haymes, and Kidd also made an explicit mention of solidarity in arguing that associating allows those seen as strong to learn from the marginalized and weakest, "to allow the weak to give something to the strong . . . this is solidarity in covenant with each other and with Christ."[74]

68. *Baptist Times* (Apr. 29, 1993), 5. See sec. 4.2.2.
69. *Baptist Times* (Apr. 29, 1993), 5.
70. Bruce, "Exploring the Far Country," 12–13. See sec. 5.3.
71. See sec. 5.3.
72. *Baptist Times* (Apr. 21, 2005), 13. See sec. 4.2.3.
73. Kidd, *Something to Declare*, 35.
74. Kidd, *Something to Declare*, 35–36. See sec. 5.3.

Fiddes, Haymes, and Kidd's writing demonstrates the most extensive links with the six principles. Fiddes understands that covenant and participation are held together, a covenant not just with God, but in God. For Fiddes, the Baptist understanding of covenant, centered in the language of walking together, is relational language and implies openness and trust and being on a journey together. Thus, the focus is on covenant theology that is about relationships and journeying together with others which can be related to the principles of solidarity, listening and centering the margins.

In section 6.4, I will develop further the connections we can make between these principles and covenantal relationships. I will also examine how focusing on covenantal relationships can strengthen both a Baptist theological ethic for social justice and community organizing. However, before this, in the next section we will examine how practicing the six principles can strengthen a Baptist theological ethic.

6.3 How the Six Principles Can Strengthen a Baptist Theological Ethic for Social Justice

The synthesis of chapters 4–5 underlines the lack of a shared methodology for listening to people and communities—particularly those that are impoverished and marginalized—to discover their priorities and their solutions on issues of social injustice. It also underlines the lack of a shared understanding of, and approach to, working with other churches and other organizations in civil society. This synthesis also demonstrated that, when these themes were being recognized as important for Baptist engagement, strong links were made with the principles of centering the margins, listening, solidarity and the common good. Thus, in section 6.3.1 we will focus on how listening to impoverished and marginalized people, and ensuring that their perspectives are central to discussions, can strengthen a Baptist theological ethic. In section 6.3.2, we will focus on how bringing listening and centering the margins together with the principles of solidarity and the common good when Baptists assemble together locally can also strengthen a Baptist theological ethic.

6.3.1 Listening

In this part of the argument, we will consider how listening can strengthen a Baptist theological ethic. First, as noted earlier, listening is of central importance in community organizing. Having brought together a broad alliance of churches and other institutions, the next step in making social change through organizing is listening.[75] This listening identifies issues on which to act together. A key quote used by Citizens UK when talking about listening is from Dietrich Bonhoeffer: "The first service that one owes to others in the fellowship consists in listening to them. . . . Those who cannot listen long and patiently will always be talking past others, and finally will no longer even notice it. . . . The death of the spiritual life starts here."[76] Bonhoeffer's thinking about this way of listening is in the context of fellowship understood as sharing and holding in common with a diverse community, rather than a specific church fellowship group. While Bonhoeffer wrote this in 1939, it seems just as relevant today.

Second, listening well is about solidarity, neighborliness, and restoring and building relationships in our communities. From engaging with Fiddes, all six principles involve thinking about relationships.[77] The reason for listening is theological. It starts from a belief that God is already in the situation. We are seeking to hear what God has to say through people and through a situation, based on an understanding that God is involved in the world. So, it is important to listen and through listening we might learn something more about God and about how we should act in a situation.[78]

Third, engaging with the understanding of listening through theological reflection on community organizing strengthens an understanding of to whom Baptists should be listening. Bretherton understands the importance of listening, which "assumes the poor have something to teach the privileged about how to live and that a common life between them is necessary to the flourishing of each and the flourishing of all."[79]

In *God of the Oppressed*, Cone argues that "one's social and historical context decides not only the questions we address to God but also the mode or form of the answers given to the questions."[80] Cone explores this with particular reference to the contrasting ways that Black and white people think about God. Cone reveals that when Black and white people are speaking about God and Jesus they are not referring to the same reality as they are experiencing life

75. See sec. 1.3, 2.4.

76. Bonhoeffer, *Life Together*.

77. See sec. 5.4.

78. In ch. 1 of *Outside-In*, John Weaver, UK Baptist theologian and former BUGB president, outlines three key questions for theological reflection: What does this say about God; what does it say about God's desire for our life; and what does it say about the ways in which God works in the world?

79. Bretherton, *Christ and the Common Life*, 78. See sec. 3.6.

80. Cone, *God of the Oppressed*, 14.

and the world differently.[81] Cone highlights that "after being told six days of the week that they were nothings by the rulers of white society, on the Sabbath, the first day of the week, black people went to church in order to experience another definition of their humanity."[82] From this, I understand we should listen to those with direct experience of an issue. Finding these people will come from listening and building relationships. This section therefore builds on the earlier analysis in section 6.2.2.1 on listening to those at the margins.

A good example of listening to the voices of marginalized people is seen in Bob Holman's book *Faith in the Poor*, where he records the voices of poor people telling their own stories of dealing with poverty in Easterhouse, Glasgow. In doing so they find power and dignity as they themselves tell their own story. This approach to listening is seeking to address the challenge, where Baptists were not listening to marginalized and impoverished people, that was highlighted by Marchant, George, Searle, and Coleman.

I argue that a Baptist social ethic will be strengthened through listening well to people from within Baptist churches and particularly to those on the margins, both within congregations and the wider community. It is through listening to the margins that we discover where God is at work and where he desires us to focus.

I also argue that it is important to have more reflection from the experiences and perspectives of Black Baptist churches in Britain. This will support the strengthening of a theological ethic to overcome social injustices experienced by marginalized and impoverished people. Anthony Reddie, a UK theologian focused on Black theology, notes that "it has been this [Baptist] form of radical egalitarianism and collectivism that has seen the Baptist tradition become the repository for the development of Black Liberation Theology in the United States and in Jamaica."[83] However, British Baptists have produced very little leadership on Black theology in Britain.[84] So, as Bretherton notes, listening to the margins can profoundly redirect our understanding and how we describe what is going on in a situation.[85] Listening is thus about centering the margins.

It is very important that this listening to people on the margins is practiced, and not just talked or written about. Rowlands argues that we need to be able to hard wire the experiences of those at the margins into decision-making

81. Cone, *God of the Oppressed*, 10.

82. Cone, *God of the Oppressed*, 12. This quote was also used earlier in sec. 3.8.

83. Reddie, "Baptist Identity," 228.

84. Reddie, "Baptist Identity," 229.

85. Bretherton, *Primer in Christian Ethics*, 76.

processes.[86] As Willie James Jennings underlines, "We should work towards a design that aims at an attention that forms deeper habits of attending to one another and to the world around us."[87] And so for Jennings this means being "open toward more intense listening and learning from one another."[88] As Sîan and Stuart Murray-Williams, UK Baptist theologians, argue, being Baptist is about being multivoiced. Listening will seek to draw out the reticent, including the marginalized, listen for the prophetic minority, and develop processes to ensure all are heard.[89] They argue that the weakest voices are often the most important and their voice may well be the prophetic voice in the congregation. The Murray-Williamses understand that a multivoiced approach to discerning "means being open to hearing the voice of God through many different voices," being attentive to quieter and weaker voices as well as more confident voices.[90]

Fourth, what we do with what we have heard is important. When people say they are centering the margins, where do these people think they are positioned?[91] It can be argued that the social structures we are part of have us at the center. So, we need to act intentionally to center the perspectives of those people not currently at the center.

However, there is still a power imbalance at play here. If we say we will make space for you, we are still the ones able to decide who is in and who is out. Looking to the margins is to change how we are living in the empire as Baptists. Hence, Bob Holman enabled marginalized people to write their own stories in their own words.[92]

When Roman Catholic and Anglican theologians write about centering the margins, it appears that they are still considering themselves to be in the center. The Roman Catholic Church in the UK is disestablished, as is the Church in Wales, but both still use the language of the parish with an understanding that they are at the center of the parish.

We might learn from the fact that Baptists in Wales and England were not originally in the center, but they then sought acceptance and recognition.[93]

86. Rowlands, "Mixing Religion and Politics."

87. Jennings, *After Whiteness*, 51.

88. Jennings, *After Whiteness*, 67.

89. Murray-Williams and Murray-Williams, *Multi-Voiced Church*, 7.

90. Murray-Williams and Murray-Williams, *Multi-Voiced Church*, 116.

91. Miguel de la Torre, in his book *Doing Christian Ethics from the Margins*, self-describes himself as at the margins. This is different than us describing other people as on or at the margins.

92. Holman, *Faith in the Poor*, 25–27.

93. See sec. 4.3.1.

Baptists went from being a marginalized and oppressed group to seeking acceptance to then having some degree of power and influence in communities. Many Baptists still practice an understanding of church where they are at the center of things and are able to act alone. However, Baptists in Wales and England do not have the power and influence that they once had. This should encourage Baptists to consider who else is marginalized and does not currently have power within society.

Thus, centering the margins is not just about listening to people currently marginalized and impoverished, but is about seeking the common good through acting to reduce the injustices they face and reducing their economic exploitation by people currently in the center. Being able to assemble and work together with them and others will then be important in making change. This is the challenge for Baptists.

6.3.2 Assembling Together

We will consider how the way Baptists understand assembling together can strengthen a theological ethic. We can therefore build on the earlier analysis in section 6.2.2.2 on the experience of Baptists working together with others. First, let us consider who assembles together. Community organizing assemblies are held in churches, mosques, schools and other settings. Therefore, "community organizing literally draws you out of what is familiar and invites those who are unfamiliar into your sacred spaces."[94] They are about looking outwards rather than inwards. Accountability assemblies in community organizing seek to enable the public accountability of powerful decision-makers as well as demonstrating the people-power of organized civil society.[95] These public assemblies enable people who are too often silenced in political discussions to share their experiences of an injustice and speak truth directly to powerful decision makers who can help make change on this issue. This chimes well with a quote from Thurman, and highlighted by Gushee, that

> fearless truthfulness might also have a surprisingly transformative effect on the oppressor. Powerful people who are not accustomed to being told the truth by those who are "beneath" them can be thrown off balance by no longer being able to validate themselves based on their power.[96]

94. Bretherton, *Christianity and Contemporary Politics*, 103.
95. See sec. 2.4.
96. Gushee, *Introducing Christian Ethics*, 49.

Doing justice with others, in the context of injustice in communities, and holding powerful people accountable, is emphasizing acting for the world as it should be in the world as it is.

Second, we can contrast this understanding of assembling in community organizing with how Baptists assemble when they are gathered together. In writing about Baptist assemblies of churches, Fiddes, in *The Nature of the Assembly*, suggests distinguishing between *a church* (the local congregation), *the church* (universal) and *being church* when Baptists are together in a wider union.[97] Fiddes highlights the importance of listening to one another in assembly and seeking to speak a prophetic word to the principalities and powers of our society.[98] So, this causes Baptists to consider who they assemble with, and what Baptists should do when they assemble. Fiddes understands that when Baptists speak of a *gathered church* this is in response to the Christ who has gathered them.[99] Later, Fiddes argues that this understanding of gathered church "means that the local church is a community which gathers together a whole range of people, cutting across barriers of age, class, culture and temperament. . . . Its strength comes from being a gathering of the 'unlike,' people quite different from each other."[100] This is important in the context of how Baptist churches then gather with others, for example in a wider community organizing assembly or alliance.

Fiddes highlights that what binds people together in this community is not what people have in common, but it is a community of difference. So, it is not what people have in common that brings people together apart from belonging to Christ. However, this only too rarely reflects the reality of local Baptist church congregations. Many Baptist churches consist of people from across a wide area rather than from a local community. In addition, larger churches are often more middle class whereas the smaller churches are often those that gather people from the local area and have proportionally more people from economically deprived backgrounds. Thus, many larger Baptist churches are largely homogenous rather than churches of the "unlike" coming together. In contrast, we might expect smaller churches to be proportionally more heterogeneous. Practicing a stronger theological ethic may mean that when Baptist churches gather and assemble with others, this better reflects the "unlike" coming together and building relationships across difference. However, in reality, the cost of attending assemblies negates the representation of

97. BUGB, *Nature of the Assembly*, 10. See sec. 5.3.

98. BUGB, *Nature of the Assembly*, 24–27.

99. Fiddes, *Tracks and Traces*, 233. See sec. 5.4.

100. Fiddes, *Tracks and Traces*, 254. See sec. 5.4.

marginalized people. This is a challenge for how assemblies are organized, and how impoverished and marginalized people are able to participate.

Third, let us consider why churches assemble together with other organizations. I argue that they should assemble in solidarity, to build relationships, to listen, to center the margins and to seek the common good. It can be argued that Baptist churches should be challenged to do this. Ivereigh linked solidarity with accountability assemblies and had a chapter in *Faithful Citizens* entitled "Assembling in Solidarity."[101] He described an assembly as "a 'civic congregation' where people of different faiths and none who live alongside each other express the hopes and frustrations they share for the city, commit to working in solidarity with each other for the common good, and hold people with power to account."[102] People who are on the margins of their communities or institutions play central roles in these assemblies and relationships are built across difference. Thus, this builds on the analysis in 6.2.2.1 on bringing the experience of impoverished and marginalized people into the center through assemblies and social justice campaigns.

It can be argued that the gathering of the "unlike" does not address the challenges people and communities experiencing injustices face. Similarly, it can also be argued that solidarity, centering the margins and the common good are not just about the 'unlike' coming together. Instead, these principles are about working for social justice for all, making change with people, and not just accepting them as part of a local church. Thus, I argue this will mean giving central importance to hearing from those on the margins. Assembling in solidarity will also then mean coming together to tackle social injustices.

So, it can be seen that a key question is how we enable Baptists to engage in assemblies with others, and encourage Baptist churches to see that this is part of the church's mission of being Christ in and for the world. Community organizing focuses on solidarity and can increase the sense of community and so counter the ever-increasing sense of individualism. It can be argued that Baptists need this perspective to deepen the understanding of what it means to be part of a union of Baptist churches. Community organizing focuses on commonality and community rather than individualism, and the building of reciprocal relationships and "political friendships" between churches and other organizations. It can cause us to consider how churches join in a life that is greater than their own. I suggest that a key area for Baptist churches is to

101. See sec. 3.2.

102. Ivereigh, *Faithful Citizens*, 71. In this chapter Ivereigh focuses on the same London Citizens assembly in Nov. 2009 that Bretherton uses powerfully in the opening chapter of his book *Resurrecting Democracy*.

recognize that they do not have to rely on their own power and organization alone in seeking to be involved in transforming communities. As Lee argues,

> Christians are tasked with the responsibility to work with others in order to organise institutions and society afresh. Christians do not have to rely on their own power and organisation alone. . . . They need to build coalitions with non-Christians. Bridging work in community organizing is a concrete way to practice the covenantal principle of unity-in-diversity [solidarity], the vision of a life together.[103]

Thus, it can be argued that assembling with others in solidarity should be at the center of a Baptist theological ethic. The challenge is to enable marginalized and impoverished people to participate, and when they do attend to enable their voices to be heard.

In this section, we have noted how the principles can all come together to strengthen a Baptist theological ethic, particularly in relation to listening and assembling together with others. In the next section, I will bring together the six principles with covenantal relationships. I will argue that the community organizing practices of listening and accountability assemblies can help Baptists understand how to act in covenantal relationships.[104] I will argue that this can also help us move from what can be seen as a static form of assembling together to something more dynamic.

6.4 How Covenantal Relationships Can Strengthen a Baptist Theological Ethic for Social Justice and Strengthen Community Organizing

We examined in the previous section how listening and assembling together, two key practices in community organizing, can help strengthen a Baptist theological ethic for social justice. We noted the need to find a way to move beyond a "static" view of assembling together to a more "dynamic" understanding.

Bretherton draws on covenant language in writing about community organizing.[105] Covenant language was developed by Baptists and other early dissenters in the seventeenth century, in focusing on building strong relationships between members of an individual congregation in the context of

103. Lee, *Christian Ethics*, 95.

104. It is important to emphasize that community organizing does not stop with accountability assemblies. Instead, these are just one important milestone on a long road to building relationship and making change.

105. See sec. 1.4.

persecution and oppression. These Baptist churches also brought together people who were "unlike," and they formed covenants across difference. Baptists adopted a covenantal life to walk together and watch over each other in love.

The writings of Paul Fiddes provide a precedent for Baptist thinking in exploring covenantal relationships and integrating the six principles. From our analysis in chapters 4–5, Fiddes emerged as the most promising of the interlocutors quoted in our analysis of Baptist thinking and writing from the period studied. I will propose that an understanding of covenantal relationships based on the writing of Fiddes helps enable us to move to a more dynamic understanding of assembling, building relationships with others, and organizing together in communities.

In this understanding, part of a church's covenant is always an engagement with its neighbors and the wider world and not just with its own church community. I will demonstrate how this can be brought together and strengthened by incorporation of the additional understanding of covenant ethics presented by Bretherton and Lee. I will outline how this understanding of covenantal relationships can help weave together the six principles extrapolated from current theological reflection on community organizing. Through bringing together community organizing theological reflections and Baptist theological reflections, I therefore argue that covenantal relationships can strengthen both a Baptist theological ethic and also the understanding and practice of community organizing. Thus, I build on Fiddes's thinking on covenant relationships and integrate this theme into community organizing.

The recovery of the term covenantal relationships is relatively recent among UK Baptists. Fiddes, Haymes, and Kidd were among a group who wrote *Bound to Love* in 1985.[106] This considered how the concept of covenant provides a theological basis for Baptist life and mission. Now, almost forty years on from the recovery of the term's use, Baptists in Wales and England do talk about churches being covenanted together. Covenant language is embedded at the level of the BUGB. However, there is often a relatively weak understanding of covenant at the level of local Baptist churches.

For Fiddes, in *Bound to Love*, to speak of covenant is not to speak of something static, but dynamic.[107] Thus, rather than a fixed relationship between a specific group of people in a specific place, covenantal relationships formed by God are open ended and wide ranging. We also observed that "walking together and watching over each other" was a common way in the seventeenth

106. See sec. 5.2.

107. Fiddes, *Bound to Love*, 5. See sec. 5.2.

century for Baptists to talk about fellowship together.[108] Covenants helped Baptists gather together across difference. Covenantal relationships recover this idea today.

Below is part of the wording in Welsh and English of the covenant for Coleg y Bedyddwyr Caerdydd/Cardiff Baptist College where I am a tutor:

> *Heddiw, rydyn ni'n ymrwymo ein hunain unwaith eto i'n gilydd ac i'n Harglwydd ni.*
> *Rydyn ni'n cyfamodi i wylio ein gilydd gyda chariad, ac i gerdded gyda Duw, mewn ffyrdd adnabyddus, yn ogystal â'r rhai sydd anhysbys eto.*
> *Rydyn ni'n rhoi popeth sydd gennym a phopeth yr ydym i fwriadau datblygol cariad Duw*
>
> This day we give ourselves again to each other and to our Lord.
> We covenant to watch over one another and to walk together with God, in ways known and still to be made known.
> We commit all that we have and all that we are to God's unfolding purposes of love.

These words are not exclusive to this Baptist college. They are used weekly in college prayers to express together how we seek to live together as a college community.

However, the language of covenant and walking together and watching over each other in Baptist churches has often been understood as focused on relationships within a local church, rather than about walking together with the whole of society. Thus, it can be seen as an inward-focused idea rather than as something connected to strengthening Baptist church engagement in working together with others on social justice issues.

But this is not how Fiddes understands covenantal relationships. In these relationships God is drawing people together and binding people together.[109] People do not choose who they are gathering with. Churches should become places for the marginalized, and as groups of the "unlike" gathered together in relationship for participation in the gathered Christian community as well as wider society. Only seeing covenantal relationships as something formed within church congregations also speaks to a "cramped" Baptist vision where all the action of what God is doing in the world is in the life of the local congregation. This vision is too small.

Fiddes underlines that while "the church offers the context for a 'particular' covenant . . . others outside the community of the church will . . . be

108. See sec. 5.4.

109. See sec. 5.4.

living in another covenant."[110] Thus, Fiddes develops an understanding of covenantal relationships in which churches can join in with covenantal relationships that God forms in the wider community. Fiddes is keen to highlight that this does not mean that this is the same kind of covenant that God makes with churches, nor does it take away responsibility for churches to be involved in mission. These relationships should encourage Baptist churches in their relationships with others beyond the church, and Fiddes understands that "God has many covenant relationships of which we are scarcely aware."[111]

Fiddes highlights how the idea of covenant makes sense of complicated and challenging relationships in a community. Covenant theology can be understood as weaving strands together. Through merging the Trinitarian theology of "participating in God" with the ecclesiology of "covenant," Fiddes understands that we can see how there are different kinds of covenant between God and created beings, just as human persons participate in God in different ways and at different depths of commitment. Not all relations are the same, and not all covenants are the same.[112] Fiddes, Haymes, and Kidd have all brought concerns for peace and justice in the wider world into a theology of covenant. They led the revival of covenant theology and took it in new directions. They proffer a more expansive and open-ended approach to covenantal relationships, and provide the grounding for working together with others. They develop covenant theology in asking how it can be made much more outward-focused. Their understanding of covenant, which enables churches to act with others for change in wider society, aligns with Bretherton and Lee's use of covenant as we will explore next.

Covenant has been used as a theme in thinking about community organizing, not just from a Christian perspective, but also from a Muslim perspective. In chapter 1 we observed that there was a Citizens UK publication in 2012 entitled *A New Covenant of Virtue: Islam and Community Organizing.*[113] Bretherton picked up on this covenant language from Jewish and Muslim leaders as well as from Christian leaders engaged in community organizing in London. Although Bretherton does not specify covenant as a framework of community organizing for Christians, he understands "the term 'community' in the term 'community organising' to denote a coming together by mutual agreement of distinct institutions for a common purpose without loss of each

110. Fiddes, "Participation," 162.

111. Paul S. Fiddes, in Goodliff, "*Renewing a Modern Denomination* Launch." See sec. 5.4.

112. Fiddes, preface to *Covenant and Church*, 1–2.

113. Ali et al., *New Covenant of Virtue*. See sec. 1.4.

of their specific identities or beliefs and practices."[114] Bretherton concludes in *Resurrecting Democracy* that "community organising is one form covenantal citizenship may take."[115] In *Christ and the Common Life*, Bretherton again brings a covenantal approach and focus on covenantal associations. Bretherton understands that "a person-in-relation or covenantal approach [to democratic politics] envisages politics not as a domain of self-expression but as one arena among others in which we discover how we are always already constituted through relationship with others."[116]

Bretherton recognizes that we need to reorder these relationships so that all may flourish. Bretherton then argues that "community organising exemplifies a politics that prioritises the relationship between distinct but reciprocally related 'consociations' or covenantal associations."[117] Through this, politics can then contribute to flourishing lives and communities. We should do this because we are called to love our neighbors. So, as Bretherton argues, "politics is not merely an arena for practicing neighbour love; it can of itself be a form of neighbour love."[118] Where Bretherton's understanding of covenant comes closest to Fiddes is when Bretherton understands that "we are always already entangled in and constituted through the lives of others,"[119] and "our lives are interwoven in seen and unseen ways."[120] The implication for Baptists covenanting together is that they should think, listen and speak more widely.

Let us now consider how Hak Joon Lee's understanding of covenantal ethics relates to Fiddes and Bretherton. I have used the metaphor of weaving to explore how a church engages with the wider community beyond the church congregation, where others may also be involved in the mission of God without acknowledging this as the source and motivation of their actions. This understanding of community organizing as reweaving civil society is also picked up by Lee, who argues that a covenantal approach to organizing is "instrumental in reconstituting and interweaving civil society."[121] Lee understands this reweaving of civil society to be a constant work in progress, to repair the damage done, to receive new members, and to adapt to ongoing political and cultural changes.

114. Bretherton, *Resurrecting Democracy*, 241.
115. Bretherton, *Resurrecting Democracy*, 284.
116. Bretherton, *Christ and the Common Life*, 429.
117. Bretherton, *Christ and the Common Life*, 430.
118. Bretherton, *Christ and the Common Life*, 4.
119. Bretherton, *Primer in Christian Ethics*, 82.
120. Bretherton, *Primer in Christian Ethics*, 88.
121. Lee, *God and Community Organizing*, 199.

Lee brings covenantal theology into dialogue with Alinsky's model of community organizing and uses this to model a Christian communal response to contemporary challenges facing society.[122] In contrast to Bretherton, in *God and Community Organizing* Lee argues that covenant can be a framework for community organizing for Christians. Lee compares organizing based on an understanding of God's covenant, what he terms *covenantal organizing*, with community organizing. He understands that both see organizing as key to a common life, both are focused on justice, and both are about gathering and bringing people together. In addition, both see marginalized people as the subjects of organizing, and both are focused on empowerment of marginalized people and a transformation of their situation.[123] Both also focus on building broad alliances or coalitions.

Lee agrees with Bretherton that organizing is "an indispensable aspect of a common life and politics, and the task of politics is to organise a common life according to the principles of justice."[124] Lee presents "covenant as the primary method of God's organizing of a new just community. . . . By entering God's covenant, humans become God's co-workers in building a new community."[125] In covenants, people are bound to God and to each other. Lee highlights that

> from a covenantal perspective, the Creation Covenant and the Noahic Covenant offer theological grounds for compact and coalition with non-Christians; both are inclusive covenants that God made with the representatives of all humanity . . . binding the entire human population regardless of faith response, beyond particular religious communities.[126]

From this it can therefore be seen that Lee, like Fiddes, understands that God forms covenants with people and institutions beyond the church. However, what Lee then does is to outline how covenantal relationships, and ethics built on covenant, enable churches to be able to participate with others. This is something which Fiddes hints at in highlighting the connection between

122. It is important to highlight that in his exploration and analysis, Lee constantly refers to "Alinsky's community organizing" (*God and Community Organizing*). He does not give the sense that he has engaged with how community organizing and its approach was reshaped by Chambers, Cortes, Gecan, and Graf following Alinsky's death as we observed in ch. 1. Nor does Lee recognize the importance of Black Baptist churches to community organizing alliances in the US.

123. Lee, *God and Community Organizing*, 162.

124. Lee, *God and Community Organizing*, 172.

125. Lee, *God and Community Organizing*, xiv.

126. Lee, *God and Community Organizing*, 171.

covenantal relationships and acting for justice. Then Lee, partly drawing on Bretherton, makes this explicit. Gushee then links this to acting together with others in democratic participation.

Lee makes the case that covenant is the central organizing category of Jewish and Christian theology and ethics. In *Christian Ethics: A New Covenant Model* Lee brings together ethics, community organizing, and covenant thinking. It presents new covenant ethics "as a plausible paradigm of Christian ethics."[127] As Lee notes, "The new covenant of Jesus was radical . . . he redefined the boundaries, structure and meaning of the community by including people previously excluded." Thus, for Lee, covenant is liberating and focused on relationships.[128] Here Lee agrees with Bretherton and Fiddes. Lee defines covenant as "a communicative mechanism that *justly* organizes the *powers* and commitment of people into a *loving* fellowship, with shalom as the ultimate goal."[129] As with Fiddes, Lee's understanding of ethics based on covenant "applies not only to the church but also society and its institutions." He highlights that the ecumenical and public engagement of this ethic "takes place through its dialectic relationship with the Noah covenant that was given to all humanity without any religious prerequisite for membership . . . its primary purpose is to preserve the minimal order of justice and human flourishing."[130] We can add to this the flourishing of all creation.

There are resonances and shared understanding between Fiddes, Bretherton and Lee on covenantal relationships. Importantly, for all three of them, these covenant relationships are for working together for justice. Bretherton and Lee have perhaps developed this further in that they focus on working together with others for social justice. However, it can be argued that they are writing about different things. Fiddes's writing on covenantal relationships that exist beyond the church is a far more dynamic view of covenant relationships than is presented by Bretherton and Lee. Fiddes is writing about living dynamic covenants that God makes with local churches and with communities beyond the churches, rather than ones formed in the past with Noah and Abraham. Therefore, it can be argued that the challenge to Baptist churches is to learn from community organizing, and from Fiddes's theology, to work with other churches, other faith groups, and further organizations, as part of

127. Lee, *Christian Ethics*, x. Nowhere in *God and Community Organizing* and *Christian Ethics* does Lee give a sense of where he has encountered broad-based community organizing nor his experience of engagement in it. So, his theological reflection is based on the theory rather than from the experience of practicing it. Despite this, I do not think we should discount Lee's thinking and analysis.

128. Lee, *Christian Ethics*, xi.

129. Lee, *Christian Ethics*, 15; emphasis in original.

130. Lee, *Christian Ethics*, 85.

these dynamic covenants. If Baptists do not, it can be understood that they will miss where God is at work in the world.

Through Fiddes's understanding of covenantal relationships beyond the local church, we can now explore the argument for what covenantal relationships can offer to community organizing. This broader understanding of covenantal relationships enables Baptist churches to build relationships with others. It also has implications for the type of relationships formed and with whom they are formed. If people are gathered or called into covenant with others in a local church, then they do not choose who they are gathering with. Thus, church becomes a place for the marginalized rather than being a self-selecting group. Groups of the "unlike" gather together and through this participate in God's mission.[131] This participation is then about participation in the gathered community and also outwards to the world. It is important to highlight that this is about covenantal relationships that lead to action, that change things, and that right wrongs. Thus, solidarity and the common good are important for these relationships. An understanding of covenantal relationships can thus both strengthen a Baptist theological ethic and the practice of community organizing.

Lee recognizes that "communities and institutions are increasingly fragmented and depleted as people's commitment to them is fluid and thin."[132] Thus, community organizing's focus on reweaving civil society is helpful through strengthening relationships between institutions. However, these relationships should remain dynamic so that they continue to allow the institutions to be influenced by, and to influence, others. As Lee highlights, "Covenant is not static, but an evolving and adapting mechanism of community organizing. This means that its organizing method is still open and relevant to a new social context."[133]

It can be argued that bringing covenantal relationships together with community organizing expands its goal. As Lee argues, "The goal of covenantal organizing is not only to achieve just and fair relationships . . . liberation from oppression is not the ultimate goal. Rather, it is just the beginning of the task of building a just, righteous, and peaceful community that fulfils God's original intention for humanity."[134] Thus, covenantal relationships move the focus from community as a neighborhood or physical space to focusing on working toward a common communal vision, such as that of the beloved

131. I am emphasizing here what I argued earlier in sec. 6.3.2.

132. Lee, *God and Community Organizing*, 2.

133. Lee, *God and Community Organizing*, 10.

134. Lee, *God and Community Organizing*, 176.

community.[135] As Lee concludes, new covenant ethics "is uncompromisingly Jesus-centered but equally politically relevant" and so is "applicable to the church as well as to the public realm."[136] So, what Lee is proposing is the same as the understanding of CST as something offered to the whole world and not just to the Roman Catholic Church.[137]

The concept of covenant has the potential to be the Organizing framework bringing community organizing and Baptist social ethics together. It can be argued that it is possible to weave together all six of the principles we have extrapolated from current theological reflection on community organizing with thinking about covenantal relationships and so strengthen a Baptist theological ethic. Churches and other institutions involved in organizing can therefore enter into a shared covenant together following all six of the principles. This can be understood as the central feature of the challenge I am presenting to Baptist churches and to community organizing.

Churches enter into a covenant to pursue the common good. They are covenanting at the local level and so will be engaged in subsidiarity through addressing issues at the most appropriate level, and often this is the local level.

Covenant is an intrinsically relational and communal concept, rather than an individual concept. Acting in a neighborly fashion opens the doors to all our neighbors. So, neighborliness is key because you are entering into a covenant with neighbors on equal terms to pursue the common good together.

Churches cooperate with others in listening to the local community, and to other institutions who are already working within it, to advance the common good in covenant with others. Churches and other organizations are therefore also entering into a listening covenant because part of the covenant effort is to listen to one another and discover what the common issues of injustice are.

In an unjust world, people are pushed to the margins and the church that is listening to the community will be less centered on itself and more on those on the margins. Churches and others who are used to being in the center may also end up on the margins, and as more of a marginal player, as they work with other institutions in civic society and are invited as a guest into alliances rather than being at the center as the host.

It is important to note that we do not have to identify the margins on our own. We choose to build relationships. In covenant we hear each other's testimonies of pain and suffering and it is then in the empathy we have committed

135. Lee, *God and Community Organizing*, 177.

136. Lee, *Christian Ethics*, 496.

137. See sec. 3.9.

to in covenant that we discover together where action on injustices needs to be taken. Then in solidarity churches act with others to address these issues.

It can be argued that a theological ethic of social justice requires Baptists to consider what it means to be a local Baptist church covenanted together and also acting in covenantal relationships with others. It necessitates Baptists to act together through the covenant that they hold together with others in a local church. It also requires Baptists to act together as an institution and to covenant with other key civil society institutions in their local community, including institutions that are different to them. This sense of working together as institutions is important for community organizing. Institutions, rather than individuals, can join an alliance. So, this is about how the institution—in this case a local Baptist church—works together across difference with others in covenantal relationships.

What we observed in many of the Baptist assembly resolutions and addresses is that the local church is still seen as the center of God's action in the world. This view leads the church to have a navel-gazing, inward focus. However, if the church is invited to join the trade unions, mosques, universities, colleges and other groups to address specific issues, the church has the opportunity to enter into a shared covenant with these other institutions for the common good. This will broaden the church's understanding of mission and develop its engagement with the community it seeks to serve. Local churches do not control the covenant, but are able to participate in it.

Engaging with Fiddes's thinking on covenant allows us to take the covenant theology out from a local church into wider society. As I highlighted earlier in section 6.4, Fiddes is concerned with how we might engage in covenantal relationships formed by God beyond those formed by church communities. Covenantal relationships enable Baptists to be able to listen better, center the margins, act together in solidarity, be neighborly, take decisions at the most appropriate level, and act together for the common good. It can be argued that this understanding of covenantal relationships also enables a move to a more dynamic understanding of community in community organizing. It also engages more fully with an understanding of participating in God's mission in the world.

We will now consider the implications for a Baptist theological ethic of not limiting God's mission in the world to the local church.

6.5 The Mission of God in the World

We will explore how social justice and covenant discussions relate to an understanding of the mission of God in the world which is much broader than a church-centered understanding. Fiddes suggested that mission and covenant are intertwined.[138] He understands that the missionary God is also the covenant-making God. Mission is "essentially relational, essentially a matter of making communion and community."[139] Again, as we noted in chapter 5, Fiddes concludes,

> Mission is a sharing in the mission of God . . . and so it will also involve partnership with those who are fostering human health and welfare whether or not they are professing Christians. . . . If we are truly to carry through God's "preferential option for the poor," then we shall have to discern where the grace of God is at work in the world, and seek to cooperate with movements and structures which are in tune with the purpose of God.[140]

Fiddes is interpreting mission in terms of Christ's mission in and for the world, not as the church's mission. God's mission in the world is bigger than the local church. Joining in with the intentional covenants that God forms means joining in with God's mission in the world and God's focus on justice for oppressed and marginalized people. Thus, joining in with the mission of God in the world involves interrupting systems of injustice and seeking a transformed world. From the analysis in this research, we can conclude that the struggle for solidarity and justice is at the heart of the mission of God in the world. Therefore, as we highlighted earlier in section 6.3.2, solidarity should be at the center of a Baptist theological ethic. When we engage with the world and its communities we are seeking to work where God is already at work, or desires to be at work.

The risk Baptists need to take is in understanding that God is more concerned with the mission of Christ in and for the world than in the perpetuation of particular expressions of church. God can act and speak in all the most unlikely places, and we need to be ready to listen. The church needs to go beyond being inward looking and needs to understand that it assembles for a purpose that goes beyond its own life and that of its participants. The church is assembling in part to participate in the mission of God in the world. Thus, it needs to open its doors and its vision beyond itself.

Again, as we highlighted in section 6.3.2, the church is one actor invited to join the assembly who are gathering in solidarity to advance the mission of God in the world. So, the assembly is not just for the church. Instead, it is for God's mission in the world. We assemble in solidarity because this is what

138. See sec. 5.4.

139. Fiddes, *Tracks and Traces*, 253.

140. Fiddes, *Tracks and Traces*, 265.

God wants us to do in the world. The church then develops an understanding of the priority to be outward looking. In addition, the church develops an understanding that it is not the only community that is seeking to do the will of God in the world. This is challenging and humbling. However, it is healthy because it keeps churches from only focusing on internal issues. It is also recognizing that God is working out God's purposes in the world, outside of church organizations and maybe even in spite of them.

From this analysis, it can be seen that joining in with the mission of God in the world is the first step. The second step is to recognize that the church is one actor invited to join the assembly as a guest, rather than being the host. Community organizing, through drawing together people from across a community, making space for all people, and enabling especially those on the margins to have a voice, offers crucial insights to the church in understanding its mission. Those participating in community organizing are participating in the mission of God in the world, even if they may not realize they are doing it, and in covenantal relationships which God forms with all kinds of people and organizations. Baptists are invited to enter into a broader covenant with this community and with God for the common good and the flourishing of all.

We are involved in the mission of God in the world whenever we are going out and offering something to others in the world. Covenantal relationships and community organizing can help Baptists rethink what God's purpose is in the world and how this shapes their understanding of mission, community and relationships.

6.6 Disentangling and Re-Entangling

Chambers and Alinsky, in their understandings of community organizing, focused on what it means to be radical and what it means for an institution to act from its roots.[141] It can be argued that Baptists can come to ethics based on covenantal relationships from their roots.

Baptists will need to renew their understanding of what it means to be radical and rediscover their roots in covenantal relationships. As we noted earlier, in contrast to the Church of England, Baptist churches and unions of Baptist churches are not part of the establishment and are not entangled with the state in the same way as the Church of England.[142] However, it can be argued that Baptist churches are entangled with empire and with the market which sustains and increases injustice. So, the question, as Graham Adams

141. See sec. 1.2—1.3.

142. See sec. 6.3.1.

notes, is whether to go with the flow of empire or whether to resist. In Walter Brueggemann's terms the alternative to the thinking of empire is the prophetic imagination which calls forth a different reality.[143] It can be concluded that we need to develop communities of resistance in the context of empire, having a prophetic imagination for the world as it should be with others in community.[144] But as Adams underlines, it is often difficult for us to imagine anything but the system we are living in, and so we cannot imagine any alternatives when we are entangled in it.[145] So, Baptists will need to find ways to disentangle themselves from the place they have got themselves into, however awkward this process might feel.

Baptists need to disentangle themselves from this by focusing on their roots. It can be argued that this focus would enable Baptists to disentangle themselves from systems of domination and control. Then, through covenantal relationships and community organizing, they will be able to entangle themselves with impoverished and marginalized people to act together for the liberation of all. Based on their experiences, Baptists should then do more theological reflection together as churches, associations and unions on actions for social justice using community organizing. This is the challenge for Baptists embedded in and wanting to be embedded in empire.

6.7 Conclusions

I have brought together all that we have learned in the previous five chapters. I have also offered a synthesis of where this can be combined to help strengthen a Baptist theological ethic for the practice of social justice to enable Baptists to act with others across difference.

Section 6.2.1 highlighted a number of separate strands in the thinking and practice of Baptists in Wales and England during the period studied which contributed to there not being a strong shared Baptist theological ethic for the practice of social justice in Wales and England.

Section 6.2.2 summarized where the writings of the four major UK Baptist theologians and Baptist assembly resolutions and presentations picked up on the six principles that represent current theological reflections on community organizing and so, at least to some extent, I have woven together these various Baptist discussions and writing.

143. Adams, *Holy Anarchy*, 76–81; drawing on Brueggemann, *Prophetic Imagination*. See also Walsh and Keesmat, *Colossians Remixed*, which also makes this argument.

144. Freeman, *Undomesticated Dissent*, 224–26.

145. Adams, *Holy Anarchy*, 82.

Section 6.3 demonstrated how the principles can all come together to strengthen a Baptist theological ethic, with a particular focus on how understandings and practices of listening and assembling together can be strengthened from an engagement with community organizing.

Section 6.4 then brought together the six principles with covenantal relationships. I have sought to find a Baptist language to talk about and act together with others for social justice. This has led me to the language of covenant and covenantal relationships. Strengthening a Baptist theological ethic through covenantal relationships is to some extent recovering an earlier Baptist practice. Covenant ethics enriches a Baptist response to the six principles drawn from the current theological reflection on community organizing and can be part of a Baptist theological ethic for the practice of social justice. Covenantal relationships can help us move from a static form of listening and assembling together to something more dynamic. The concept of covenant thus has the potential to be the organizing framework bringing community organizing and Baptist social ethics together. Through engaging with community organizing, we have taken a liberational approach to ethics, and developed a fruitful engagement with covenantal relationships and covenant ethics.

Section 6.5 then considered the implications for a Baptist theological ethic of not seeing the local church as the center of God's mission in the world. Thus, I focused on the mission of God in the world, and the church understanding itself as one actor in this mission. I have connected covenantal relationships, as Fiddes does, with acting for social justice as part of mission. As part of this mission, the church enters into a shared covenant.

Finally, section 6.6 considered the implications for Baptists in Wales and England of engaging in covenant ethics, and through this of engaging in the mission of God in the world. I focused on the need for Baptists to disentangle themselves from empire to then be able to entangle themselves with others in covenantal relationships.

The research question in this investigation started from the perspective of how community organizing can strengthen a Baptist theological ethic of social justice. Through examining current theological reflection on community organizing and the work of major UK theologians during the period, I have found a focus on covenant theology and ethics, and the call to participate in the mission of the triune God, very helpful both to strengthen a Baptist theological ethic as well as something Baptists can offer other churches and other institutions engaging in community organizing. I have woven covenant language together with community organizing, and demonstrated how covenant language can strengthen community organizing. Covenantal relationships bring a Baptist theological understanding to community organizing and provide a dynamic way to weave institutions together in acting for justice. Through this I have developed the rudiments of a Baptist theology and practice for social justice that brings both community organizing and Baptist thinking together in a new synthesis, and that is the breakthrough in this thesis.

Thus, in this chapter I have answered the overall research question for my investigation by drawing the strands together from the previous chapters. The synthesis in this chapter has provided a way forward for Baptist social justice theology and ethics.

Throughout the research I have shown the contribution that community organizing makes to the practice of social justice and of listening to other voices, especially those from the margins.

I have explored the theological contribution especially of Fiddes and shown his ability to clearly define a Baptist theological basis for social justice. Listening, assembling in solidarity, and covenantal relationships may be the root for strengthening a Baptist theological ethic.

Gathering with others outside of the church is what Bretherton, Fiddes, and Lee develop with understanding covenant in terms of committed, intentional relationships that are open to listening for the voice of God.

Fiddes, Haymes, and Kidd understand that "certain insights which have been important in the Baptist story remain significant for the whole church of God."[146] The synthesis in this chapter has shown how a Baptist understanding of covenant relationships can strengthen both a Baptist theological ethic and can be significant for everyone engaging in community organizing. Haymes notes that a Baptist way of doing theology will be reflection on practice and will be done together in community, as a gathered church.[147] Fiddes builds on this in highlighting that theology will be shaped from the experience of the community, its stories of dissent, and the relationships between people. Fiddes highlights that in seeking to center the margins, Baptists need to pay attention to the hidden stories, such as those of women, in how they do church. The Baptist way of community will then mean that from a local identity, "we are called into as wide a fellowship as is possible."[148] Fiddes understands that Baptist identity is about an ongoing shared life and is held in community. Baptist identity is not something static but instead it is dynamic and able to draw on its past and also through its engagement with other church denominations and the wider community. Community organizing asks Baptists to work not just with other Baptists or other churches but with a much broader

146. Haymes, "Theology and Baptist Identity." See sec. 5.4.

147. Haymes, "Theology and Baptist Identity." This is also what John Weaver explored in *Outside-In*.

148. Fiddes, "Theology and Baptist Way," 30.

group of institutions. The development of covenant language can culminate in this theological ethic and pull all the threads together. Thus, I argue that covenantal relationships can be an organizing framework bringing community organizing and Baptist social ethics together.

What we have sought to do is to offer to Baptists in Wales and England a drawing together of theology with the experience and practice of those engaged in community organizing. It brings together the theological principles and the practical experience, alongside the Baptist understanding of assembly and covenantal relationships, to give a clear challenge to Baptist churches to become involved in rebuilding and strengthening local communities and to be facilitators of the mission of Christ wherever God has placed them. Considering how community organizing can strengthen a Baptist theological ethic has also brought us back to a focus on covenantal relationships as well as expanding the boundaries of what many Baptist churches understand these to mean and what it means to be involved in the mission of God.

Baptists and community organizing have for the most part been on parallel tracks since community organizing was introduced to Wales and England in the late 1980s. Acting for justice starts with listening to others and seeking to discern what the common good is in this context. It involves building solidarity across lines of difference, moving outwards from what is familiar and where we feel comfortable. This is not easy to do. Rather than continuing to follow parallel tracks, Baptists can come to acting for justice based on covenant relationships from their radical roots. Through these Baptists can help recover solidarity between people and institutions by walking together and watching over each other in love, and so renew their understanding of what it means to be radical in covenantal relationships with others. This is the challenge for Baptists.

The Rule of the Iona Community includes the statement "Our commitment on justice and peace is . . . a point of departure. It will remain no more than a pious hope (and a false witness) unless we seek, separately and together, to put it into practice."[149] Thus, it is not enough to have a Baptist theological ethic for the practice of social justice. It must be translated into reality; it must be practiced through action in the world as it is and that aims to more fully bring about the world as it should be.

Baptists can and should be part of coming together with others to win change on justice issues with a strengthened theological ethic for the practice of social justice. Weaving relationships together with others in distinctive ways should produce new patterns and reconfigure the quality and character of both Baptist churches and other organizations. The result will be patterns in

149. Gardiner, *Melodies of a New Monasticism*, 116.

communities that are beautiful and inspiring to others. We have a long way to go before our communities resemble the beloved community of Christ.

Postscript

People and relationships are central to Christian ethics. It considers what course of action cares best for others and strengthens relationships in seeking the common good. In this book, I have sought to explore the relationship between Baptists and community organizing and to weave together strands to propose a way forward for Baptist social justice theology and ethics. Continuing the metaphor of weaving, in this final part of the book I will present a brief synthesis of the pattern formed so far through bringing together community organizing and Baptist understandings and practice of social justice. I will outline some issues and questions, or loose threads, that we are left with. I will then highlight where these threads could be explored and developed, and potentially woven into the developing pattern through further research.

What We Have Discovered Through This Research

I sought to answer the question of what community organizing is and how it has developed in the United States and in Wales and England. We discovered an approach that was developed by Saul Alinsky first among people and organizations who were oppressed and marginalized in the Back of the Yards area of inner-city Chicago in the 1930s. These initially included trade unions and Roman Catholic churches consisting of large numbers of recent immigrants to the US.

We then discovered that community organizing, as it developed in the US, involved many Black Baptist churches. These churches were central to the alliances formed through the "unlike" coming together and gathering together across difference in citywide alliances. Through the leadership of Ed Chambers, Ernesto Cortes, Mike Gecan, and Arnie Graf, the alliances in the US often became predominantly made up of churches of various denominations, particularly Roman Catholic churches with large proportions of people from Latin American immigrant communities and Black Baptist churches. Both churches were made up of people, and were meeting in communities, that were often impoverished, marginalized, and oppressed. Through organizing, churches were able to come together to bring about change on the issues that affected people in their churches and communities, such as low wages, poor public transport, poor public services, and a lack of good housing.

We discovered that community organizing developed in specific places and contexts and in specific civil society institutions. Community organizing in the US was influenced at least to some extent by the theology and practices of Latin American and Black liberation theologies, and by the continued influence of the US civil rights movement on Black Baptist churches. Despite the central involvement of Black Baptist churches, the Baptist experience and theological engagement in broad-based community organizing is not dealt with in any depth in the current literature.

We then explored how community organizing was introduced first into England and then into Wales, under the leadership of Neil Jameson, and thus into very different contexts to those of the US. Despite the new contexts, we discovered that again the approach and practices of community organizing had been embraced by churches and other faith institutions, initially in East London, and then in many other places. As we observed in the US, this was mainly in economically impoverished places where people and their institutions perceived that they were often oppressed and marginalized. In addition, these institutions felt they had no power to make change on the issues that were affecting them and that, through coming together, they were able to make positive changes locally. Black Baptist churches have played a central role in several Organizing alliances and key campaigns in the US. However, the major involvement of Baptist churches was not translated into community organizing in Wales and England.

I then sought to answer the question of how churches that have embraced community organizing understood it and what it means for their practice of social justice. Black Baptist and Roman Catholic churches, their traditions and practices, had a strong influence on community organizing in the US. Our explorations revealed the importance that, for many churches, their understanding of community organizing and theological reflection on it has come from their experience and practice of it rather than the other way round. This is the same methodological commitment found in Black and Latin American liberation theology. The *hallmarks of an organized church*, developed in the UK by Angus Ritchie, are based on churches' experience and use of community organizing, rather than as a theoretical framework to engage churches in organizing.[1] Through their engagement in organizing, churches have made social justice a bigger priority by moving it to the center of the life of the church congregation and integrating social justice into all aspects of a church.

Exploring this further, and building on the emerging themes, I next sought to answer the question of what can be learned from theological reflection on community organizing by theologians and organizers in the US and UK. In addition, I sought to answer the questions of who they reference and who has influenced them. We discovered, in particular, the influence of CST principles in current reflections mainly done by Luke Bretherton, Anna Rowlands, Austen Ivereigh, and Angus Ritchie. Ivereigh argued that the fuel and road map offered by CST have found a perfect vehicle for translating them into action in community organizing.

Our analysis also revealed the importance placed on building relationships across difference in communities. Through exploring and critiquing current theological reflections, I produced a synthesis working definition of six principles; solidarity, subsidiarity, the common good, neighborliness, listening, and centering the margins. However, the current theologians of community organizing are not particularly diverse and have blind spots. Thus, the current theological reflection did not give us everything we need in developing a strengthened Baptist theological ethic for the practice of social justice.

We then turned to consider the Baptist response to current theological reflection on community organizing. In dialogue with my working definitions of the six principles, I sought to answer the question of to what extent a theological ethic for the practice of social justice within Baptist churches in Wales and England had developed during the period when community organizing was developing in England and Wales from the late 1980s to 2010. We focused on what was being discussed at assemblies of the BUW and the BUGB. We discovered some examples in presidential addresses and public resolutions at these assemblies where there was a focus on social justice and how Baptists should practice it. However, it was not prioritized at the national level in the two unions. We considered the impact of whose voices are being heard in the assemblies. The context and location of the majority of Baptist congregations often meant they were facing different issues to Roman Catholic and Anglican churches in inner cities. In addition, the perspectives and voices of Black Baptist churches and other churches meeting in economically impoverished communities were largely not heard by the wider union. Listening closely to these and working from their perspective may have led to an increased priority on social justice and a stronger Baptist theological ethic of social justice.

1. Ritchie, *People of Power*.

In answering this question on the development of a theological ethic within Baptist churches in Wales and England, we then explored the main themes in the writing of four UK Baptist theologians, during the period when community organizing was developing in England and Wales, and how these themes engage with the six principles. We were primarily concerned with how their focus and arguments can help in strengthening a Baptist theological ethic for the practice of social justice.

Paul Fiddes, Brian Haymes, and Richard Kidd's writings demonstrated the most extensive links to the six principles, particularly in their writing on covenantal relationships. In contrast, Nigel Wright demonstrated few connections with the six principles in his writing. For Fiddes, the Baptist understanding of covenant, centered in the language of walking together is relational language and implies openness and trust and being on a journey together. Fiddes's writing engages with and challenges what is the center and what are the margins. The writings of Haymes and Kidd have been much influenced by theologies of liberation. However, it appears that much of the writing of these three Baptist theologians was not widely read in Baptist churches, nor have their proposals yet been taken up by Baptists to any significant extent. Their writings can contribute to strengthening a Baptist theological ethic for the practice of social justice. However, more diverse sources will be needed to strengthen this. Overall, examining these Baptist sources has not provided us with a sense that there is a strong shared Baptist theological ethic for the practice of social justice.

I then sought to answer the question of what Baptist churches in Wales and England could learn from the practice of community organizing. Finally, I sought to answer the question of what Baptist social justice theology and ethics would look like if it included lessons learned from community organizing. I demonstrated how the six principles can all come together to strengthen a Baptist theological ethic, with a particular focus on how understandings and practices of listening and assembling together can be strengthened from an engagement with community organizing.

I have sought to find a Baptist language to talk about and act together with others for social justice. This has led me to the language of covenant and covenantal relationships. Strengthening a Baptist theological ethic through covenantal relationships is to some extent recovering an earlier Baptist practice. Covenant ethics helps a Baptist response to the six principles drawn from the current theological reflection on community organizing and can be part of a Baptist theological ethic for the practice of social justice. I have found that covenantal relationships can help us move from what can be seen as a static form of listening and assembling together to something more dynamic. The concept of covenant thus has the potential to be the organizing framework bringing community organizing and Baptist social ethics together.

The overall research question for my book asked how an investigation of the theory and practice of community organizing can help form a more adequate theological ethic for the practice of social justice by Baptist churches in Wales and England. Through examining current theological reflection on community organizing and the work of Baptist theologians, I have found a focus on covenant theology and ethics very helpful both to strengthen a Baptist theological ethic as well as something Baptists can offer other churches and other institutions engaging in community organizing. I have woven covenant language together with the principles and practice of community organizing, and demonstrated how covenant language can strengthen community organizing. Covenantal relationships bring a Baptist theological understanding to community organizing and provide a dynamic way to weave institutions together in acting for justice. Through this, I have developed the rudiments of a Baptist theology and practice for social justice that brings both community organizing and Baptist thinking together in a new synthesis, and that is the breakthrough in this research.

Issues and Questions We Are Left With

We are left with several issues and questions for those engaged in community organizing and for Baptists in Wales and England. These have been raised through the exploration in this book. We highlighted several challenges for Baptist churches in chapter 6. These challenges connect to the reasons why Baptists in Wales and England have not developed a strong shared theological ethic for the practice of social justice so far, nor engaged significantly in community organizing in these nations. These challenges also connect to how community organizing can strengthen a Baptist theological ethic.

At the level of local church practice, Baptists in Wales and England are challenged to recognize how the mission of God in the world is much broader than local church activities.

In addition, only seeing covenantal relationships as something formed within church congregations also speaks to a "cramped" Baptist vision where all of the action of what God is doing in the world is confined to the life of the local congregation. There is thus a challenge here for Baptists to expand their vision and be immersed in their wider communities.

In the understanding of covenantal relationships, the challenge to Baptist churches is to learn from community organizing, and from Fiddes's theology, to work together with others as part of dynamic covenants. Both Baptist churches and community organizing should understand that they enter into a shared covenant following all of the six principles.

At the level of ethical reflection, the challenge is for Baptists to listen to impoverished and marginalized people. Centering the margins means starting from the perspective of those currently impoverished and on the margins, and for their priorities to be the basis for action together.

At the level of Baptist associations and assemblies, the challenge for Baptists is to be able to assemble together as Baptists, as interdependent with others rather than independent churches, and to re-entangle themselves with others to make change on social justice issues.

When they assemble, the challenge that faces Baptists is to provide opportunities to enable impoverished and marginalized people to participate, to listen to them, and to again be able to discuss and agree public resolutions on social justice issues in national assemblies based on their priorities. Then, to engage in community organizing as an approach to take action on these injustices, through assembling with other groups and covenanting with them in bringing about social change.

Some words from Idris Davies's poem "The Angry Summer," about the General Strike in 1926 and its impact in the South Wales Valleys, are helpful here:

> Tis very embarrassing, say what you like,
> To be a good vicar in a valley on strike
> And preach Christian fellowship on Sunday night
> To men and women who are forced to fight
> For bread and cheese. How shall I handle this text from St. Paul?
> (There's that meeting outside the vicarage wall.
> O dear, O dear, these politics! Drat them, I say!
> I would I were living much farther away.)
> And some of these leaders quote scripture with ease
> As though they had spent all their nights on their knees.
> (That's Margaret upstairs singing love songs again!)
> I must make up my mind, make the issue plain,
> I must be honest with honest men,
> Bless them in battle, and speak on their side,
> And gather my courage, and envy their pride![2]

As Davies appears to be arguing, there is the need for churches and their leaders to show up and assemble together in solidarity with others in local communities who are already acting to tackle social injustices. I have argued that

2. "The Angry Summer," in Davies, *Collected Poems*, 91.

this is a key challenge for Baptists and should be the next step for Baptists in Wales and England.

This book is a literature-based study examining what we can draw on from community organizing and Baptist thinking to strengthen a Baptist theological ethic for the practice of social justice. However, a nonnegotiable in theological reflection on community organizing is that you cannot reflect theologically about community organizing without being involved in the practice. In other words, first you have do community organizing and then reflect theologically on it. As we have discovered, there is little literature by Black Baptists with their reflections on community organizing. Therefore, a question that we are left with is what more could Baptists in the UK learn from the experiences and reflections of Black Baptists in the US, and of Black Baptists in Wales and England. It would be good to explore how listening to and learning from fellow Baptists in another context might strengthen the work of Baptist churches in social justice in Wales and England in their own contexts.

It is not enough to have a strengthened Baptist theological ethic for the practice of social justice in theory. It must be translated into reality, it must be practiced and then reflected on. To borrow the title of a publication about CST and community organizing, "realities are greater than ideas."[3] Thus, further reflection together as churches, associations and unions on how community organizing can support and strengthen a Baptist theological ethic for the practice of social justice will come from further Baptist engagement in community organizing and then from reflecting theologically on that experience in specific social and economic contexts. This is the same methodological commitment found in Black and Latin American theologies of liberation.

Theologies of liberation, community organizing (in the US) and a Baptist approach to being church (in Wales and England) were all forged and developed in the context of communities of people experiencing impoverishment, marginalization and oppression. A key theme in this book has been the need to listen to and act from the perspective of people currently at the margins; in community organizing, in theological reflection, and in strengthening a Baptist theological ethic for the practice of social justice in Wales and England. I have argued that covenantal relationships enable Baptists and others to do this.

Perhaps what I have done in this book is similar to what Austen Ivereigh sought to do in *Faithful Citizens*. In this book, he argued that CST provides the fuel and community organizing the vehicle for Roman Catholic Church engagement in, and action for, social justice. Instead of the heritage and teaching of CST, Baptists have covenant theology. However, in the same way as

3. Rodrigues, *Realities Are Greater*.

Luke Bretherton asserts that community organizing is little understood either within or outside of the church,[4] it can be argued that the same is true of both CST and covenant theology.

Further Research That Could Be Explored

As we come to the end of the journey of this investigation, and plan where and in what ways we can best travel on, let us briefly consider what we can now observe from this vantage point might be some areas for further research.

It can be argued that covenant theology is not well understood, and future research would include further exploration of it. In this investigation, we have explored the engagement in the literature with recovering and developing Baptist understandings of covenantal relationships. We have considered how the concept of covenantal relationships and the writings of Paul Fiddes can help us in exploring this as something that Baptists can offer to community organizing. We have discovered that the concept of covenant has the potential to be the organizing framework bringing community organizing and Baptist social ethics together. We have examined and critiqued how the focus on covenantal relationships connects both in the life within local church congregations and as a contribution Baptists ought to be able to make to community organizing through joining in with broader covenantal relationships formed in the wider community.

We have also observed that community organizing supports democratic practices. The original purpose of the IAF in the US was "to restore the democratic way of life to modern industrial society."[5] Membership of community organizing alliances in both the US and in Wales and England enables churches to participate with other institutions in democratic practices. David Gushee has recently brought together Christian engagement in democratic politics with ethics built on covenant.[6] Having explored the relationship between an individual church covenant and covenant ethics in wider community, he has helpfully linked covenant ethics to acting together with others in democratic politics. This then provides a framework for thinking about and reclaiming or improving democracy, and Christian engagement in democracy through covenant ethics. Further engagement and research engaging in covenant ethics and community organizing and how it strengthens Christian engagement

4. Bretherton, "Recovering Democratic Politics."

5. Rogers, *Cold Anger*, 83.

6. Gushee, *Defending Democracy*. In this Gushee has also engaged with the writings of Luke Bretherton and Hak Joon Lee.

in democratic politics has the potential to help us to continue to think through and strengthen a Baptist theological ethic for the practice of social justice.

Current theological reflection on community organizing is based predominantly on Roman Catholic and Anglican perspectives and has been done mostly by white men. As a result, we can conclude that more diverse voices are much needed. Therefore, in addition to this research, there is need for further theological reflection by Black Baptist churches on their experience, and by churches in Wales and England which have engaged in community organizing as part of Citizens UK alliances. Qualitative and ethnographic research methods could be used to research what theological reflections can be developed from the experience and practice of these Baptist churches.[7] In addition, Wales has a different history, culture and society, and a different relationship between churches and wider society compared to England. The Welsh context is distinct to the English context for Baptist churches as well as for community organizing. This too could be explored further in ongoing research on Baptist church engagement in organizing.

Briefly, three additional areas for future research are on worship, leadership, and institutions. Craig Gardiner connects the social justice work that a church is involved in with worship in a church.[8] This is not something that I have focused on in this book to any extent. An additional area for research could therefore be to explore how churches engaged in community organizing understand the connection between this and church worship, and how their worship has changed as a result of their involvement.

Developing leaders within churches and other civil society institutions is an important focus of community organizing but has not been a focus of this investigation. Future research could focus on understandings of leadership in Baptist churches and how this is changed through engagement in organizing. Paul Fiddes and Nigel Wright, among other UK Baptist theologians, have written about Baptist church leadership. Further research could engage in what Baptists can contribute to understandings and approaches to leadership development in organizing as well as vice versa.

Community organizing focuses on building broad-based alliances of institutions such as churches and trade unions. However, as we have observed in this research, these intermediary or "people's institutions" are currently in

7. During the period studied, Paul Fiddes was not focusing on qualitative and ethnographic research on church practice. This approach has come to be more important for his research and writing more recently, including that with Pete Ward, a UK practical theologian, and the Ecclesiology and Ethnography Network.

8. Gardiner, *Melodies of a New Monasticism*.

decline.[9] Community organizing assumes the importance to people and to civil society of these institutions and focuses on strengthening these institutions. The roots of so much past action and social justice campaigns, such as Chartism, action against the transatlantic slave trade, Jubilee 2000, and Make Poverty History, were in churches and trade unions. Future research could focus on how engagement in social justice can strengthen Baptist churches. However, if these institutions continue to decline, future research could also explore what that means for a Baptist theological ethic and how Baptists should be and act in the world.

To conclude, we have followed the story of the development of community organizing, and the story of Baptist engagement in social justice from the late 1980s to 2010. We have learned some community organizing stories, such as an early living wage action in East London, the story of assemblies in South London and Wales, and the Nando's campaign in Cardiff. The importance of including stories in this book returns to Jeffrey Stout's argument; that the details of the stories are important in drawing out organizing principles and what is going on in community organizing.[10] My hope is that there might be many more stories that can be told in the future of Baptist engagement in community organizing in Wales and England, as Baptists seek to be radical in covenanting with God and with others in seeking justice. This will mean Baptists disentangling and re-entangling themselves in their relationships with others, learning from each other, and with the prophetic imagination to confront and bring down the ideas and structures of empire. Through this, they will walk together in ways known and still to be made known and commit all that they have and all that they are to God's unfolding purposes of love.

9. Gecan, *People's Institutions in Decline.*

10. Stout, *Blessed Are the Organized.*

Bibliography

Adams, Graham. *Holy Anarchy: Dismantling Domination, Embodying Community, Loving Strangeness*. London: SCM, 2022.

Ali, Ruhana, et al. *A New Covenant of Virtue: Islam and Community Organising*. London: Citizens UK, 2012.

Alinsky, Saul. *Reveille for Radicals*. New York: Vintage, 1989.

———. *Rules for Radicals: A Pragmatic Primer for Realistic Radicals*. New York: Vintage, 1989.

Arendt, Hannah. *On Revolution*. Penguin Classics. London: Penguin, 2006.

———. *On Violence*. Penguin Modern Classics. London: Penguin, 2023.

Baptist Union of Great Britain [BUGB]. https://www.baptist.org.uk/.

———. *Annual Report 1988*. Didcot, UK: Baptist Union of Great Britain, 1988.

———. *Annual Report 1989*. Didcot, UK: Baptist Union of Great Britain, 1989.

———. *Annual Report 1990*. Didcot, UK: Baptist Union of Great Britain, 1990.

———. *Annual Report 1992*. Didcot, UK: Baptist Union of Great Britain, 1992.

———. *Annual Report 1994*. Didcot, UK: Baptist Union of Great Britain, 1994.

———. *Annual Report 1995*. Didcot, UK: Baptist Union of Great Britain, 1995.

———. *Baptist Union Directory, 1989–1990*. Didcot, UK: Baptist Union of Great Britain, 1989.

———. *Baptist Union Directory, 1990–1991*. Didcot, UK: Baptist Union of Great Britain, 1990.

———. *Baptist Union Directory, 1991–1992*. Didcot, UK: Baptist Union of Great Britain, 1991.

———. *Baptist Union Directory, 1993–1994*. Didcot, UK: Baptist Union of Great Britain, 1993.

———. *Baptist Union Directory, 1994–1995*. Didcot, UK: Baptist Union of Great Britain, 1994.

———. *Baptist Union Directory, 1995–1996*. Didcot, UK: Baptist Union of Great Britain, 1995.

———. *Baptist Union Directory, 1996–1997*. Didcot, UK: Baptist Union of Great Britain, 1996.

———. *Baptist Union Directory, 1997–1998*. Didcot, UK: Baptist Union of Great Britain, 1997.

———. *Baptist Union Directory, 1998–1999*. Didcot, UK: Baptist Union of Great Britain, 1998.

———. *Baptist Union Directory, 1999–2000*. Didcot, UK: Baptist Union of Great Britain, 1999.

———. *Baptist Union Directory, 2000–2001–2002*. Didcot, UK: Baptist Union of Great Britain, 2001.

———. *Baptist Union Directory, 2003–2004*. Didcot, UK: Baptist Union of Great Britain, 2003.

———. *Baptist Union Directory, 2004–2005*. Didcot, UK: Baptist Union of Great Britain, 2004.

———. *Baptist Union Directory, 2005–2006*. Didcot, UK: Baptist Union of Great Britain, 2005.

———. *Baptist Union Directory, 2007*. Didcot, UK: Baptist Union of Great Britain, 2007.

———. *Baptist Union Directory, 2008*. Didcot, UK: Baptist Union of Great Britain, 2008.

———. *Baptist Union Directory, 2009*. Didcot, UK: Baptist Union of Great Britain, 2009.

———. *Baptist Union Directory, 2010*. Didcot, UK: Baptist Union of Great Britain, 2010.

———. *Baptist Union Directory, 2011*. Didcot, UK: Baptist Union of Great Britain, 2011.

———. *Baptist Union Directory, 2012*. Didcot, UK: Baptist Union of Great Britain, 2012.

———. *Covenant 21: Covenant for a Gospel People*. London: Baptist Union, 2000.

———. *Five Core Values for a Gospel People*. Didcot: Baptist Union of Great Britain, 1998.

———. *The Nature of the Assembly and the Council of the Baptist Union of Great Britain*. Didcot, UK: Baptist Union of Great Britain, 1994.

Baptist Union of Wales [BUW]. https://buw.wales/.

———. *The Annual Report 2005–2006*: *The Baptist Union of Wales English Assembly*. N.p.: N.p., n.d.

———. *The Annual Report 2006–2007*: *The Baptist Union of Wales English Assembly*. N.p.: N.p., n.d.

———. *The Annual Report 2007–2008*: *The Baptist Union of Wales English Assembly*. N.p.: N.p., n.d.

———. *The Annual Report 2008–2009*: *The Baptist Union of Wales English Assembly*. N.p.: N.p., n.d.

———. *The Annual Report 2009–2010*: *The Baptist Union of Wales English Assembly*. N.p.: N.p., n.d.

———. *The Annual Report 2010–2011*: *The Baptist Union of Wales English Assembly*. N.p.: N.p., n.d.

———. "Appendix 1 [1989]: Annual Conference of the English Assembly at North Road Baptist Church, Milford Haven on Tuesday and Wednesday, 16th and 17th May, 1989." In *The Baptist Union of Wales: The English Assembly 1990*. Carmarthen, Wales: Baptist Union of Wales, 1990.

———. "Appendix 1 [1988]: Annual Conference of the English Assembly at Tabernacle, Llandrindod on Tuesday and Wednesday, 17th and 18th May, 1988." In *The Baptist Union of Wales: The English Assembly 1989*. Carmarthen, Wales: Baptist Union of Wales, 1989.

———. "Appendix 1 [1990]: Annual Conference of the English Assembly at the Penbryn Campus, Aberystwyth on Tuesday, Wednesday and Thursday 10, 11, 12 July 1990." In *The Baptist Union of Wales: The English Assembly 1991*. Carmarthen, Wales: Baptist Union of Wales, 1991.

———. “Appendix 1 [1992]: Annual Conference of the English Assembly Held at Trinity College, Carmarthen on 1st–3rd July 1992.” In *The Baptist Union of Wales: The English Assembly, 1993*. Carmarthen, Wales: Baptist Union of Wales, 1993.

———. “Appendix 1 [1993]: Annual Conference of the English Assembly Held at Knighton Baptist Church on 25–26 May, 1993.” In *The Baptist Union of Wales: The English Assembly, 1994*. Carmarthen, Wales: Baptist Union of Wales, 1994.

———. “Appendix 1 [1994]: Annual Conference of the English Assembly Held at Bethel Baptist Church, Loveston on 21–22 June, 1994.” In *The Baptist Union of Wales English Assembly Conference 11–12 July 1995*. Carmarthen, Wales: Baptist Union of Wales, 1995.

———. “Appendix 1 [1995]: Annual Conference of the English Assembly Held at Trefeca Conference Centre, Talgarth Tuesday and Wednesday 11–12 July 1995.” In *The Baptist Union of Wales English Assembly Conference 21–22 May 1996*. Carmarthen, Wales: Baptist Union of Wales, 1996.

———. “Appendix 1 [1996]: Annual Conference of the English Assembly Held at Moriah, Risca Tuesday and Wednesday 21–22 May 1996.” In *The Baptist Union of Wales English Assembly Conference 16–17 May 1997*. Carmarthen, Wales: Baptist Union of Wales, 1997.

———. “Appendix 1 [1997]: Annual Conference of the English Assembly Held at Maesyrhelem Baptist Church Friday and Saturday 1997.” In *The Baptist Union of Wales English Assembly Conference June 5th–7th, 1998*. Carmarthen, Wales: Baptist Union of Wales, 1998.

———. “Appendix 1 [1999]: Annual Conference of the English Assembly Held at Presteigne Baptist Church Monday and Tuesday 28–29 June 1999.” In *The Baptist Union of Wales English Assembly Conference July 9–11 2000*. Carmarthen, Wales: Baptist Union of Wales, 2000.

———. “Appendix 1 [2000]: Annual Conference of the English Assembly Held at Brackla, Bridgend on Monday and Tuesday 10–11 July 2000.” In *The Baptist Union of Wales English Assembly Conference 11–12 September 2001*. Carmarthen, Wales: Baptist Union of Wales, 2001.

———. “Appendix 1 [2001]: Baptist Union of Wales Annual Conference of the English Assembly Held at Nantgwyn Chapel, Panty Dwr. The Meetings Were Held on Tuesday and Wednesday 11–12 September 2001.” In *The Baptist Union of Wales English Assembly 2002*. Carmarthen, Wales: Baptist Union of Wales, 2002.

———. “Appendix 1 [2002]: Annual Conference of the English Assembly Held at Llanwenarth Baptist Church on Tuesday and Wednesday 11 and 12 June, 2002.” In *Programme for BUW (English Wing) Assembly, Broad Haven Friday/Saturday 27th/28th June 2003*. Carmarthen, Wales: Baptist Union of Wales, 2003.

———. “Appendix 1 [2003]: The Annual Conference of the English Assembly held at Hephzibah, Broad Haven on Friday/Saturday 27th/28th June 2003.” In *Baptist Union of Wales Assembly Programme 15–16 June 2004*. Carmarthen, Wales: Baptist Union of Wales, 2004.

———. “Appendix 1 [2009]: The Baptist Assembly in Wales 2009.” In *The Annual Report 2009–2010: The Baptist Union of Wales English Assembly*. Carmarthen, Wales: Baptist Union of Wales, 2009.

———. “Assembly Programme.” June 15–16, 2004, Wales.

———. “Atodiad 1 [1999]: Cyfarfodydd Blynyddol, Adran Gymraeg Undeb Bedyddwyr Cymru, Cylch Bae Colwyn 25–29 Gorffennaf 1999” [Appendix 1: Annual meetings,

Welsh wing of the Baptist Union of Wales, Colwyn Bay Circle, 25–29 July 1999]. In *Cyfarfodydd yr Undeb 2000, Yr Adran Gymraeg*. N.p.: Welsh Wing of the Baptist Union of Wales, 2000.

———. "Atodiad 1 [2000]: Cyfarfodydd Blynyddol, Adran Gymraeg Undeb Bedyddwyr Cymru, Hermon Abergwaun Glandwr a'r Fro Mehefin 25–29 2000" [Appendix 1: Annual meetings, Welsh wing of the Baptist Union of Wales, Hermon Fishguard Glandwr and Vale, June 25–29 2000]. In *Cyfarfodydd yr Undeb 2001, Yr Adran Gymraeg*. N.p.: Welsh Wing of the Baptist Union of Wales, 2001.

———. *The Baptist Union of Wales: The English Assembly, 1990*. N.p.: N.p., n.d.

———. *The Baptist Union of Wales: The English Assembly, 1992*. N.p.: N.p., n.d.

———. *The Baptist Union of Wales English Assembly 1998*. N.p.: N.p., n.d.

———. *The Baptist Union of Wales English Assembly 2001*. N.p.: N.p., n.d.

———. *The Baptist Union of Wales English Assembly 2004*. N.p.: N.p., n.d.

———. *The Baptist Union of Wales English Assembly Conference, Hephzibah, Broadhaven, June 5th–7th, 1998*. N.p.: N.p., [1998].

———. *The Baptist Union of Wales English Assembly Conference, 11–12 September 2001*. N.p.: N.p., n.d.

———. *Cyfarfodydd yr Undeb 1988, Yr Adran Gymraeg, at Ebenezer, Llandeilo, July 24–27, 1988*. N.p.: Welsh Wing of the Baptist Union of Wales, 1988.

———. *Cyfarfodydd yr Undeb 1989, Yr Adran Gymraeg, at Bethel, Caergybi, July 23–27, 1989*. N.p.: Welsh Wing of the Baptist Union of Wales, 1989.

———. *Cyfarfodydd yr Undeb 1990, Yr Adran Gymraeg*. N.p.: Welsh Wing of the Baptist Union of Wales, 1990.

———. *Cyfarfodydd yr Undeb 1991, Yr Adran Gymraeg*. N.p.: Welsh Wing of the Baptist Union of Wales, 1991.

———. *Cyfarfodydd yr Undeb 1992, Yr Adran Gymraeg*. N.p.: Welsh Wing of the Baptist Union of Wales, 1992.

———. *Cyfarfodydd yr Undeb 1993, Yr Adran Gymraeg*. N.p.: Welsh Wing of the Baptist Union of Wales, 1993.

———. *Cyfarfodydd yr Undeb 1994, Yr Adran Gymraeg*. N.p.: Welsh Wing of the Baptist Union of Wales, 1994.

———. *Cyfarfodydd yr Undeb 1995, Yr Adran Gymraeg*. N.p.: Welsh Wing of the Baptist Union of Wales, 1995.

———. *Cyfarfodydd yr Undeb 1996, Yr Adran Gymraeg*. N.p.: Welsh Wing of the Baptist Union of Wales, 1996.

———. *Cyfarfodydd yr Undeb 1997, Yr Adran Gymraeg*. N.p.: Welsh Wing of the Baptist Union of Wales, 1997.

———. "Programme for BUW (English Wing) Assembly, Broad Haven Friday/Saturday 27th/28th June 2003." June 27–28, 2003, Broad Haven, Wales.

Baptist World Alliance. "Covenant on Intra-Baptist Relations." Baptist World Alliance, 2013.

Barclay, David. *Making Multiculturalism Work: Enabling Practical Action Across Deep Difference*. London: Theos, 2013.

Bebbington, David W. *Baptists Through the Centuries: A History of a Global People*. Waco: Baylor University Press, 2010.

Biggs, John. "My Presidential Year." *Fraternal* 232 (1990) 9–14.

Blond, Phillip. *Red Tory: How Left and Right Have Broken Britain and How We Can Fix It*. London: Faber and Faber, 2010.

Boff, Leonardo, and Clodovis Boff. *Introducing Liberation Theology.* London: Orbis, 1986.

Bolton, Matthew. *How to Resist: Turn Protest to Power.* London: Bloomsbury, 2017.

Bonhoeffer, Dietrich. *Life Together.* Translated by J. W. Doberstein. Rev. ed. London: SCM, 2015.

Bosch, David J. *Transforming Mission: Paradigm Shifts in Theology of Mission.* American Society of Missiology. Maryknoll, NY: Orbis, 1991.

Bradstock, Andrew, and Christopher Rowland, eds. *Radical Christian Writings: A Reader.* Oxford: Blackwell, 2002.

Bretherton, Luke. "The Ability to Act: Power Over and Power With." *Listen, Organize, Act!*, season 1, episode 4, Mar. 9, 2021. https://listenorganizeact.buzzsprout.com/1646254/episodes/8101073-s1-e4-the-ability-to-act-power-over-and-power-with.

———. "Campaigns as Public Action." *Listen, Organize, Act!*, season 1, episode 11, May 5, 2021. https://listenorganizeact.buzzsprout.com/1646254/episodes/8386941-s1-e11-campaigns-as-public-action.

———. *Christ and the Common Life: Political Theology and the Case for Democracy.* Grand Rapids: Eerdmans, 2019.

———. *Christianity and Contemporary Politics: The Conditions and Possibilities of Faithful Witness.* Oxford: Wiley-Blackwell, 2010.

———. "How Community Organising Helps Christians Connect Democracy and Faith." Presentation at Citizens UK online workshop, June 24, 2021.

———. "Institutions: Why They're Vital for Democratic Politics." *Listen, Organize, Act!*, season 1, episode 6, Mar. 25, 2021. https://listenorganizeact.buzzsprout.com/1646254/episodes/8161409-s1-e6-institutions-why-they-re-vital-for-democratic-politics.

———. "The Other Basic Tool of Democratic Organizing: House Meetings." *Listen, Organize, Act!*, season 1, episode 3, Mar. 2, 2021. https://listenorganizeact.buzzsprout.com/1646254/episodes/8063827-s1-e3-the-other-basic-tool-of-organizing-house-meetings.

———. *A Primer in Christian Ethics: Christ and the Struggle to Live Well.* Cambridge: Cambridge University Press, 2023.

———. "Recovering Democratic Politics." Breaking Ground, [May 7, 2021]. https://breakingground.us/recovering-christian-faithfulness-through-recovering-democratic-politics/.

———. *Resurrecting Democracy: Faith, Citizenship, and the Politics of a Common Life.* Cambridge: Cambridge University Press, 2015.

———. "Saul Alinsky—Part 2." *Listen, Organize, Act!*, season 2, episode 2, July 23, 2022. https://listenorganizeact.buzzsprout.com/1646254/episodes/11005222-s2-e2-2-saul-alinsky-part-2.

———. "What Is Community Organizing? And Why Is It Needed?" *Listen, Organize, Act!*, season 1, episode 1, Feb. 14, 2021. https://listenorganizeact.buzzsprout.com/1646254/episodes/7867726-s1-e1-what-is-community-organizing-and-why-is-it-needed.

Briggs, John. *The English Baptists of the 19th Century.* History of the English Baptists. Didcot, UK: Baptist Historical Society, 1994.

Bruce, Andy. "Exploring the Far Country: A Contextual Approach to Social Action." In Finamore, *On Earth as in Heaven.*

Brueggemann, Walter. *Interpretation and Obedience: From Faithful Reading to Faithful Living.* Minneapolis: Fortress, 1991.

———. *Journey to the Common Good*. Louisville: Westminster John Knox, 2010.

———. *The Land: Place as Gift, Promise and Challenge in Biblical Faith*. 2nd ed. Minneapolis: Fortress, 2002.

———. *Reality, Grief, Hope: Three Urgent Prophetic Tasks*. Grand Rapids: Eerdmans, 2014.

———. *A Social Reading of the Old Testament: Prophetic Approaches to Israel's Communal Life*. Minneapolis: Fortress, 1994.

Catholic Church. *Catechism of the Catholic Church*. Vatican, 1993. https://www.vatican.va/archive/ENG0015/_INDEX.HTM#fonte.

Center for Action and Contemplation. "Edge of the Inside: The True Center." Center for Action and Contemplation, Sept. 10, 2023. Adapted from publications by Richard Rohr. https://cac.org/daily-meditations/the-true-center-2023-09-10/.

Chambers, Edward. *Roots for Radicals: Organizing for Power, Action, and Justice*. With Michael Cowan. New York: Continuum, 2004.

Chilton, Amy, and Steven Harmon, eds. *Sources of Light: Resources for Baptist Churches Practicing Theology*. Perspectives on Baptist Identities. Macon: Mercer University Press, 2020.

Clarke, Anthony, ed. *For the Sake of the Church: Essays in Honour of Paul S. Fiddes*. Oxford: Regent's Park College Press, 2014.

Cloke, Paul, and Mike Pears, eds. *Mission in Marginal Places: The Praxis*. Milton Keynes: Paternoster, 2016.

———. *Mission in Marginal Places: The Stories*. Milton Keynes: Paternoster, 2019.

———. *Mission in Marginal Places: The Theory*. Milton Keynes: Paternoster, 2016.

Citizens Cymru Wales. "The Governance of Wales Accountability Assembly 17 March 2016." Unpublished manuscript, last modified Mar. 17, 2016. Microsoft Word file.

Citizens UK. *Annual Report 2020: Organising and Global Impact*. Citizens UK, [2021]. https://citizensuk.contentfiles.net/media/documents/Citizens_UK_2020_Annual_Report.pdf.

Clifton, John, et al. *Marching Towards Justice: Community Organising and the Salvation Army*. London: Centre for Theology and Community, 2015.

Coffey, David. *Build That Bridge: The Presidential Address Delivered at the Baptist Assembly 28th April 1986 Westminster Chapel, London*. London: Baptist Union of Great Britain, 1986.

Coleman, Kate. *Being Human: A Black British Christian Woman's Perspective*. Oxford: Whitley, 2006.

Coles, Romand. *Beyond Gated Politics: Reflections for the Possibility of Democracy*. Minneapolis: University of Minnesota Press, 2005.

Commission on Urban Priority Areas. *Faith in the City: A Call for Action by Church and Nation*. London: Church House, 1985.

Commission on Urban Life and Faith. *Faithful Cities: A Call for Celebration, Vision and Justice*. London: Church House, 2006.

Cone, James H. *God of the Oppressed*. Rev. ed. Maryknoll, NY: Orbis, 1997.

Cortes, Ernesto, Jr. *Rebuilding Our Institutions*. Chicago: ACTA, 2010.

———. "Toward a Democratic Culture." *Kettering Review* 24 (2006) 46–57.

Davie, Grace. *Europe: The Exceptional Case; Parameters of Faith in the Modern World*. London: Darton, Longman & Todd, 2002.

———. *Religion in Britain Since 1945: Believing Without Belonging*. Oxford: Blackwell, 1994.

Davies, Idris. *The Collected Poems of Idris Davies*. Edited by Islwyn Jenkins. Llandysul, Wales: Gomer, 2003.

Davis, Rowenna. *Tangled Up in Blue: Blue Labour and the Struggle for Labour's Soul*. London: Short, 2011.

Day, Dorothy. *Loaves and Fishes: The Inspiring Story of the Catholic Worker Movement*. Maryknoll, NY: Orbis, 1997.

———. *The Long Loneliness: The Autobiography of the Legendary Catholic Social Activist*. London: Harper Collins, 2009.

Fiddes, Paul S. "Communion and Covenant." In *Baptists and the Communion of Saints: A Theology of Covenanted Disciples*, by Paul S. Fiddes et al. Waco: Baylor University Press, 2014.

———. "Covenant and Participation: A Personal Review." *Perspectives in Religious Studies* 44 (2017) 119–37.

———. *The Creative Suffering of God*. Oxford: Clarendon, 1988.

———, ed. *Doing Theology in a Baptist Way*. Oxford: Whitley, 2000.

———. "Introduction." In *Bound for Glory? God, Church and World in Covenant*, edited by Anthony Clarke. Oxford: Whitley, 2002.

———. *Participating in God: A Pastoral Doctrine of the Trinity*. London: Darton, Longman & Todd, 2000.

———. "Participation." In *Communion, Covenant, and Creativity: An Approach to the Communion of Saints through the Arts*, edited by Paul S. Fiddes et al. Eugene, OR: Cascade, 2020.

———. *Past Event and Present Salvation: The Christian Idea of Atonement*. London: Darton, Longman & Todd, 1989.

———. Preface to *Covenant and Church for Rough Sleepers: A Baptist Ecclesiology in Conversation with the Trinitarian Pastoral Theology of Paul S. Fiddes*, by Daniel Sutcliffe-Pratt. Centre for Baptist Studies in Oxford. Oxford: Whitley, 2017.

———, ed. *Reflections on the Water: Understanding God and the World Through the Baptism of Believers*. Regent's Study Guide 4. Oxford: Regent's Park College Press with Smyth and Helwys, 1996.

———. "Theology and a Baptist Way of Community." In *Doing Theology in a Baptist Way*.

———. *Tracks and Traces: Baptist Identity in Church and Theology*. Carlisle: Paternoster, 2003.

———, ed. *Under the Rule of Christ: Discussions of Baptist Spirituality*. Oxford: Regent's Park College Press, 2008.

Fiddes, Paul S., et al. *Bound to Love: The Covenant Basis of Baptist Life and Mission*. London: Baptist Union, 1985.

———. "Doing Theology Together, 1979–1999: A Shared Story." In *Doing Theology in a Baptist Way*.

Finamore, Steve, ed. *On Earth as in Heaven: A Theology of Social Action for Baptist Churches*. Didcot, UK: Baptist Union of Great Britain, 1996.

Follett, Mary Parker. *Creative Experience*. New York: Longmans Green, 1930.

Francis. "*Evangelii Gaudium*: On the Proclamation of the Gospel in Today's World." Vatican, Nov. 24, 2013. https://www.vatican.va/content/francesco/en/apost_exhortations/documents/papa-francesco_esortazione-ap_20131124_evangelii-gaudium.html.

———. "*Fratelli Tutti*: On Fraternity and Social Friendship." Vatican, Oct. 3, 2020. https://www.vatican.va/content/francesco/en/encyclicals/documents/papa-francesco_20201003_enciclica-fratelli-tutti.html.

———. "*Laudato Si'*: On Care for Our Common Home." Vatican, May 24, 2015. https://www.vatican.va/content/francesco/en/encyclicals/documents/papa-francesco_20150524_enciclica-laudato-si.html.

———. *Let Us Dream: The Path to a Better Future*. In conversation with Austen Ivereigh. London: Simon and Schuster, 2020.

———. "A Politics Rooted in the People." Vatican, Apr. 15, 2021. https://www.vatican.va/content/francesco/en/messages/pont-messages/2021/documents/papa-francesco_20210415_videomessaggio-conferenza-londra.html.

Freedman, Samuel G. *Upon This Rock: The Miracles of a Black Church*. New York: Harper Collins, 1993.

Freeman, Curtis. *Undomesticated Dissent: Democracy and the Public Virtue of Religious Nonconformity*. Waco: Baylor University Press, 2017.

Freire, Paulo. *Pedagogy of the Oppressed*. Penguin Classics. London: Penguin, 1996.

Furbey, R., et al. "Breaking with Tradition? The Church of England and Community Organizing." *Community Development Journal* 32 (1997) 141–50.

Gardiner, Craig. *Melodies of a New Monasticism: Bonhoeffer's Vision, Iona's Witness*. London: SCM, 2018.

Gecan, Michael. "Change Maker Chat." Change Makers, Sept. 20, 2020. https://changemakerspodcast.org/mike-gecan-changemaker-chat/.

———. *Effective Organizing for Congregational Renewal*. Chicago: ACTA, 2011.

———. *Going Public: An Organizer's Guide to Citizen Action*. Boston: Beacon, 2002.

———. *People's Institutions in Decline*. Chicago: ACTA, 2018.

General Superintendency Review Group. *Transforming Superintendency*. Didcot, UK: Baptist Union of Great Britain, 1996.

Goodliff, Andy. *Renewing a Modern Denomination: A Study of Baptist Institutional Life in the 1990s*. Eugene, OR: Wipf & Stock, 2021.

———. "*Renewing a Modern Denomination* Launch." YouTube, Mar. 16, 2021. https://www.youtube.com/watch?v=aFlKpimFFZg. Link discontinued.

Gouldbourne, Ruth. *Reinventing the Wheel: Women and Ministry in English Baptist Life*. Whitley Lecture. Oxford: Whitley, 1997.

Graf, Arnie. *Lessons Learned: Stories from a Lifetime of Organizing*. Chicago: ACTA, 2020.

Graham, Elaine. "Practical Theology as Transforming Practice." In *The Blackwell Reader in Pastoral and Practical Theology*, edited by James Woodward and Stephen Pattison. Oxford: Blackwell, 2000.

Green, Beth. *Church Growth in East London: A Grassroots View*. With Angus Ritchie and Tim Thorlby. London: Centre for Theology and Community, 2016.

Gregory, David. "Towards a Baptist Eco-Theology." In *One Earth, One Love: Orthodox and Baptist Theologians in Conversation About the Natural Environment*, edited by Paul S. Fiddes. Oxford: Firedint, 2025.

Gushee, David P. *Defending Democracy from Its Christian Enemies*. Grand Rapids: Eerdmans, 2023.

———. *Introducing Christian Ethics: Core Convictions for Christians Today*. Canton, MI: Front Edge, 2021.

Gutiérrez, Gustavo. *A Theology of Liberation: History, Politics, and Salvation*. London: Orbis, 1972.

Hauerwas, Stanley, and Romand Coles. *Christianity, Democracy and the Radical Ordinary: Conversations Between a Radical Democrat and a Christian.* Cambridge: Clarke and Co., 2010.

Haymes, Brian. "Baptism as a Political Act." In Fiddes, *Reflections on the Water.*

———. *The Fullness of Christ: The Presidential Address. The Baptist Assembly 1993, 19 April 1993.* Didcot, UK: Baptist Union of Great Britain, 1993.

———. *A Question of Identity: Reflections on Baptist Principles and Practice.* Leeds: Yorkshire Baptist Association, 1986.

———. "Still Blessing the Tie That Binds." In Clarke, *For the Sake of the Church.*

———. "Theology and Baptist Identity." In Fiddes, *Doing Theology in a Baptist Way.*

Haymes, Brian, et al. *On Being the Church: Revisioning Baptist Identity.* Studies in Baptist History and Thought. Milton Keynes: Paternoster, 2008.

Hochschild, Adam. *Bury the Chains: The British Struggle to Abolish Slavery.* London: Pan Macmillan, 2005.

Holman, Bob. *Faith in the Poor: Britain's Poor Reveal What It's Really Like to Be "Socially Excluded."* Oxford: Lion, 1998.

Hunt, Rosa. "Unity in Translation: The Role of Translation in Building Up the Unity of the Body of Christ." *Journal of European Baptist Studies* 23 (2023) 1–18. https://doi.org/10.25782/jebs.v23i1.1125.

Ivereigh, Austen. *Faithful Citizens: A Practical Guide to Catholic Social Teaching and Community Organising.* London: Darton, Longman & Todd, 2010.

Jacobs, Jill. *Where Justice Dwells: A Hands-On Guide to Doing Social Justice in Your Jewish Community.* Woodstock, VT: Jewish Lights, 2012.

Jacobsen, Dennis. *Doing Justice: Congregations and Community Organizing.* Minneapolis: Fortress, 2001.

Jamoul, Lina, and Jane Wills. "Faith in Politics." *Urban Studies* 45 (2008) 2035–56.

Jenkins, Roy. *Cry Freedom! The Presidential Address Given at the Baptist Assembly Bournemouth, 22 April 1991.* Didcot, UK: Baptist Union of Great Britain, 1991.

Jennings, Willie James. *After Whiteness: An Education in Belonging.* Theological Education Between the Times. London: SPCK, 2020.

Jones, Keith. *A Believing Church: Learning from Some Contemporary Anabaptist and Baptist Perspectives.* Didcot, UK: Baptist Union of Great Britain, 1998.

Kidd, Richard. "Baptists and Theologies of Liberation." In Fiddes, *Doing Theology in a Baptist Way.*

———. "On Realising the Dance." In Clarke, *For the Sake of the Church.*

———, ed. *On the Way of Trust.* Oxford: Whitley, 1997.

———, ed. *Something to Declare: A Study of the Declaration of Principle.* Oxford: Whitley, 1996.

King, Martin Luther, Jr. *Where Do We Go from Here: Chaos or Community?* New York: Harper and Row, 1967.

———. *Why We Can't Wait.* London: Penguin Random House, 2018.

Krehbiel, Jeffrey. *Reflecting with Scripture on Community Organizing.* Chicago: ACTA, 2010.

Lange, Jonathan, and Michael Gecan. *Using the Tools of Effective Organizing to Build Your Union's Local Strength.* Chicago: ACTA, 2016.

Larner, Luke, ed. *Confounding the Mighty: Stories of Church, Social Class and Solidarity.* London: SCM, 2023.

Lee, Hak Joon. *Christian Ethics: A New Covenant Model.* Grand Rapids: Eerdmans, 2021.

———. *God and Community Organizing: A Covenantal Approach.* Waco: Baylor University Press, 2020.

Leech, Kenneth. *The Sky Is Red: Discerning the Signs of the Times*. London: Darton, Longman & Todd, 1997.

Leo XIII. "*Rerum Novarum*: On Capital and Labour." Vatican, May 15, 1891. https://www.vatican.va/content/leo-xiii/en/encyclicals/documents/hf_l-xiii_enc_15051891_rerum-novarum.html.

Lewis, Barry J., et al. *A History of Christianity in Wales*. Cardiff: University of Wales Press, 2022.

Long, Michael, ed. *I Must Resist: Bayard Rustin's Life in Letters*. San Francisco: City Lights, 2012.

Loomer, Bernard. "Two Conceptions of Power." *Process Studies* 6 (1976) 5–32.

Louis, Eleasah, and Andy Goodliff, eds. *Voicing New Questions for Baptist Identity*. Oxford: Regents Park College Press, 2023.

MacLeod, Jay. *Community Organising: A Practical and Theological Evaluation*. London: Christian Action, 1988.

Marchant, Colin. "My Presidential Year." *Fraternal* 228 (1989) 19–24.

McClintock Fulkerson, Mary. *Places of Redemption: Theology for a Worldly Church*. Oxford: Oxford University Press, 2007.

Miliband, Ed. *Go Big: How to Fix Our World*. London: Bodley Head, 2021.

Miller, Mike. *Community Organizing: A Brief Introduction*. Milwaukee: Enclid Avenue, 2012.

Morgan, D. Densil. *The Span of the Cross: Christian Religion and Society in Wales, 1914–2000*. Cardiff: University of Wales Press, 1999.

Murray, Stuart. *A Vast Minority: Church and Mission in a Plural Culture*. Milton Keynes: Paternoster, 2015.

Murray-Williams, Stuart, and Sian Murray-Williams. *Multi-Voiced Church*. Milton Keynes: Paternoster, 2012.

Paul VI, promulgator. "*Gaudium et Spes*: On the Church in the Modern World." Vatican, Dec. 7, 1965. https://www.vatican.va/archive/hist_councils/ii_vatican_council/documents/vat-ii_const_19651207_gaudium-et-spes_en.html.

Payne, Charles M. *I've Got the Light of Freedom: The Organizing Tradition and the Mississippi Freedom Struggle*. Oakland: University of California Press, 2007.

Pierce, Gregory F. Augustine, ed. *Reveille for a New Generation: Organizers and Leaders Reflect on Power*. Chicago: ACTA, 2020.

Randall, Ian. *The English Baptists of the Twentieth Century*. Didcot, UK: Baptist Historical Society, 2005.

Reddie, Anthony. "Baptist Identity? A Response." In Louis and Goodliff, *Voicing New Questions for Baptist Identity*.

Rich, Hannah. *Growing Good: Growth, Social Action and Discipleship in the Church of England*. London: Church of England, 2020.

Richards, Peter Dewi. "Llythyr o Lundain Anerchiad yr Llywydd 2008/09." Paper distributed at the BUW Assembly, 2008.

Ritchie, Angus. *Inclusive Populism: Creating Citizens in the Global Age*. Notre Dame, IN: University of Notre Dame Press, 2019.

———. *People of Power: How Community Organising Recalls the Church to the Vision of the Gospel*. London: Centre for Theology and Community, 2018.

Ritchie, Angus, and Paul Hackwood. *Just Love: Personal and Social Transformation in Christ*. Watford, UK: Instant Apostle, 2014.

Ritchie, Angus, and Sarah Hutt, eds. *From Houses to Homes: Faith, Power and the Housing Crisis*. London: Centre for Theology and Community, 2016.

Ritchie, Angus, et al. *Just Church: Local Congregations Transforming Their Neighbourhoods*. London: Centre for Theology and Community, 2013.

Rodrigues, Dunstan. *Realities Are Greater Than Ideas: Evangelisation, Catholicism and Community Organising*. With Angus Ritchie and Anna Rowlands. London: Centre for Theology and Community, 2018.

Rogers, Mary Beth. *Cold Anger: A Story of Faith and Power Politics*. Denton: University of North Texas Press, 1990.

Rowlands, Anna. "Mixing Religion and Politics: Rethinking the Common Good." Theos, Feb. 1, 2022. https://www.theosthinktank.co.uk/events/2021/11/25/mixing-religion-and-politics-rethinking-the-common-good.

———. *Towards a Politics of Communion: Catholic Social Teaching in Dark Times*. London: T&T Clark, 2021.

Sobrino, Jon. *The Principle of Mercy: Taking the Crucified People from the Cross*. New York: Orbis, 1994.

Stout, Jeffrey. "Blessed Are the Organized." Princeton, June 1, 2011. Interview by Jarrett Kerbel. https://princeton.edu/~stout/stout_hmp.htm. Link discontinued.

———. *Blessed Are the Organized: Grassroots Democracy in America*. Princeton, NJ: Princeton University Press, 2012.

Sutcliffe-Pratt, Daniel. *Covenant and Church for Rough Sleepers: A Baptist Ecclesiology in Conversation with the Trinitarian Pastoral Theology of Paul S. Fiddes*. Oxford: Whitley, 2017.

Task Group on Associating. *Relating and Resourcing*. Didcot, UK: Baptist Union of Great Britain, 1998.

Thurman, Howard. *Jesus and the Disinherited*. Boston: Beacon, 1996.

Tidball, Derek. "My Presidential Year." *Fraternal* 236 (1991) 15–19.

Tocqueville, Alexis de. "*Democracy in America*" *and* "*Two Essays on America*." Edited by Isaac Kramnick. Translated by Gerald Bevan. Penguin Classics. London: Penguin, 2003.

Torre, Miguel de la. *Doing Christian Ethics from the Margins*. New York: Orbis, 2004.

Von Hoffman, Nicholas. *Radical: A Portrait of Saul Alinsky*. New York: Nation, 2010.

Walsh, Brian J., and Sylvia C. Keesmaat. *Colossians Remixed: Subverting the Empire*. Downers Grove, IL: IVP Academic, 2004.

Warren, Mark. "Community Organizing in Britain: The Political Engagement of Faith-Based Social Capital." *City and Community* 8 (2009) 99–127.

———. *Dry Bones Rattling: Community Building to Revitalize American Democracy*. Princeton, NJ: Princeton University Press, 2001.

Weaver, John. *Outside-In: Theological Reflections on Life*. Oxford: Regents Park College Press with Smyth and Helwys, 2006.

Williams, Rowan. *On Christian Theology*. Oxford: Wiley-Blackwell, 2000.

———. "Solidarity." YouTube, Nov. 15, 2021. Third Ken Leech Memorial Lecture. https://www.youtube.com/watch?v=LyuJS-J2ork.

Wills, Jane. "Faith in Action: Lessons from Citizens UK's work in East London." In *Theology and Civil Society*, edited by Charles Pemberton. Routledge Studies in Religion. London: Routledge, 2017.

Wink, Walter. *Engaging the Powers: Discernment and Resistance in a World of Domination.* Minneapolis: Fortress, 1992.

———. *Naming the Powers: The Language of Power in the New Testament.* Minneapolis: Fortress, 1984.

———. *The Powers That Be: Theology for a New Millennium.* New York: Bantam Doubleday Dell, 2000.

———. *Transforming Bible Study: A Leader's Guide.* Eugene, OR: Wipf & Stock, 2009.

———. *Unmasking the Powers: The Invisible Forces That Determine Human Existence.* Minneapolis: Fortress, 1986.

Wood, Jason. "The Power to Act: Dissecting Distinctive Elements of Power and Ownership in Community Organising in England and Wales." *Community Development Journal* 60 (2025) 200–217. https://doi.org/10.1093/cdj/bsad023.

Wood, Richard. *Faith in Action: Religion, Race and Democratic Organizing in America.* Chicago: University of Chicago Press, 2002.

Wright, Nigel G. *Challenge to Change: A Radical Agenda for Baptists.* Eastbourne, UK: Kingsway, 1991.

———. *Free Church, Free State: The Positive Baptist Vision.* Eugene, OR: Wipf & Stock, 2005.

———. *New Baptists, New Agenda.* Carlisle: Paternoster, 2002.

———. *Power and Discipleship: Towards a Baptist Theology of the State.* Whitley Lecture. Oxford: Whitley, 1996.

———. *The Radical Kingdom: Restoration in Theory and Practice.* Eastbourne, UK: Kingsway, 1986.

www.ingramcontent.com/pod-product-compliance
Lightning Source LLC
LaVergne TN
LVHW050613100826
845148LV00011B/1576

* 9 7 9 8 3 8 5 2 5 3 9 1 3 *